Intimacy in Cinema

Intimacy in Cinema

Critical Essays on English Language Films

Edited by DAVID ROCHE *and* ISABELLE SCHMITT-PITIOT

McFarland & Company, Inc., Publishers
Jefferson, North Carolina

LIBRARY OF CONGRESS CATALOGUING-IN-PUBLICATION DATA

Intimacy in cinema : critical essays on English language films / edited by David Roche and Isabelle Schmitt-Pitiot.

p.   cm.

Includes bibliographical references and index.

ISBN 978-0-7864-7924-5 (softcover : acid free paper) ∞
ISBN 978-1-4766-1711-4 (ebook)

1. Intimacy (Psychology) in motion pictures.   I. Roche, David, 1976– editor.   II. Schmitt-Pitiot, Isabelle, editor.

PN1995.9.I57I58 2014
791.43'653—dc23   2014027546

BRITISH LIBRARY CATALOGUING DATA ARE AVAILABLE

© 2014 David Roche and Isabelle Schmitt-Pitiot. All rights reserved

No part of this book may be reproduced or transmitted in any form or by any means, electronic or mechanical, including photocopying or recording, or by any information storage and retrieval system, without permission in writing from the publisher.

On the cover: Keira Knightley and James McAvoy in *Atonement* (2007); photographer Alex Bailey (Focus Features/Photofest)

Printed in the United States of America

McFarland & Company, Inc., Publishers
  Box 611, Jefferson, North Carolina 28640
  www.mcfarlandpub.com

Acknowledgments

The following essays comprise a selection of talks given at the 17th annual SERCIA conference, "Cinema of Intimacy and/or the Intimacy of Cinema in English-Speaking Film," held at the Université de Bourgogne, in Dijon, France, in September 2012. The conference benefited from the support of the Centre Interlangues (EA 4182) and the Conseil Régional de Bourgogne. Special thanks are due to Sylvie Crinquand and Myriam Segura-Pineiro for helping us organize this conference.

We would also like to thank Thomas Elsaesser for accepting our invitation to the conference and participating in this book, and Gilles Menegaldo for the part he played in organizing the keynote lecture.

Warm thanks are due to the other members of the reading committee for their time and input: Jean-François Baillon, Christophe Chambost, Nicole Cloarec, Raphaëlle Costa de Beauregard, Yves Carlet, Wendy Everett, Pierre Floquet, Christophe Gelly, Georges-Claude Guilbert, Xavier Lemoine, Céline Murillo, Mark Niemeyer, Anne-Marie Paquet-Deyris, Dominique Sipière, Penny Starfield, Melvyn Stokes, Patricia-Laure Thivat and Shannon Wells-Lassagne. Additional thanks to Mark who knows why.

Love to our families and friends.

Table of Contents

Acknowledgments   v

*"I feel different inside": An Introduction to Intimacy in
English Language Cinema*
       DAVID ROCHE and ISABELLE SCHMITT-PITIOT   1

Touch and Gesture: On the Borders of Intimacy
       THOMAS ELSAESSER   17

Exposing and Threatening Female Intimacy and Sexuality: How
Traffic in Souls Depicts the White Slave Trade in New York
       CLÉMENTINE THOLAS-DISSET   34

Fictions of Intimacy and the Intimacy of Fiction: "Going into
people's houses" and the Remediation of 1920s Film Reception
       FABRICE LYCZBA   46

The Impossible Sex Life of Couples in the Screwball Comedy
       GRÉGOIRE HALBOUT   61

Intimacy Shared in Laughter and Tears: *Brief Encounter* and
The Seven Year Itch
       RAPHAËLLE COSTA DE BEAUREGARD   73

The Intimate Gaze: (Deviant) Uses of the Subjective Camera in
Lady in the Lake and *La Femme défendue*
       CHRISTOPHE GELLY   84

Shooting Stars and Poet Friends in My Bedroom: Domestic and
Poetic Intimacy in *Pull My Daisy*
       CÉLINE MURILLO   94

Public Confessions in *American Revolution 2*
       ZACHARY BAQUÉ   105

The Limits of Hypermasculinity: Intimacy in American Science
   Fiction Films of the 1980s
      MARIANNE KAC-VERGNE   119
"I've got you under my skin": No Exit from Insane Intimacy in *Bug*
      CHRISTOPHE CHAMBOST   133
Filming Fantasy, Imitating the Intimate in *Eyes Wide Shut*
      YANN ROBLOU   146
J. Edgar: Staging Secrecy
      ANNE-MARIE PAQUET-DEYRIS   156
Intrusions of the Other: Intimacy in the Films of Atom Egoyan
      JEAN-FRANÇOIS BAILLON   165
Hidden Worlds and Unspoken Desires: Terence Davies and
   Autobiographical Discourse
      WENDY EVERETT   179
"Extimacy" and Embodiment in *Hunger* and *Shame*
      ISABELLE LE CORFF   192
Keira's Kiss: The Affordance of "Kissability" in the
   Film Experience
      ADRIANO D'ALOIA   202
Melancholy, Empathy and Animated Bodies: Pixar vs.
   Mary and Max
      RICHARD NEUPERT   215

About the Contributors   225
Index   229

"I feel different inside"
An Introduction to Intimacy in English Language Cinema

DAVID ROCHE AND
ISABELLE SCHMITT-PITIOT

Intimacy has been a main concern in the humanities for many years now, particularly in France. In 1998, Elisabeth Lebovici, editor of a volume entitled *L'Intime*, stated that "intimacy had established itself in cultural space" (12, our translation), thus suggesting that it had become closely woven into the fabric of contemporary experience. In any case, the turn of the 21st century saw an upsurge of writings on intimacy. Approaches have mainly been historical (Wahl 1999; Giddens 2004; Stoler 2006; Bromley 2012), psychological (Kristeva 1997; Alper 1998; Tisseron 2002; Amselek 2006), sociological (Berlant et al. 1998; Jeudy 2007; Gabb 2008; Ballantyne, Burton et al. 2009), feminist and gender-oriented (Sanger 2010; Pratt, Rosner et al. 2012), or have combined several approaches (Hatfield and Rapson 1993; Clam 2007). Studies in the aesthetics of intimacy have mainly concerned literature, particularly autobiographical writings. Gaston Bachelard (1957) and Maurice Blanchot (1959) evoked intimacy when discussing, respectively, the poetics of space and diaries (*journal intime* in French), while, more recently, scholars like Daniel Madelénat (1989, 2008) have made it the heart of their concerns on autobiographical writings. Case studies have been conducted on Elizabeth Bishop (Harrison 1993), First World War literature (Das 2005), the Bloomsbury group (Wolfe 2011) and the representation of intimacy in contemporary literature (Cooke et al. 2013).

As this quick overview suggests, intimacy is often associated with the couple, the family and sexuality (Berlant 281). Intimacy has to do with depth

(Murat 117), with one's inner life and one's relation to, and expression of, one's self and emotions, an enigmatic essence that can be a source of spontaneity (Clam 18–19); for Blanchot, "intimacy is our everyday self" (230, our translation), while Lauren Berlant reminds us that "to intimate is to communicate" (281). Intimacy has to do with "something shared" (Berlant 281; Lebovici 15), and, consequently, with one's relationship with the Other; for anthropologist Edward T. Hall (1966), intimacy is the mode of relationship where two people are closest, a mode where the senses of touch and smell are predominant, i.e., the space of parents and children, lovers and fighters (Lebovici 13). Intimacy, as Bachelard and Hall emphasized, has to do with one's handling of space: "intimacy builds worlds; it creates spaces and usurps places meant for other kinds of relation" (Berlant 283). Thus, as a concept, intimacy is problematic— and stimulating—because it begs to be defined and delineated in terms of binaries that are themselves unstable, such as inside and outside (Lebovici 18; Clam 11), hidden depth and visible surface (Clam 20), public and private (Boyer 72), self and other, or from a Lacanian perspective, the intimate and the extimate.[1] Indeed, the borders between these binaries are inevitably blurred by intimacy's potential for sharing, i.e., what Berlant refers to as people's "attachments" (Berlant 283). Given to evolve in time and space, intimacy is, then, a most unstable term that deconstructs the very terms it contributes to define and is itself partly defined by. In so doing, it reveals how tenuous and arbitrary the foundations of power (from a Foucauldian perspective) are. As Berlant concludes in her introduction, intimacy ultimately provides another angle from which to examine normative discourses and practices, and the modes by which they attempt to impose hegemony and exclude difference:

> Rethinking intimacy calls out not only for redescription but for transformative analyses of the rhetorical and material conditions that enable hegemonic fantasies to thrive in the minds and on the bodies of subjects while, at the same time, attachments are developing that might redirect the different routes taken by history and biography [286].

Intimacy is, thus, a productive entry point to consider subjection and resistance.

Our overview also indicates that aesthetic approaches to intimacy have mainly involved literary studies of the representation of intimacy—i.e., the couple, the family, sexuality—and its expression—i.e., staging the intimate "I" (Lebovici 16), especially in "intimate" forms like autobiography, diaries and letters. Comparatively, little has been written on the subject of intimacy in film studies, particularly when dealing with English Language cinema. It is in order to make up for this lack that the 17th SERCIA conference was organized in 2012. This book contains a selection of presentations from it. The conference theme, "Cinema of Intimacy and/or the Intimacy of Cinema in English-Speaking Cinema," was meant as an invitation to consider the relationship between cinema and intimacy from two angles: (1) what is intimacy in film and how is it represented in terms of aesthetics and politics? and (2) to what extent is cinema an intimate medium? Most scholars, as the essays in this book testify, tackled the first question. Answers to the second question were, however, provided by several presentations, including Thomas Elsaesser's, Fabrice Lyczba's and Richard Neupert's.

It is necessary to distinguish, first, between cinema as an institution (i.e., production, distribution and exhibition) and cinema as a medium (i.e., the actual films), both of which have evolved in time and will continue to do so. Apparatus theory of the 1970s conceived spectatorship as an individual, and thus particularly intimate, experience of immersion: though a member of an audience, the spectator, according to Christian Metz (1977), related fantasmatically with the imaginary signifier that tapped into unconscious processes involving primary and secondary identifications (i.e., with the apparatus and the characters). Materialist reception studies employing the methodologies of history and sociology have, since, called into question this model by drawing attention to the importance of movie-going as a social experience, one that involves acknowledgment of, and often interaction with, other members of the audience (Stokes 47). In this respect, cinema is probably not the most intimate medium developed in the 20th century, radio, television, video game stations and Internet having succeeded in "going into people's houses," to cite Lyczba.

In her 2004 preface to *L'Intime*, Elisabeth Lebovici points to the advent of reality TV in the late 1990s as symptomatic of a shift in paradigm to a world where intimacy is closely (self-)monitored, notably with the multiplication of surveillance cameras and webcams (9–10). It comes as no surprise that a book like *The Intimate Screen* by Jason Jacobs deals not with film, but with British television drama from the 1930s to the 1950s. According to Jacobs, "'[i]ntimacy' for early television drama was understood by critics and producers in terms of the reception of television in the private 'intimate' sphere of the home, something shared by all television programmes" (7), and, presumably, by radio at the time and by Internet today. Accordingly, this intimate address begged for a more intimate style. The utilization of closeups, zoom-ins and forward tracking shots, "a more restrained performance style—the conversational rather than the declarative" (7), were, according to Jacobs, instrumental in television producers' ambition "to 'get in closer' to the dramatic action, to become intimate with it" (6): "[i]ntimacy meant the revelation and display of the character's inner feelings and emotions, effected by a close-up style of multi-camera studio production" (8). Jacobs thus concludes that getting closer to the subject is the historical function of television, and because of that it is part of the definition of the subject. [...] the visualization of interior subjective states is a part of the intimate—drawing room—address of some television drama from the beginning [159].

If cinema could not compete with TV in terms of its address, in the U.S., it did end up competing in terms of content and style.² Following the Miracle Decision (1952), Hollywood turned to technology (3D and CinemaScope) and to more adult and transgressive subjects to rival TV (Sklar 283–85, 294–96). With the advent of new technology, modes of consuming films have, since, changed, arguably lending the consumer a greater deal of control and intimacy. As Olivier Séguret noted in 1998, "the VCR encourages the intimate consumption of films," notably pornography (95). American audiences, for instance, have gone from watching films on TV from the 1950s on, to renting them at a video store from the 1980s on, to streaming them on the Internet from the 2000s on, each mode by no means canceling the others, but adding to the possibilities. Interestingly enough, iPhones and iPads now provide, as Beugnet (2013) has remarked, one-on-one viewing experiences similar to those experienced by spectators in the days of peep-shows. In order to ensure that audiences will continue to go to the movie theaters, and thus to guarantee that production costs will be quickly made up for, the industry's reaction has been to develop technology that reinforces the conception of spectatorship apparatus theory developed: Dolby Surround Sound, iMax theaters and 3D all aim at facilitating the spectator's immersion in the spectacle (Elsaesser and Hagener 175). The film experience has, perhaps, never been as diverse *and* intimate as it is today. Nor, perhaps, as physical. As Elsaesser has remarked, the body and the senses are heavily engaged, whether watching films on an iPhone or in an Imax theater (Elsaesser and Hagener 171).

No doubt prompted by the increasing intimacy of the movie-watching experience, film theory has witnessed a paradigm shift from the "ocular-centered" theories that were dominant from the 1920s to the 1970s (Elsaesser and Hagener 109), to contemporary approaches, influenced by cognitive psychology, Gilles Deleuze and the phenomenology of Maurice Merleau-Ponty, that emphasize other senses: hearing in the works of Michel Chion, who provocatively argues that "it is the ear that renders the image visible" (Elsaesser and Hagener 145); and touch in the writings of Vivian Sobchak (1992, 2004) and Laura Marks (2000, 2002). We have seen that, for Hall, touch is one of the main senses engaged in the intimate sphere, sight becoming more relevant when distances increase. A theory that favors touch rather than sight could, then, offer a possible model for the theory of the intimacy of film. Yet these approaches are not without their own share of limitations. Elsaesser has cautioned that "the haptic turn and other body-based approaches to the cinematic experience are sometimes in danger of celebrating a big-tent, inclusive feel-good-theory of sensory empowerment" (127–28). Moreover, many of the case studies grounded in these approaches focus on films that could be described as especially intimate, so that the relevance of these approaches might concern these and similar films, and may not be valid for film experience in general. Finally, emphasis on touch should not make us forget that the signs we are dealing with are visual and aural. For instance, when Sobchack describes the effect a scene from *The Piano* (Jane Campion, 1993) had on her as a viewer (see Elsaesser in this book), though she does note that the scene involves a closeup of Ada's stocking (Fig. 4), she fails to point out that it is combined with a zoom-in, while closeups of Ada's face and foot pressing the foot pedal draw attention to the music which expresses her sensual titillation [43:59]. In other words, the effects described by Sobchack are, at least in part, triggered by the film's aesthetics of intimacy and, consequently, limited by the visual and aural signs that make up the film. Before the "haptic gaze" became fashionable, *Videodrome* (David Cronenberg, 1983) had drawn attention to its potential limitations, which consumers of pornography are blissfully[3] aware of. When the image of Nikki Brand on Max Renn's television comes to life and invites him to "come to [her]," Max ends up caressing a fleshy image as opposed to an image made flesh [34:20] (Fig. 1): the screen remains impenetrable, the "real" Nikki Brand out of reach.

Intimacy in film is not readily associated with English language cinema—Olivier Séguret's "Cinéma intime" offers an overview of French cinema and traces the legacy of "intimate cinema" to the Nouvelle Vague and even further back to Jean Renoir (92), while Tim Palmer's *Brutal Intimacy* is concerned with contemporary French filmmakers like Claire Denis and Gaspar Noé. Intimacy is even less associated with mainstream and Hollywood cinema—Lebovici sees Andy Warhol's 1963 films *Sleep*, *Kiss*, *Eat* and *Blow Job* as intimate films (14), Séguret evokes Derek Jarman and Jon Jost when mentioning intimacy in British and American cinema (91), while Palmer points out that filmmakers like Noé are, in fact, influenced by the body horror of David Cronenberg (86) and avant-garde directors like Stan Brakhage (76). Recently, in a book called *Hollywood and Intimacy*, Steven Peacock has endeavored to explore intimacy in more mainstream productions. He argues that, in films like *The Age of Innocence* (Martin Scorsese, 1993), *The Bridges of Madison County* (Clint Eastwood, 1995), *The Straight Story* (David Lynch, 1999) and *The Insider* (Michael Mann, 1999), the grandeur of Hollywood cinema is deployed to express intimacy, thereby articulating "the big" and "the little" (3). One could, no doubt, object that these films are not typical Hollywood

Fig. 1. Max Renn (James Wood) embraces Nikki Brand's (Deborah Harry) lips on his TV screen made flesh in David Cronenberg's *Videodrome* (1983).

fare, as their directors are often seen as auteurs. Moreover, although many of the scenes analyzed could, indeed, be described as intimate, Peacock's definition of intimacy is, above all, stylistic: "This tightness of synthesis is a form of intimacy in and of itself. This book is a close study of closeness. Intimacy is found in the close, significant relationships of style, and in the close, significant relationships between characters. Both are bound" (12). In other words, intimacy, for Peacock, ultimately means "qualities of organisation and coherence" (148), one of the main criteria film critics (including ourselves) brandish when assessing the value of a film (Jullier 15, 89). That said, Peacock's study does succeed in foregrounding some of the stylistic means utilized to express intimacy in film: frame-within-the-frame composition (44–45), iris effects (116), voiceovers (reading letters, for instance) (121), eyeline matches (128), gestures of affection (150) or the singling out of two characters in a crowd thanks to camerawork and sound design (73).

Peacock's analyses also suggest that intimacy requires time or "moments," as the subtitle of his book indicates. It seems to us that this is exactly where intimacy may appear in classical and mainstream Hollywood films: in moments that disrupt the classical narrative logic analyzed by David Bordwell and Kristin Thompson (1985, 1988). At the 2012 conference, Dominique Sipière (2015) drew attention to an intimate moment from *Vertigo* (Alfred Hitchcock, 1958) that occurs in Scottie's apartment after he has rescued Madeleine from drowning at the foot of the Golden Gate Bridge [42:09]. The camera tracks left over Scottie, who is stoking the fire in the hearth, offers a glimpse of her clothes dry-ing in the bathroom—and thus a glimpse of her intimacy which nonetheless points back to the last stage in the narrative—then stops on the bedroom doorway through which we can see her sleeping.[4] These glimpses hint at another intimate gaze: one that occurred in the interval between two scenes when Scottie undressed Madeleine. The phone rings, Scottie answers, but tells the person on the other end of the line he will "call" her or him back. In other words, the phone call fails to revitalize the detective plot; it is, in this respect, "useless" apart from the fact that it stands for his (and possibly our) desire to enjoy this moment and make it last. After Scottie has woken Madeleine up, she joins him in the living room, the full shot revealing an intimate detail: she may be dressed in a red dressing gown that reflects Scottie's fantasmatical desire (he has lent it to her), but she is barefoot, almost on tiptoe, as if she were reacting to a chill. As Sipière has noted, adopting an approach similar to Marks's and Sobchack's, our knowledge of what it feels like to walk on a carpet allows us to share in Madeleine/Judy's experience. This glimpse of spontaneity and intimacy thus appears to offer Scottie (and the viewer) a glimpse of the "real," i.e., intimate, woman (Fig. 2). Yet, as we all know, therein lies the film's "real" plot: in the woman's "reality," or more precisely in the coexistence of the real woman and the fabrication. In the end, *Vertigo* can be seen as a mystery, disguised as a psychological melodrama, disguised as a mystery plot, so that it is impossible to decide whether the potential for intimacy stems from the mystery or the melodrama.

Clearly, a cinema of intimacy is both a matter of content and form. Some

Fig. 2. Barefoot, Madeleine Elster (Kim Novak) enters Scottie's (James Stewart) living room in Alfred Hitchcock's *Vertigo* (1958).

subjects are particularly intimate: couples, families, sex and sexuality, secrecy. Some genres are particularly intimate: autobiographical films and documentaries like *Distant Voices, Still Lives* (Terrence Davies, 1988) and *Tarnation* (Jonathan Caouette, 2003), or Linda Williams's body genres (melodrama, horror and pornography). The acting can be particularly intimate, with actors speaking in low voices. The camerawork can be particularly intimate, with closeups,[5] zoom-ins, forward tracking shots, frame-within-the-frame composition, long takes. And the soundtrack can be particularly intimate, through the utilization of voiceovers, amped-up bodily noises and music.[6] A film like *Intimacy* (Patrice Chéreau, 2001), which Palmer includes in his corpus of French films (65), contains many of these features: family, adultery, "real" sex scenes, closeups, handheld camera, lovers that hardly speak (in the first part of the film), but moan and grunt instead. These features, as will become clear in the following essays, can also be found in American, British and Canadian cinemas.

A movie like *The Fountain* (Darren Aronofsky, 2006) shares many characteristics of the *cinéma du corps* (Roche 2015): it revolves around a couple, deals with the negotiation of love and death, utilizes closeups and expresses intimacy aurally, for instance, when the characters whisper, or the sound design evokes Tommy Creo's shutting out the outer world by eliminating surrounding sounds as he walks down the snowy streets until a car braking and honking pulls him out of his torpor [42:50]. What makes *The Fountain* particularly interesting is the way it bravely tackles one of the main challenges of film: expressing a subject's intimate depths. When Tommy realizes his wife Izzi has lost all hot/cold sensation, she offers by way of explanation: "Because I feel different ... inside. I feel different. Every moment. Each one" [22:10]. Expressing a character's inner life through an actor's body, through gestures and voice, and thus metonymically, is what cinema, as a visual, aural and part-performance art, is very much at ease with. But *The Fountain*'s complex narrative structure also attempts to express what the characters feel inside, notably their coming to terms with death, metaphorically, through two other narratives that seem to be subordinate to the main narrative (Tommy and Izzi facing her cancer):

1. the scenes that relate the events in Izzi's manuscript evoke the intimacy of "ideation," i.e., the process of perceiving mentally what one is reading or writing;
2. the scenes that depict a Buddhist-looking Tom traveling through space aboard a bubble evoke Tommy's subjectivity (Fig. 3); these scenes constitute what Deleuze calls a "crystal-image," an image that conflates both "the actual image and *its* virtual image," without it being possible to determine which is which (105, our translation), an image capable

of expressing that "the only subjectivity" is "non-chronological time" [110, our translation].

Thus, the problem posed by *The Fountain* is not that of depicting a mental image on film—the "crystal-image" is ample proof that it is possible to do so— but that posed by metaphor in film, and perhaps, more generally, in the visual arts: the stereotypical approach to historical and Mayan imagery in Izzi's narrative is justified by Izzi's lack of knowledge evidenced in the main narrative; the new age imagery of the bubble scenes is, however, never justified by the other narratives, so that the viewer is expected to accept the metaphor for what it is, an image, without irony, an effect amplified by the music score, which could have tempered this impression instead of amplifying it in the final scenes [74:25].

The essays that follow seek to reveal the intimate potential of English language cinema even where it is less expected, including in mainstream Hollywood cinema. They approach the relationship between intimacy and cinema from angles that are thematic, aesthetic, historical and/or theoretical. They focus on an array of topics and motifs: couples (Chambost, Costa de Beauregard, Gelly, Halbout, Kac-Vergne, Roblou), sex (Everett, Costa de Beauregard, Halbout, Le Corff, Paquet-Deyris, Roblou, Tholas-Disset), the respect or violation of the boundary between self and other (Baillon, Baqué, Paquet-Deyris, Tholas-Disset), the relationship between the personal and political (Baqué, Halbout), forms that are conducive to self-expression (Baqué, Everett,

Fig. 3. Tom (Hugh Jackman) travels through space toward the Mayan underworld aboard his bubble in Darren Aronofsky's *The Fountain* (2006).

Murillo), body genres (Chambost, Costa de Beauregard, Kac-Vergne), devices that invite or discourage an intimate mode of spectatorship (Baqué, Chambost, Gelly, Murillo, Neupert, Paquet-Deyris, Roblou) or the intimate relationship viewers may have with films and stars (D'Aloia, Baillon, Lyczba).

Thomas Elsaesser begins the collection by noting that Berlant's definition of intimacy seems to point to an obvious association between intimacy and cinema. He sees today's interest in this relationship as symptomatic of contemporary debates in film theory and correlates the appearance of phenomenological approaches, with their interest in skin, body and touch,[7] to that of a cinema of intimacy in Europe, East Asia and the U.S. (directors of the "new sincerity"); he nonetheless cautions against the lure of pre-symbolic fusion implicit, to some degree, in these approaches. Further symptomatic of this crisis of the body is the increasing representation of deprivation and deficit in contemporary films. Elsaesser then turns to the intimacy of cinema by paying attention, first, to the bodily involvement of the spectator, particularly when consuming body genres like pornography, horror and melodrama, and second, to the intimacy of new modes of viewing films on Internet. He concludes that, in the spectator-screen relationship, "intimacy situates itself between identification and empathy," thus inviting a possible convergence between psychoanalytic and cognitive approaches.

The next five essays investigate intimacy in Hollywood cinema during the silent and classic eras. Clémentine Tholas-Disset focuses on the representation of the white slave trade in *Traffic in Souls* (George Loan Tucker, 1913), a film that, instead of merely pursuing the potential of motion pictures to exhibit sexuality onscreen, proposes a cautionary tale, in this respect reminiscent of the 18th century novel, that takes us inside the lives of ordinary people and reveals how male desire works to subject, debase and consume female bodies. Taking his cue from a 1929 article in which Irving Thalberg reflected on the advent of sound, Fabrice Lyczba investigates the way Hollywood in the 1920s resorted to more intimate media (radio and magazines) to "go into people's houses," not only to promote its products, but also to create or reinforce a sense of intimacy between audiences and "film imaginaries." Grégoire Halbout tackles a popular genre of the 1930s and 1940s, the screwball comedy, which, though not obviously intimate, resorted to an aesthetics of suggestion in order to deal with intimate matters (marriage and sex), thus taking part in the public debate on marriage by promoting a vision of marriage based on sexual contentment. Raphaëlle Costa de Beauregard and Christophe Gelly offer comparative analyses of classical Hollywood films and foreign films that do not belong to the same genre. Costa de Beauregard reads David Lean's melodrama *Brief Encounter* (1945) as a structuring intertext for Billy Wilder's comedy *The Seven Year Itch* (1955), paying particular attention to structure, language and music, all of which serve to dramatize the elusive quality of the intimacy the characters feel is lacking in married life. Gelly's comparative study concerns experiments with the subjective camera in a classic film noir based on Raymond Chandler, *Lady in the Lake* (Robert Montgomery, 1947), and a contemporary French film about adultery, *La Femme défendue* (Philippe Harel, 1997): a technique that was meant to establish an intimate relationship), grounded in an ideal of truth, between the spectator and the main character (Philip Marlowe) is used in 1997 to draw the spectator's attention to the main character's (François's) duplicity.[8]

Céline Murillo and Zachary Baqué deal with more obviously intimate forms of cinema: underground and documentary film. Murillo argues that *Pull My Daisy* (Robert Frank and Alfred Leslie, 1959) functions much like a home movie by constructing the Beat poets as a family and establishing a closeness with the bodies and voices depicted, and ultimately, foregrounds the problematic relationship between text and body, notably in the intimate expression of bodily experience, that was a central concern of Jack Kerouac and the Beat poets. Baqué discusses the relationship between the public and the personal by paying particular attention to the problematic treatment of voice and gaze in a militant documentary, *American Revolution 2* (Howard Alk and Mike Gray, 1969), that depends on its filmic subjects' intimate vision of the world.

The next three essays return to Hollywood cinema, yet deal mainly with filmmakers that are seen as auteurs and that are not all American (David Cronenberg and Paul Verhoeven). Marianne Kac-Vergne foregrounds the way certain intimate scenes undercut the exhibition of a "hypermasculine" ideal, in Hollywood science-fiction films of the 1980s like *The Fly* (Cronenberg, 1986) and the first two installments of *RoboCop* (Verhoeven, 1987; Irvin Kershner, 1990), by exposing the male characters' vulnerability and alienation from (female) others, and thus from the possibility of "sharing something" which is at the basis of intimacy. Christophe Chambost sees *Bug* (William Friedkin, 2006), with its focus on excessive physicality and grotesque bodies, as participating in the "brutal intimacy" critics have recently attributed to French cinema, the mad couple's hysterical flesh emerging from a sense of "extimacy" that remains ultimately inexpressible. Yann Roblou offers an in-depth analysis of a key scene from *Eyes Wide Shut* (Kubrick, 1999) that is both paradigmatic of the film's aesthetic terms and informs the rest of the film. Anne-Marie Paquet-Deyris analyzes *J. Edgar* (Clint Eastwood, 2011), the portrayal of a man who spent his life violating the intimacy of others in order to manipulate them while concealing the intimate secrets he could not assume, as a biopic that both exposes the FBI director's endeavor for secrecy and participates in his own self-mythologizing project, notably by tapping into other film genres.

Jean-François Baillon, Wendy Everett and Isabell Le Corff turn their attention to contemporary British and Canadian auteurs: Atom Egoyan, Terrence Davies and Steve McQueen. Baillon argues that the violation of the Other's intimate space depicted in Egoyan's films, from *Next of Kin* (1984) to *Adoration* (2008), reflects the filmmaker's own view of the intimacy of cinema as being founded on the ethically problematic relationship between filming and filmed subjects, a question inherited from *Peeping Tom* (Michael Powell, 1960) and *Videodrome* (Cronenberg, 1983). Everett reveals how the autobiographical material present in Davies's openly autobiographical films like *The Long Day Closes* (1992) persists in his recent adaptation of Terence Rattigan's play *The Deep Blue Sea* (2011), both on a thematic level (the homosexual themes underlying an explicitly heterosexual narrative) and on a formal level (his very personal use of music and camerawork to create a sense of intimacy). In her study of the treatment of the body in Steve McQueen's first two feature films (a comparison encouraged by the presence of Michael Fassbender in both), Le Corff relies on the concept of "extimacy" to circumscribe the protagonists' experience, suggesting that, if the actor's experience can be considered from a phenonemological perspective, the films invite neither empathy nor identification on the part of the spectator.

The final two essays return to the question of the intimacy of cinema by resorting to cognitive approaches that emphasize bodily and emotional cues and responses. Adriano D'Aloia makes the bold claim that British actress Keira Knightley's lips are particularly "kissable," and are exploited as such in the films she stars in, grounding his analysis in psychologist James J. Gibson's notion of "affordance." Richard Neupert compares a selection of Pixar shorts and the Australian claymotion film *Mary and Max* (Adam Elliot, 2009) in order to gauge the efficacy of strategies and techniques (notably 3D as opposed to stop-motion) utilized in animated films to convey emotions as complex as a character's melancholy to viewers through cognitive cues.

We hope that the following essays will ultimately inspire further research on the relationship between intimacy and cinema.

Notes

1. Though coined by Jacques Lacan in 1969 (249), the "extimate" was developed by Jacques-Alain Miller in his 1986 seminar, where it is delineated in relation to other concepts—for instance, extimacy is what the Other that is language lacks—and further defined by Serge Tisseron (2001), for whom extimacy is the desire to make visible some aspects of one's self (52).

2. Michel Chion (1995) has even suggested that music in film became increasingly intimate under the influence of TV series (143).
3. We have in mind the Lacanian notion of *jouissance*, which involves both the pleasure and trauma of transgression.
4. All these open doors are, however, highly symptomatic of the transparency of classical Hollywood cinema.
5. In Elsaesser's words, "the close-up's relation to intimacy and monumentality [...] is based on an inherent tension: does the close-up exhibit an intimate monumentality or a monumental intimacy?" (Elsaesser and Hagener 79).
6. Michel Chion (1995) has emphasized the important role played by music in evoking intimacy in film, notably to "translate the characters' subjectivity" (108), through the usage of songs (281) or by relying on specific modes of orchestration like chamber music (116), while Elsaesser has pointed out that Dolby technology increases the potential intimacy of contemporary cinema, "allowing the film to 'transgress' the boundaries of the screen and 'enter' into the spectator's space" (Elsaesser and Hagener 141).
7. We could even add taste and smell, e.g., the films of Claire Denis.
8. The subjective camera has similarly been utilized in *Maniac* (Franck Khalfoun, 2012), a remake of William Lustig's 1980 film, to emphasize the main character's psychosis. and thus distance the spectator from the character.

WORKS CITED

Alper, Gerald. 1998. *Blind Alleys: Obstacles Along the Road to Intimacy*. San Francisco, CA: International Scholars Publications.
Amselek, Alain. 2006 [2010]. *Le livre Rouge de la psychanalyse (Tome 1: L'Écoute de l'intime et de l'invisible)*. Paris: Desclée de Brouwer.
Bachelard, Gaston. 1957. *La Poétique de l'espace*. Paris: PUF.
Ballantyne, Tony, and Antoinette Burton, eds. 2009. *Moving Subjects: Gender, Mobility and Intimacy in an Age of Global Empire*. Urbana: University of Illinois Press.
Berlant, Lauren. 1998. "Introduction." *Critical Inquiry* 24.2 "Intimacy: A Special Issue" (Winter): 281–88.
Bernard-Griffiths, Simone, Françoise Le Borgne and Daniel Madelénat, eds. 2008. *Jardins et intimité dans la littérature européenne (1750–1920)*. Clermont-Ferrand: PU Blaise Pascal.
Beugnet, Martine. 2013. "Miniature Pleasures: On Watching Films on an iPhone." *Cinematicity in Media History*. Eds. Jeffrey Geiger and Karin Littau. Edinburgh: Edinburgh University Press. 196–211.
Blanchot, Maurice. 1959. "Le Journal intime et le récit." *Le Livre à venir*. Paris: Gallimard. 224–30.
Bordwell, David. 1985. *Narration in the Fiction Film*. Madison: University of Wisconsin Press.
Bordwell, David, Janet Staiger, and Kristin Tompson. 1988. *The Classical Hollywood Cinema: Film Style and Mode of Production to 1960*. London: Routledge and Kegan Paul.
Boyer, Charles-Arthur. 1998 [2004]. "Architecture, intimité, promiscuité: L'évolution de l'espace domestique en France du Moyen Âge au XIXe siècle." *L'Intime*. Ed. Elisabeth Lebovici. Paris: Ecole nationale supérieure de beaux-arts. 69–88.
Bromley, James M. 2012. *Intimacy and Sexuality in the Age of Shakespeare*. Cambridge: Cambridge University Press.
Chion, Michel. 1990 [2013]. *L'Audio-vision : Son et image au cinéma*. Paris: Nathan.
———. 1995. *La Musique au cinéma*. Paris: Fayard.
Clam, Jean. 2007. *L'Intime : Genèses, régimes, nouages. Contributions à une sociologie et une psychologie de l'intimité contemporaine*. Paris: Ganse.

Cooke, Jennifer G., ed. 2013. *Scenes of Intimacy: Reading, Writing and Theorizing Contemporary Literature*. London: Bloomsbury.
Das, Santanu. 2005. *Touch and Intimacy in First World War Literature*. Cambridge: Cambridge University Press.
Deleuze, Gilles. 1985. *Cinéma 2: L'Image-temps*. Paris: les Éditions de Minuit.
Elsaesser, Thomas, and Malte Hagener. 2010. *Film Theory: An Introduction through the Senses*. New York: Routledge.
The Fountain. 2006 [2007]. Dir. Darren Aronofsky. With Hugh Jackman (Tommy Creo/Tomas), Rachel Weisz (Izzi Creo/Isabel) and Ellen Burstyn (Dr. Lillian Guzetti). Protozoa Pictures, Regency Enterprises, Warner Bros. DVD. TF1.
Gabb, Jacqui. 2008. *Researching Intimacy in Families*. Basingstoke: Palgrave Macmillan.
Giddens, Anthony. 2004. *La Transformation de l'intimité: Sexualité, amour et érotisme dans les sociétés modernes*. Rodez: Les Editions du Rouergue.
Hall, Edward T. 1996. *The Hidden Dimension*. Garden City, NY: Doubleday.
Harrison, Victoria. 1993. *Elizabeth Bishop's Poetics of Intimacy*. Cambridge: Cambridge University Press.
Hatfield, Elaine and Richard L. Rapson. 1993. *Love, Sex, and Intimacy: Their Psychology, Biology, and History*. New York: HarperCollins.
Jacobs, Jason. 2000. *The Intimate Screen: Early British Television Drama*. Oxford: Oxford University Press.
Jeudy, Henri-Pierre. 2007. *L'Absence de l'intimité: Sociologie des choses intimes*. Belval: Circé.
Jullier, Laurent. 2002. *Qu'est-ce qu'un bon film?* Paris: La Dispute.
Kristeva, Julia. 1997. *La Révolte intime*. Paris: Fayard.
Lacan, Jacques. 2006. *Le Séminaire livre XVI: D'un Autre à l'autre*. Ed. Jacques-Alain Miller. Paris: Seuil.
Lebovici, Elisabeth, ed. 1998 [2004]. *L'Intime*. Paris: Ecole nationale supérieure des beaux-arts.
Madelénat, Daniel. *L'Intimisme*. Paris: PUF, 1989.
_____, ed. 2008. *Biographie et intimité : Des Lumières à nos jours*. Clermont-Ferrand: PU Blaise Pascal.
Marks, Laura U. 2000. *The Skin of the Film: Intercultural Cinema, Embodiment, and the Senses*. Durham: Duke University Press.
_____. 2002. *Touch: Sensuous Theory and Multisensory Media*. Minneapolis: University of Minnesota Press.
Metz, Christian. 1977 [2002]. *Le Signifiant imaginaire : Psychanalyse et cinéma*. Paris: Christian Bourgeois.
Miller, Jacques-Alain. "Extimité." May 28, 1986. http://ttyemupt.unblog.fr/2012/09/07/jacques-alain-miller-extimite-28-mai-1986. Retrieved on 3/1/2014.
Murat, Laure. 1998 [2004]. "Écriture : intimité d'une pratique." *L'Intime*. Ed. Elisabeth Lebovici. Paris: École Nationale Supérieure des Beaux-Arts. 113–22.
Palmer, Tim. 2011. *Brutal Intimacy: Analyzing Contemporary French Cinema*. Middletown, CT: Wesleyan University Press.
Peacock, Steven. 2012. *Hollywood and Intimacy: Style, Moments, Magnificence*. Basingstoke, UK: Palgrave Macmillan.
The Piano. 1993 [2003]. Directed and written by Jane Campion. With Holly Hunter (Ada McGrath), Harvey Keitel (George Barnes) and Sam Neill (Alisdair Stewart). Australian Film Commision, CiBy. DVD. TF1 Video.
Pratt, Geraldine, and Victoria Rosner, eds. 2012. *The Global and the Intimate: Feminism in our Time*. New York: Columbia University Press.
Roche, David. (2015). "Exprimer l'intime dans *The Fountain* de Darren Aronofsky." *CinémAction* 153 "De l'intimité dans le cinéma anglophone" Forthcoming.
Sanger, Tam. 2010. *Trans People's Partnerships: Towards an Ethics of Intimacy*. Basingstroke and New York: Palgrave Macmillan.

Séguret, Olivier. 1998 [2004]. "Cinéma intime." *L'Intime*. Ed. Elisabeth Lebovici. Paris: Ecole nationale supérieure des beaux-arts. 89–96.

Sklar, Robert. 1975 [1994]. *Movie-Made America: A Cultural History of American Movies (Revised and Updated)*. New York: Vintage.

Sipière, Dominique. 2015. "Petite grammaire de l'intime." *CinémAction* 153 "De l'intimité dans le cinéma anglophone." Forthcoming.

Sobchack, Vivian. 1992. *The Address of the Eye: A Phenomenology of Film Experience*. Princeton: Princeton University Press.

_____. 2004. *Carnal Thoughts: Embodiment and Moving Image Culture*. Berkeley: University of California Press.

Stokes, Melvyn. 2012. "Audiences in Cinema History." *Cinéma et théories de la réception / Approaches to Film and Reception Theories*. Eds. Christophe Gelly and David Roche. Clermont-Ferrand: PU Blaise Pascal. 31–53.

Stoler, Ann Laura. 2006. *Haunted by Empire: Geographies of Intimacy in North American History*. Durham: Duke University Press.

Tisseron, Serge. 2001. *L'Intimité exposée*. Paris: Ramsay.

Vertigo. 1958 [2003]. Dir. Alfred Hitchcock. With James Stewart (John "Scottie" Ferguson) and Kim Novak (Madeleine Elster/Judy Barton). Paramount Pictures. DVD. Universal Pictures.

Videodrome. 1983 [2002]. Written and directed by David Cronenberg. With James Woods (Max Renn), Sonja Smits (Bianca O'Blivion) and Deborah Harry (Nicki Brand). Canadian Film Development Corporation. DVD. Universal Pictures.

Wahl, Elizabeth Susan. 1999. *Invisible Relations: Representations of Female Intimacy in the Age of Enlightenment*. Stanford: Stanford University Press.

Wolfe, Jesse. 2011. *Bloomsbury, Modernism and the Reinvention of Intimacy*. Cambridge: Cambridge University Press.

Touch and Gesture
On the Borders of Intimacy

Thomas Elsaesser

If the Internet might well claim to be the medium of public intimacy par excellence, with humans exposing their most intimate moments to legions of strangers and often receiving such warm and welcoming responses that it feels like one really could be close to half of the world, my own interest in the subject of intimacy is less "intimate." Partly symptomatic and partly generic, it situates itself more on the meta-level of the discipline of film studies and does not attempt to explore intimacy in the context of family, domestic space and the inner life. Instead, I shall explore the intricate relationship between the cinema of intimacy and the intimacy of cinema.

Why "Intimacy" Now?

My main definition of intimacy I borrow from Laura Berlant:

> To intimate is to communicate with the sparest of signs and gestures, and at its root intimacy has the quality of eloquence and brevity. But intimacy also involves an aspiration for a narrative about something shared, a story about both oneself and others that will turn out in a particular way. Usually, this story is set within zones of comfort: friendship, the couple, and the family, animated by expressive and emancipating kinds of love. Yet the inwardness of the intimate is met by a corresponding publicness [281].

Berlant here suggests an inherent tension, if not a willed paradox and contradiction, namely that intimacy is a closeness that demands or desires to be opened up, either from within, by those who seek this proximity and want to share and show it. Or it is opened up from without, by those who want to intrude on it, who feel threatened by it or envy it. This is why I associate borders and edges with intimacy, and why it can already imply its own negation, its own vulnerability and its transience. In fact, one might say that at the outer boundary of intimacy (and thus its always looming horizon) is "shame": when exposed from without, and—when exposed from within—its implicit and ever-present obverse is a transgressive self-abandon, bordering on abjection. Berlant hints at something similar when she goes on:

> intimacy builds worlds; it creates spaces and usurps places meant for other kinds of relation. Its potential failure to stabilize closeness always haunts its persistent activity, making the very attachments deemed to buttress "a life" seem in a state of constant if latent vulnerability. [...] it becomes clear that virtually no one knows how to do intimacy; [...] and that the mass fascination with the aggression, incoherence, vulnerability, and ambivalence at the scene of desire somehow escalates the demand for the traditional promise of intimate happiness to be fulfilled in everyone's everyday life [282].

This suggests that intimacy should be a cinematic topic par excellence, since the very definition of intimacy as proposed by Berlant implies a tension and mutual interdependence between public and private that is nothing less than foundational and constitutive for the cinema, which is, after all, our last public sphere, where the private is depicted, experienced and negotiated *as private*. This in contrast to television, where the private becomes a public performance, when we think of sitcoms with their laugh track, or of politicians who have to stage huge multi-million spectaculars for the TV networks, in order to show off the real person, the intimate family man, the private self. As Thomas Friedman of the *New York Times* put it in 2012: "this is a presidential election where both candidates are running as 'I'm not Mitt Romney.'"

So why has "intimacy" not been a major concern in film studies? My own answer is in response to a slightly different question: why "intimacy" now? The special issue of *Critical Inquiry* from which I just quoted, as well as several conferences besides the 2012 SERCIA conference in Dijon, testify to a special interest, and maybe even a particular urgency inherent in the topic. This is why I said that my interest in "intimacy" is as a symptom: symptom of a shift, a crisis, and a change in register and attention. To be more specific, I venture that, in the context of the cinema, the topic of "intimacy" has possibly become symptomatic, thanks to four current preoccupations in film studies. First, we can think of a *cinema of intimacy* in light of the revival of phenomenology, itself a reaction to both Lacanian psychoanalysis and Anglo-American cognitivism. Second, a *cinema of intimacy* may be an inadvertent and unintended, but nonetheless distinct response to several tendencies in contemporary cinema, notably the "cinema of the new extremity" in France and Europe, and the "cinema of the new sincerity" in the U.S. And third, a cinema of intimacy could be seen as a promising initiative in the debate over spectatorship, since it offers another possibility of understanding the affective bond linking film and spectator. In this case, intimacy would be a concept somewhere between identification and empathy, two terms that have been heavily theorized by both psychoanalytic and cognitivist film theory.

Cinema of Intimacy from the Film Theory Perspective: The Revival of Phenomenology

It will not come as a surprise if I say that, over the past decade, film studies has witnessed a rise in the number of approaches which, under the auspices of phenomenology, have promoted forms of perception other than those that concentrate exclusively on the visual register, i.e., which privilege the look and the gaze. This has often implied not so much a negation of the visual sense in itself, but a way of thinking of the visual in a different mode, such as that of hearing and especially touch—hence the extraordinary popularity of the term "haptic." The revival of synaesthesia, on the other hand, aims at highlighting the different senses in their interplay, while yet another group insists on the fact that all forms of perception are embodied. Each group is calling for an approach to the cinema that gives due theoretical attention to this embodiment in its full complexity: mind and body, body and brain, brain and the senses, a new post- or anti–Cartesian relation between subject and object. In the English-speaking world, it was above all Vivian Sobchack who was responsible for first proposing this shift in perspective by championing a version of Maurice Merleau-Ponty's phenomenology. Sobchack summarizes her critique as follows:

> Until quite recently, however, contemporary film theory has generally ignored or elided both cinema's sensual address and the viewer's "corporeal-material being." [...] In general, [...] most film theorists still seem either embarrassed or bemused by bodies that often act wantonly and crudely at the movies, involuntarily countering the fine-grained sensibilities, intellectual discriminations, and [traditional] vocabulary of critical reflection [55–57].

The cinema of intimacy would similarly signal the "return" to the body as a complex yet indivisible surface of communication and perception, both within the space of the film's fictional world and its protagonists, and between the screen and the audience. Cultural Studies had already advocated such positions, imagining the cinema as a space of contact, whether violent or tender, awkward or transgressive. Advancing an "ethical turn"—and speaking with Emmanuel Levinas of the cinema as the difficult but necessary encounter with the Other—has become a major platform in philosophical approaches to cinema, but also for those who study transnational cinemas or what Laura Marks has called "intercultural cinema." In a similarly trans-cultural vein, much of the French "cinéma du corps" actually originated in the films of David Cronenberg (Palmer 86), and was very much influenced by Asian cinemas, with South Korean films like *The Isle* (Ki-duk Kim, 2000) and *Old Boy* (Chanwook Park, 2003), not to mention Japanese horror films and ghost stories.

At the same time, there are films that take seriously the idea of skin as an organ of enveloping perception and try to advance cinema primarily as a tactile experience. Marks, who became a prominent theorist of a cinema of the body with her two books, *The Skin of the Film* (2000) and *Touch* (2002), both of which ingeniously if somewhat improbably managed to blend Merleau-Ponty with Gilles Deleuze, comments on the haptic-tactile move, by claiming: "Haptic images can give the impression of seeing for the first time, gradually discovering what is in the image rather than coming to the image already knowing what it is" (*The Skin* 178). She is arguing that such a move restores to the cinema its capacity for discovery and disclosure, important to film theorists of the 1920s and 1930s, such as Béla Bálazs, Jean Epstein and Siegfried Kracauer, as well as to André Bazin, but also taken up—within an explicitly Heideggerian philosophical framework—by Jean-Luc Nancy.

A movie like *The Pillow Book* (Peter Greenaway, 1996), with its closeups of ink pens running down parchment and human skin, obviously comes to mind when speaking of *The Skin of the Film*. Yet, arguably, one gets as much a sense of the sensitivity of skin, as an organ that actively interacts with the world, from Russell Crowe brushing his hand over ripening corn in *Gladiator* (Ridley Scott, 2000) as from Greenaway calligraphing a naked woman's torso. However, apart from *Hiroshima mon Amour* (Alain Resnais, 1959), it was a film like *Empire of the Senses* (Nagisha Oshima, 1976) that drew attention to the cinema's capacity to reveal the vibrancy and vulnerability of skin, giving an inner life to pure surface, and in the process, showing us intimacy as a realm not only of proximity and contact, touch and the protective envelope of human warmth and close companionship, but of risk and danger, of ecstasy, abjection and self-annihilation. It was from Oshima that directors like Claire Denis could and did learn. In *Beau Travail* (Denis, 1999), for instance, the main protagonist Galoup's pulse under his skin is the most telling index of his inner life; even Mike Leigh, in a film like *Naked* (1993), draws one of the most searing portraits of a man craving for intimacy and only able to manifest it in verbal or physical aggression.

Nearly twenty years after *Empire of the Senses*, Jane Campion, with *The Piano* (1993), took full advantage of the new fascination with body and skin, their surface tensions, potential and vulnerabilities—precisely the film that Sobchack made the centerpiece of her plea for a new cinema of intimacy in her essay "What My Fingers Knew" (2000), reprinted in her book *Carnal Thoughts*.

> As I watched *The Piano*'s opening moments—in that first shot, before I even knew there was an Ada and before I saw her from *my* side of *her* vision (that is, before I watched *her* rather than her *vision*)—something seemingly extraordinary happened. Despite my "almost blindness," the "unrecognizable blur," and resistance of the image to my eyes, *my fingers knew what I was looking at*—and this *before* the objective reverse shot that followed to put those fingers in their proper place [...]. What I was seeing was, in fact, from the beginning, *not* an unrecognizable image, however blurred and indeterminate in my vision, however much my eyes could not "make it out." From the first (although I didn't consciously know it until the second shot), my fingers *comprehended* that image, *grasped* it with a nearly imperceptible tingle of attention and anticipation and, offscreen, "felt themselves" as a potentiality in the subjective situation figured onscreen [63].

Sobchack also comments on the scene from *The Piano* where Baines lies down under the piano and touches Ada for the second time [43:59] (Fig. 4).

> Such ambient and carnal identification with material subjectivity also occurs when, for example, I "objectively" watch Baines—under the piano and Ada's skirts—reach out and touch Ada's flesh through a hole in her black woolen stocking. Looking at this "objective" image, like the reviewer cited earlier, I also felt an "immediate tactile shock when flesh first touches flesh in close-up." Yet precisely *whose* flesh I felt is ambiguous and vague—and emergent from a phenomenological experience structured on ambivalence and diffusion. That is, I had a carnal interest and investment in being *both* "here" *and* "there," in being able *both* to sense *and* to be sensible, to be *both* the subject *and* the object of tactile desire. At the moment when Baines touches Ada's skin through her stocking, suddenly my skin is both mine and not my own: the "immediate tactile shock" opens me to the general erotic mattering and diffusion of my flesh, and I feel not only my "own" body but also Baines's body, Ada's body, and what I have elsewhere called the "film's body." [...] Objectivity and subjectivity lose their presumed clarity. [...] There remains no basis for preserving the mutual exclusivity of the categories subject and object, inner and outer, I and world [65–66].

Following Sobchack and Marks, to promote a cinema of intimacy would therefore be to turn away from the self-alienating, disembodied and—according to many feminists, disempowering—theories of psychoanalysis, with their emphasis not only on vision and the gaze, but on "mis-cognition" and "disavowal" as inevitable consequences of the tyranny of the eye. A cinema of intimacy would be to experience the sensation of fusion, of erotic abandon, of

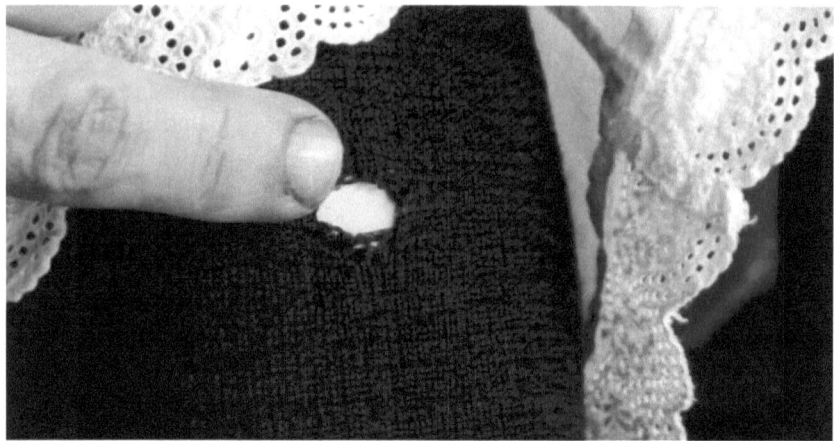

Fig. 4. The camera zooms in on Ada McGrath's (Holly Hunter) knee as Georges Baines (Harvey Keitel) pokes at a hole in her stocking in Jane Campion's *The Piano* (1993).

merging and immersion. But it could also be symptomatic of something else: a celebration of the new possibilities that the digital image brings to the screen, namely an ability of getting that much closer to the world, to bodies and skins, to the texture of any kind of surface, be it human or man-made, infinitely small or unimaginably distant, like the surface of the planet Mars captured by the rover Curiosity that so enchanted the world early in 2012.

However, in all fairness, a word of caution is also in order. Sobchack's claim that before we can comprehend film, we must make sense of it, is a clever pun, because she implies that making sense of it is to experience it with all our senses. Her targets are both semioticians and cognitivists, since "understanding how a film is understood" was Roger Odin's motto (11, my translation), just as "narrative comprehension" was the primary task for film theory, according to cognitivists such as David Bordwell and Ed Branigan, but her "making sense through the senses" also highlights a major misunderstanding. If we take "making sense" in the sense of bodily experience, we are negating or collapsing an entire strand of human evolution, which has progressed through the use of symbols and signs to represent and communicate that which is not within one's grasp, or even that which is altogether ungraspable or absent. It also undoes what Norbert Elias (1939) called the "civilizing process," with proximity senses having their functions translated into substitutes (fork for fingers, knife for teeth when eating) or symbolization (verbal aggression versus physical violence, etc.). Or as a character (Jung) says in *A Dangerous Method* (David Cronenberg, 2011), a film that portrays both him and Freud: "Law students are not normally expected to rob banks" [40:15]. This reliance on "sense" equaling sensation and sensuality thus risks becoming yet another ideology of pre-symbolic fusion, a golden age or paradise lost of immediacy and authenticity. In other words, to understand "intimacy" too much as the natural manifestation of the touchy-feely side of the new film philosophy of haptics, embodiment and tactility also has its risks—conceptually, as well as aesthetically.

For one thing, advertising has long ago discovered the lure of skin and the promise of touch. For example, in a commercial for the oh-so-subtly-named deodorant "Touch" by Axe, the harmless actions of a handsome young man—like turning on the radio or opening a book—have immediate consequences on the bodies of the beautiful young women around him.[1] And although it's all about the erotics of touch, it works by substitution and symbolization, while being up front and in your face, as well as taking its own macho posturing not quite seriously. But while it is suggesting that all kinds of pleasures of the flesh are within easy reach for the man with the Touch deodorant, the filmic construction relies entirely on semiotic play and substitutive analogy: skin and leather, heat and sweat, map reading and body tracing, opening a book and opening a blouse, buttons and nipples. In other words, it plays the tactile off against the visual, and the semiotic off against the mimetic.

Cinema of Intimacy and Other Film Movements

On a less frivolous note, I now want to briefly compare and contrast a cinema of intimacy with other parallel, but maybe also competing tendencies in contemporary cinema. It is almost impossible not to think of our topic in relation to, or in opposition to, recent scholarship devoted to contemporary French cinema, now often discussed under two complementary labels: the "New French Extremity" and, to quote a recent book title by Tim Palmer, "Brutal Intimacy." I shall not go into a description or definition of this New French Cinema, except to recall *Artforum* critic James Quandt's (2004) by now notorious definition of the New Extremity, that follows in the footsteps of Mario Bava and Pier Paolo Pasolini in including "the determinants of a cinema suddenly determined to break every taboo, to wade in rivers of viscera and spumes of sperm, to fill each frame with flesh, nubile or gnarled, and subject it to all manner of penetration, mutilation, and defilement."

Quandt wants this to be understood as a lament and a cinephile's cry of despair, asking in vain for a return to the civilized sophistication of a French cinema that was all talk and little action, all foreplay and little consummation, and associated with Éric Rohmer, Jacques Rivette, Alain Resnais, Jean-Paul Rappenau, Francois Truffaut and André Téchiné. But in response to Quandt, there have been some robust defenses of the "new exigency for reality" manifest in the films of Gaspar Noé, Bertrand Bonello, Philippe Grandrieux or Catherine Breillat, and also of the political import of this new "cinéma du corps," not least by Martine Beugnet in her book *Cinema and Sensation*.[2]

In contrast to such a cinema of extremity, the cinema of intimacy might offer a more reflexive, a more attenuated and attuned (but also a more British or Puritan) version of this new investment in the body and the senses. While acknowledging the necessity of a vital cinema to be able to break taboos, when it comes to the supposed inviolability of the body in Christian religion or Western liberal thinking, the cinema of intimacy would also re-negotiate the borders and surfaces of the gendered body, as well as the boundaries between inside and out, but do so more delicately and with greater awareness of inherent paradoxes than perhaps the cinema of extremity. What in recent years has been identified as a trend towards "contemplative cinema," characterized by slow camera movements, long takes or static shots, and become associated with directors like Pedro Costa, Hsiao-hsien Hou or Béla Tarr, might find its equivalent, in terms of tone and mood, but also as a mode of cinematic thought and of post-post-modern reflexivity, in a cinema of intimacy.

On the other hand, if we do think of the cinema of intimacy as a cinema focused on the body, then the complex and darker notion of intimacy, hinted at above, must be admitted as well, especially if one thinks of the modern body's actual expendability in civil wars and economic exploitation, its susceptibility to torture, and its pain and suffering in famines or diseases, but also its exposure to manipulation and re-assemblage thanks to modern medicine, genetics and man-machine hybridization—in short, the body under all the forms of control, calculation and coercion that Michel Foucault termed bio-power and bio-politics.

A film like *The Skin I Live In* (Pedro Almodóvar, 2011) is invested on the side of the intimacy of bodies, in the mutations and permutations of the family, but the director is equally keen to viscerally involve us in the engineering of a body's surface, as well as its gender and subjective identity. The fashionable term "brutal intimacy" might apply to this film like no other, but at the same time, Almodóvar is a far too sophisticated and self-reflexive director not to play several very different riffs on both the brutal aspect of his film and on (mediated) intimacy. For instance, he plays up to the hilt the humor and comedy inherent in filmic violence and brutality, a skill Almodóvar eminently shares with Martin Scorsese, director of *Taxi Driver* (1976), *Goodfellas* (1990) and *Casino* (1995). But *The Skin I Live In* is also a meditation on visual *mediation*, with its multiple screens, glass partitions, intercoms, windows, apertures and doors, intimating that intimacy—or at any rate, our current interest in intimacy—is, in some sense, a consequence of the new kinds of often transgressive intimacy, made possible in a world of visual *s*urveillance and up-close *m*onitoring, of micro *s*urgery and intrusive *m*edicine: some of the s/m practices (along with *s*cientific research and *m*ilitary applications) that have always been inherent in the cinematic apparatus, but that have come much more to the fore in recent years, not least through the shift to the digital, but by no means *caused* by the digital. Despite its *telenovela* melodrama and campy Grand Guignol, Almodóvar's film also gives a clinically detached assessment of what could be the consequences, if we—that is, Western middle-class culture and its cinema—are, in effect, leaving the episteme of vision and voyeurism, and are about to enter the episteme of surveillance, understood as a mode not of observing, witnessing, contemplating or even spying on, but of probing and penetrating, processing and possessing. *The Skin I Live In* makes a convincing case that "intimacy," in all its tender and cruel ambiguities, might, indeed, become a key term in the understanding of cinema and the function of images in the 21st century.

Similarly concerned with the body, but proposing a quite different reading of touch from that of either Sobchack or the world of commercials and glossy advertising, is the philosopher Jean-Luc Nancy, whom I have already mentioned in connection with a cinema of disclosure and discovery. To quote Douglas Morrey's study of Nancy and Claire Denis,

> For Nancy, in his work since *Corpus* (2000), the body is first and foremost the site of touching: it is the point of contact, the limit point between self and other and, *as such*, also between matter and signification. By extension, anything that exists on or at the limit also partakes of touching [123].

The key argument, as one would expect from a philosopher whose crucial references are deconstruction, difference and deferral, is that, for Nancy,

> a deferred touch is simply a distillation of that moment when a touch, having touched, withdraws itself. It is, for Nancy, only in this hesitation between touching and not touching that touch has its meaning, because without this tergiversation the contact between the surface touching and the surface touched would become something more akin to adhesion or agglutination [Morrey 123].

Despite the polysyllabic circumlocutions of this passage, it is easy to deduce from it that Nancy's take on the relation between vision and touch differs radically from the "haptic visuality" I discussed earlier under the names of Sobchack and Marks, since Nancy could never subscribe to their uncomplicated, not to say, naive belief in the indexicality of the image, or in the miraculously transferential access to its sensory plenitude. As another commentator (Laura McMahon) rightly remarked, "[f]or Nancy, a phenomenologically grounded model of touch would remain indebted to an intuitionist faith in immediacy and continuity, and thus [is] locked within the very metaphysics of presence which his deconstructive model seeks to resist" (cited in Morrey 123).

The filmmaker most often associated with Nancy is, of course, Claire Denis, who, to her own dismay, has occasionally been associated with the "cinema of extremity," a label that, when applied to her films, quickly loses its analytical cogency or descriptive relevance. In my argument, she exemplifies a cinema of intimacy, precisely because of the complex choreography of yielding and withdrawal, of hesitancy and abandon that characterize her scenes of sexual encounter, whether between lovers among a band of military brothers, or between strangers—the latter most impressively in *Vendredi Soir* (2002), a sort of remake of *Brief Encounter* (David Lean, 1945), now set in Paris, rather than Milford Junction, with cars rather than trains, and in a *bar tabac* called *Le Rallye* rather than a railway cafe. Sex, in Nancy's philosophy and Denis' film, is first of all a dance of glances, a back and forth of withdrawal and approach, and a diffident testing or rough handling of surfaces or points of contact, e.g., the young woman's banging away at the pinball machine [42:27], which dominates the soundtrack throughout the scene, or the waitress's robust wiping of the coffee machine [43:52]. This tentative testing of tactile matter permits at once a dispersal of self and a gathering of identity.

> Because for Nancy the key to touching is in withdrawing, it is the space between touches that gives them their sense. As he suggests in *Noli me tangere*, the touch, and especially the caress, is a giving of the self that also holds back, and in doing so invites the other to come forward and seek *more*: more touches, but also something of the secret that enfolds another soul within another body, as though within the hollow of the touch itself, as Nancy puts it, such that he or she who touches me gives of him or herself but also takes away something of myself [Morrey 125].

In a cinematic vocabulary as witty as it is understated, the condom vending machine and the green glove take on a life of their own: they tell a story of advance and protection, of self-protection and careless abandon, in short, of this couple's inner states, latent intentions and conflicted emotions at least as vividly as the characters' faces, mouths and hands.

From this perspective of a perhaps still hypothetical centrality of intimacy in contemporary cinema around a philosophy of touch in both its physical paradoxes of proximity and retreat, and its metaphoric poly-semiosis—think of the English expressions "to keep in touch" or "being out of touch," and in French, think of Stephane Mallarmé's famous "on a touché au vers," quoted by Raymond Bellour (1990) with reference to the digital: "on a touché a l'image"—from this perspective, then, the cinema of extremity—whether Japanese or South Korean, whether European or American—e.g., films like *Reservoir Dogs* (Quentin Tarantino, 1991) and *Hostel I* and *II* (Eli Roth, 2005, 2007), the latter having, along with *Saw* (James Wan, 2004) and a few other films, given rise to the snappy label "torture porn"—the cinema of extremity seems to be the very opposite of a cinema of intimacy. However, it would find itself quite close to another, possibly also "reactive" film movement, this time American, known as the "new sincerity" (Olsen 1999; Hancock 2005), and associated mainly with the films of indie director Wes Anderson, as well as with Todd Solondz and Hal Hartley. The "new" of the new sincerity would be that it is a response to postmodern irony, to teen nihilism and to "anything goes" relativism: not a rejection of it, not a nostalgic return to a simple-minded, heart-on-its-sleeve sincerity. Instead, in a further move or turn of the screw, the new sincerity incorporates cynicism, and asserts itself in conjunction with irony. It doesn't say "I love you" as if no one had ever uttered the phrase, it doesn't say "I love you" with scared quotes around the words, embarrassed at uttering a cliché. It says "I love you," fully knowing that it has been used and abused a million times, and still feels the need to say it with just these words.

What makes me bring up the new sincerity in relation to intimacy is that I think what Nancy's philosophy elaborates and Denis's cinema illustrates is eminently present in Wes Anderson, whose *Moonrise Kingdom* (2012) creates in mood and tone something of this push-pull, tug of opposites in the face of the terrifying and unlimited open space that seems so crucial to intimacy. It's the story of Sam, a twelve-year-old orphan boy, running away from a Boy Scout's summer camp and persuading Suzy, the strong-willed and wayward daughter of a lawyer couple, to elope with him. Consider a scene from their first evening together, as they pitch camp and settle for the night, but also get to know each other by inventorying what each has brought along, in their dash to freedom and a life together [24:57] (Fig. 5). Anderson's relation to his characters resonates with Berlant's vision of intimacy, combining eloquence with brevity, putting in the frame the hinted and the intimated, the gesture withheld, the tentative encounter that breaks off at the point of contact, rather than the yielding embrace. The words that come to mind when describing this aspect of his films, and in particular *Moonrise Kingdom*, are "fierce self-determination" and "chaste self-effacement," a combination that, rather than being contradictory and incompatible, actually seem a valid and necessary

Fig. 5. When inventorying their belongings in Wes Anderson's *Moonrise Kingdom* (2012), Sam (Jared Gilman) realizes the books in Suzy's (Kara Hayward) suitcase have been stolen from the library; she offers by way of explanation: "I might turn some of them back in one day; I haven't decided yet. I know it's bad. I think I just took them to have a secret to keep. Anyway, for some reason, it makes me feel in a better mood sometimes."

complement, on the side of the English-speaking world, to the continental philosophy of the body, from the Marquis de Sade and Pierre Klossowski, to filmmakers like Almodóvar and Denis.

Productive Pathologies: Blindness, Amnesia, Paralysis and the Bodiliness of Disability

At this juncture in the argument, it is worth pointing out that a certain cinema of intimacy can arise, but can also expose the risks of such a notion, when the protagonist is shown to be in some ways handicapped or has his/her perceptual register altered by the loss of one of his/her senses, at times to the advantage of another. Deprivation and deficit then function as a telling metaphor of the crisis or shift with which I began, the re-alignment of priorities, for which the metaphor offers the protagonist's handicap as the creative constraint that pushes also the subject-spectator towards a radical or a gradual re-orientation of perception and participation, as it were, re-shuffling the traditional hierarchy of the senses. Or, as Sacha Baron Cohen puts it in *Brüno* (2009): "Autism is in."

Indeed, it is remarkable how many films, both English-speaking and from world cinema, both art-house films and popular Hollywood fare, have invented stories of disability, in order to explore different forms of interaction and contact, different relations between bodies—thematizing an age gap or different skin color, apparently incompatible sexual orientations or different cultures and customs. Think of the phenomenal success of a feel-good movie like *The Untouchables* (Olivier Nakache and Eric Toledano, 2011) that already in its title hints at barriers and borders, but makes light of the real boundaries that separate not just races and classes, but neighbors and intimates.

This, too, is a symptomatic aspect of our topic, with its considerably risky politics of emancipation and empowerment. Murderous hatred of one's neighbor (or indeed one's spouse), as Slavoj Žižek never tires to point out, is a function of unbearable intimacy, not of knowing too little about the other. Ex-Yugoslavia and the director Emir Kusturica is what is on Žižek's mind, but my productive pathologies refer also to films like *Memento* (Christopher Nolan, 2000) where amnesia forces the protagonist to rely on his body as a site of inscription and memory, *Avatar* (James Cameron, 2009) where the wonders of Pandora are accessible only to a paraplegic ex–Marine, and, of course, the already discussed *Piano*, where it is the heroine's muteness that forms the basis of her quite different relationship to the world, her own sexualized body and, in effect, to the spectator: an aspect that Sobchack perhaps pays too little attention to when she expresses surprise at what her fingers knew and celebrates the eloquence of exposed flesh. Closer to home, i.e., the Anglo-Franco world of cinema I am concentrating on here, one may recall *The Diving Bell and the Butterfly* (Julian Schnabel, 2007), with Mathieu Amalric, as an example of the new kinds of intimacy that a most debilitating handicap can afford the protagonist by way of surrogate and proxy.

The Intimacy of the Cinema: Between Melodrama and Pornography

The fact that a handicap and a surrogate, especially as imagined in Mattieu Amalric's compensation fantasies, are also evident metaphors for spectatorship gives me a chance to move from the cinema of intimacy to the intimacy of cinema, that is, the amorous, ambiguous and fraught relation between screen and spectator. Here, it is worth mentioning Linda Williams's well-known 1991 essay "Film Bodies: Gender, Genre, and Excess." Williams probes quite astutely the interface between the psychic (the fantasies), the physiological (the somatic, involuntary manifestations) and the affective (emotional states and the range of feelings) that can inhabit the spectator's body when watching certain genres of movies. She pays particular attention to what she calls the body genres: melodrama, horror and pornography, each with its own specific fantasy frame: the fantasy of union with the mother in melodrama, the primal scene and the threat of castration in the horror film, and the primary fantasy of parental seduction in pornography.

Williams's thesis has been so influential, not least because she identifies three genres in which bodily integrity is, in some sense, the limit: the codes of representation are fractured, even if only momentarily, by somatic responses that are transmitted to the spectator, opening up a kind of circuit of contagion beyond empathy and close to bodily mimesis. But Williams also posits several orders of temporality, assigning not only to each of her genres one particular bodily fluid (tears, sweat and semen), but a particular time frame: too soon for horror, too late for melodrama, and the "now" of pornography. I think this is both neat and ingenious, and furthermore, these time frames help to modify the idea of a directly mimetic response that could otherwise be read out of her body genres, with their all too specific physiological, involuntary responses. While at the end of her article, Williams claimed that "more work needs to be done" on the historical context, the social parameters and the generic origins of the genres she identifies as central to a somatic theory of cinema, she might also have argued that more work should be done on these temporalities, or rather on the aspect of their failure, in relation to the affect they are supposed to produce.

For when she matches these time frames with the fantasies underpinning the three genres she discusses, she already holds the key to at least one aspect of their temporality. As every Freudian knows, it is in the very nature of fantasies that they are experiences of failure—which is why they have to be repeated, endlessly. Thus, their temporality of repetition joins those secondary elaborations in the films, which, at least in melodrama and the horror film, manifest themselves as bad timing, missed opportunities or excessively close encounters. All of these, it is true, have to do with a belatedness in the characters' responses to a given situation, but also with alternatives appearing in a flash, brief moments of bliss, smothered by the knowledge of a course of action not taken, and therefore settling into regret as the strongest affect. For melodrama, a genre often cited when one thinks of the yearning for intimacy as well as of its fragility and ultimate failure, is as much a genre of the "if-only," i.e., of the temporality of regret, as it is of the "too late," just as it is a genre of self-abandon as much as one of shame and bodily discomfort.

The Intimacy of the Internet

Regret, of course, is also one of the deeper emotions that we all know as cinema-goers: regret that the film is over, regret that we are dismissed from the company of characters we have learnt to love and become close to. In this regard, my brief survey of locating "intimacy" in film studies and contemporary cinema does actually suggest that it is more slippery and many-sided than I at first thought. As much as it has distinct qualities of its own and definable attributes, "intimacy" is also a placeholder, standing for something else. It emerges in between other terms, such as touch or gesture, and it names a togetherness that only sustains itself at the edge of being betrayed, or turning into one of its many opposites: shame, violence, aggression or embarrassment.

As spectators we are just as vulnerable, in other words, to the anxieties of intimacy as the characters in a narrative: we crave proximity, but fear disappointment, and we need distance in order to negotiate the closeness that the big screen so effortlessly seems to offer. This is why the screen-spectator relationship is most successful where it is also at its most mediated: the drama of touch and gesture, of reaching out and opening up must be shown to be also one of withholding and withdrawing, if it is to work on the spectator. We need to see in intimacy the yearning for intimacy, as well as the fear of intimacy, rather than observe bodies merely stuck together in tight embrace. As spectators, we can only experience empathy or identification, if there is an opening for us to be also present—and this opening must take the form of a gap: the semiotic gap of absence or the somatic gap of loss, rather than being faced with a plenitude that not so much eludes the spectator as it excludes the spectator.

In other words, the very indeterminacy and dividedness that I have been describing gives us an important clue to the cinema of intimacy as well as to the intimacy of the cinema, insofar as a sense of intimacy is, in effect, the most powerful bond between the spectator and the film. This is why I said that intimacy situates itself between identification and empathy, meaning that the very self-divided nature of intimacy is the ground for its efficacy in the spectator-screen relationship. We are close, but know ourselves distant; we want to fuse and merge, but know there is an unbridgeable gap in both time and space between us and the screen.

This leads me to my last point, which seemingly overturns what I have just said. I think contemporary cinema is haunted by intimacy because of the different relations that audiences now have with films, in the age of Netflix and iTunes, and which is almost the reverse of the relation in the classical cinema experience. The Internet's intimacy of instant availability, thanks to streaming video and YouTube, brings with it the freedom to appropriate the films one loves with mash-ups or by overdubbing a clip with a new soundtrack. Considering some of the Internet memes or makeovers, for instance of Jane

Campion's *The Piano*, the intimacy on display is not so much "brutal," as it is without reticence or shame, as if our love of cinema, now that the cinema is so often pronounced "dead," gave us licence to take liberties.

In this light, I am tempted to interpret the scene I mentioned from *Moonrise Kingdom* as a little allegory of the spectator-film relationship in the digital age. Although the film is set in 1965, if we substitute for the suitcase full of books and the portable record-player a laptop or an iPad, then Suzy's explanation of why she steals library books—"I think I just took them to have a secret to keep."—becomes eminently readable as a parable of piracy, peer-to-peer file-sharing, illegal downloads, and the furtive but fulfilling pleasures of doing something a little bit risky as a token of one's love.

Notes

1. This commercial can be viewed on Youtube. https://www.youtube.com/watch?v=NYOV65KBiaI. Retrieved November 29, 2013.
2. In the words of Ben McCann (2008), "Beugnet suggests that this cinema does not reproduce images of 'body horror' in the traditional sense, but instead embraces images of the corporeal and the abject in order to interrogate issues such as sexual violence, female emancipation, and the crisis of masculinity." http://tlweb.latrobe.edu.au/humanities/screeningthepast/23/cinema-and-sensation.html. Retrieved November 29, 2013.

Works Cited

Bellour, Raymond. 1990 [2002]. *L'Entre-images : Photo, cinéma, vidéo*. Paris: Éditions de la différence.
Berlant, Lauren. 1998. "Intimacy: A Special Issue." *Critical Inquiry* 24.2 (Winter): 281–88.
Beugnet, Martine. 2007 [2012]. *Cinema and Sensation: French Film and the Art of Transgression*. Edinburgh: Edinburgh University Press.
Elsaesser, Thomas. 1992. "Around Painting and the 'End of Cinema': À propos de Jacques Rivette's *La Belle Noiseuse*." *Sight and Sound* 12.1 (April): 20–23.
Elsaesser, Thomas, and Malte Hagener. 2010. *Film Theory: An Introduction through the Senses*. New York: Routledge.
Hancock, Brannon. 2005. "A Community of Characters: The Narrative Self in the Films of Wes Anderson." *The Journal of Religion and Film* 9.2 (October). http://www.unomaha.edu/jrf/Vol9No2/HancockCommunity.htm. Retrieved on 11/29/2013.
Marks, Laura U. 2000. *The Skin of the Film: Intercultural Cinema, Embodiment, and the Senses*. Durham: Duke University Press.
_____. 2002. *Touch: Sensuous Theory and Multisensory Media*. Minneapolis: University of Minnesota Press.
Moonrise Kingdom. 2012. Dir. Wes Anderson. Written by Wes Anderson and Roman Coppola. With Edward Norton (Scout Master Ward), Bob Balaban (The Narrator), Jared Gilman (Sam), Kara Hayward (Suzy), Bill Murray (Mr. Bishop) and Bruce Willis (Captain Sharp). Indian Paintbrush, American Empirical Pictures and Moonrise. DVD. StudioCanal.
Morrey, Douglas. 2008. "Listening, and Touching, Looking and Thinking: The Dialogue

in Philosophy and Film Between Jean-Luc Nancy and Claire Denis." *European Film Theory*. Ed. Temenuga Trifonova. New York: Routledge. 122–33.

Odin, Roger. 1990. *Cinéma et production de sens*. Paris: Armand Colin.

Olsen, Mark. 1999. "If I Can Dream: The Everlasting Boyhoods of Wes Anderson." *Film Comment* 35.1 (January/February): 12–17.

Palmer, Tim. 2011. *Brutal Intimacy: Analyzing Contemporary French Cinema*. Middletown, CT: Wesleyan University Press.

The Piano. 1993 [2003]. Directed and written by Jane Campion. With Holly Hunter (Ada McGrath), Harvey Keitel (George Baines) and Sam Neill (Alisdair Stewart). Australian Film Commision, CiBy 2000. DVD. TF1 Video.

Sobchack, Vivian. 2004. *Carnal Thoughts: Embodiment and Moving Image Culture*. Berkeley: University of California Press.

Vendredi Soir. 2002 [2007]. Dir. Claire Denis. Written by Emmanuèle Bernheim and Claire Denis. With Valérie Lemercier (Laure), Vincent Lindon (Jean) and Hélène de Saint-Père (Marie). Bac Films. DVD. Arte Éditions.

Williams, Linda. 1991. "Film Bodies: Gender, Genre, and Excess." *Film Quarterly* 44.4 (Summer): 2–13.

Exposing and Threatening Female Intimacy and Sexuality
How Traffic in Souls *Depicts the White Slave Trade in New York*

Clémentine Tholas-Disset

Silent motion pictures had, from the start, been associated with voyeurism (Hansen 35). As early as 1896, one of Edison's most famous—though, for some infamous—pieces was *May Irwin Kiss*, a kiss between actors May Irwin and John Rice, shot in the small vanguard studio The Black Maria. Although it was, above all, intended to be funny, *May Irwin Kiss* remains the first well-known onscreen performance of sexuality, as well as a masterpiece recording of the facial expressions of performers meant to prove the new power of cinema over stage (Sokalski 312); it even spoofed the exuberant and prolonged "Nethersole-style" stage kiss to offer evidence of motion pictures' superiority in terms of realism (Musser 2004, 112). Shown during the first public projection at Koster and Bial's the same year, this short film was much publicized, highly commented on and even started a new cinematic trend: kiss films and kissing scenes—e.g., *The Widow Jones* (1896) and *The New Kiss* (1900). Many theatergoers were outraged at what was then perceived as the bestiality and indecency of these images (Musser 2005, 33).

A new boundary had been broken by revealing, to the public eye, human behaviors that ought to remain private. Cinema became an instrument of unveiling, a sensational and daring medium dealing with new and important everyday topics and issues, including "sex, masculinity, gender relations, femininity, [and] morality" (Musser 2005, 34). At the same time, there was also a more blatant form of motion picture pornography, which started in 1893 when a nude dance by a female performer named Fatima was filmed (Slattery 69). As there was no official organized censorship providing societal control during the early years of cinema, many nudity scenes circulated in penny arcades and peep-shows. Moreover, in the U.S. in the 1900s, "whore graphs" and "whore stories" often shot by amateurs were available, as well as images of people stripping or performing sexual acts (Slattery 69–70). Audiences enjoyed watching illicit and provocative images to satisfy their voyeuristic appetites and challenge traditional Victorian moral conventions. Access to any of those pictures could be seen as a claim for freedom and a challenge to existing social codes.

So onscreen exhibition of intimacy and sexuality was not really something new when George Loan Tucker's *Traffic in Souls* came out in 1913, starring Jain Gayl (Mary Batmore), Matt Moore (Officer Burke) and William Welsh (William Trubus). The movie relates the misfortunes of Lorna Barton and other young women, abducted and forced into prostitution, and the undaunted courage of Lorna's sister to rescue her from the underworld's sinister schemes. *Traffic in Souls* was drastically different from other films of the time, insomuch as sex was not the main attraction. The aim was, rather, educative and cautionary: to inform people of the risks faced by young women in big cities. Although the movie deals with brothels and procurers, it was designed to discredit loose morality and sexual behaviors. This feature-length film challenged the erotic or pornographic one- or two-reelers that were popular at the time, by exposing some of the evils of modern urban life. Universal Manufacturing Company even advertised it as a "sermon in seven parts which every American girl and boy should see" (Olund 485) at a time when the value and suitability of "white slave" movies[1] were highly debated in New York and Chicago (Stamp 1997, 351). The movie was allowed to be screened after a series of re-viewings by the National Board of Censorship and a few minor cuts, whereas other white slavery films often ended up banned; for instance, the short film *The Inside of the White Slave Traffic* (Frank Beal, 1913), released the very same year, was unable to secure the authorization of local moral authorities (Grieveson and Krämer 2004b, 191). Scholars like Ben Brewster and Kristen Whistel have emphasized the role of *Traffic in Souls* as one of the first American feature-length movies not based on a literary classic, and a pioneering work of cinematic story-telling, "rejecting the models of narrative construction" offered in the 1910s (Brewster 226–41). Other scholars, like Tom Gunning (1997), have studied this movie to discuss issues of spectatorship and reception, while others still, for instance Shelley Stamp (1991, 1997), have focused more on the question of censorship. Richard Maltby, Kay Sloan and Janet Staiger have referred to *Traffic in Souls* in order to address the question of social order and morality (Grieveson 2004, 293).

In short, *Traffic in Souls* was widely acknowledgement as the first authorized popular movie openly dealing with the white slave trade. Though it is quite a challenge to attempt to offer a new take on this widely-discussed film, I propose to analyze why it can be labeled "an insider's motion picture" that copies, to a certain extent, "documentary style" chronicles—a reference to Walker Evans' photographic style (Chevrier 63–67). This essay starts with a journey inside what was perceived to be the reality of American big cities where private places mattered as much as public spaces, followed by an analysis of the way the movie studies the repressions faced by early twentieth-century women and attempts to raise awareness of their conditions as females and potential citizens.

An Insider's Movie

As one of the first attempts of American producers to compete with the European feature-length films praised by bourgeois spectators (Brewster 227), *Traffic in Souls* needed to stand out from other local productions in terms of both form and content. From the very first scene, when the movie opens in the heroine's apartment *in media res*, the viewer is almost commanded to observe what is going on not only behind the closed doors of deprived tenements, but also of well-off mansions, offices and even brothels, whether s/he likes it or not. The audience is taken on a tour of intimate places; interior scenes far outnumber outdoor scenes, and Tucker's choice of locations echoes the observations of contemporary critic Vachel Lindsay on the extreme receptiveness of the audience to intimacy, people's daily lives and the enhancement of ordinary routines. Lindsay has explained that cinema "viewed art as a reality, and one of our most familiar and popular realities as an art" (X). Cinema introduces viewers to places that normally remain private and hidden spaces where people do not care about public image; it highlights common-place and familiar places, elements and topics, making insignificant things relevant and remarkable by means of what Lindsay has described as

> the world's new medium for studying, not the great passions, such as black hate, transcendent love, devouring ambition, but rather the half relaxed or gently restrained moods of human creatures. It gives also our idiosyncrasies. It is gossip *in extremis*. It is apt to chronicle our petty little skirmishes, rather than our feuds [21–22].

Thus, the life of common people became the prime subject of American motion pictures, in which a strong sense of realism pervaded, even if that realism was somehow revised by the new-born cinematic system of representation.

Cinema had the ability to transform triviality and encourage people to consider their own condition as well as others. Reality had come to surpass the glorious tales and epics that mesmerized former generations. As Garth Jowett has emphasized, the rise of motion pictures occurred at a time when traditional culture was jeopardized by the repeated assaults of change; cinema was seen as an emerging artistic form matching, with more accuracy, the ideals of American democracy (95).

Traffic in Souls also takes the spectator inside the intimate sphere of several households, the Bartons' [0:26–1:28] and the Trubus's [3:23–5:53], where some of the family members feel free to be themselves and behave spontaneously, while others like William Trubus decide to hide their true nature. However, at first glance, both families seem very alike, because the apartment of the Barton family is a place of gathering and sharing where the two sisters and their father live in joyful harmony, and the house of the Trubus family conveys the same impression of domestic happiness, as the mother and daughter seem to have pleasant and affectionate interactions with the father. In both families, the young women are presented as quite free from conventional constraints; the film insists on their independence by showing them in private places like their bedroom while they are still in bed, or strolling about the house dressed in a negligee without being told off. Parental figures appear rather tolerant and benevolent, only wishing the children to be happy. Yet as the plot unfolds, the stability of both households is threatened, and the film shows that the intimate lives of these two families living in a modern American metropolis are far more complex than they seem.

Peace is shattered by the two dysfunctional fathers who end up transferring the role of "head of the family" to women, namely Mary (first intertitle) and Mrs. Trubus. The two ladies prove to be more respectable and reliable in their attempt to preserve order, Mary's father being an invalid and Trubus a villain in disguise. Moreover, the viewer may wonder about the manners and lifestyle of Trubus' daughter, who wears the same flimsy nightdress as the girls imprisoned in the brothel owned by her father. The scenes of intimacy within the two households provide a relevant illustration of social transformations in the 1910s, involving notably the family. On the one hand, the film underlines the redefinition of women's behavior as they became the "New Woman" in charge of her body, career and family, and capable of establishing a newfound leadership over men (Olund 492–94). On the other hand, it illustrates the increase of vice and criminality on all social levels, among the crooks in the slums, as well as amidst the upright bourgeoisie, like Trubus, who is ironically called "The Man Higher Up." Indeed, he may be at the top of the social ladder, but he reaches the very bottom of the ladder of morality, for having no qualms in selling the body of young innocents both in whorehouses and even in his own house when he decides to marry his daughter to a rich suitor. Trubus's only motivation is profit at any cost. Private spaces, normally thought to be protective and safe, provide the favored setting for the plot, contrary to public places that are generally associated with numerous urban perils. Moreover, *Traffic in Souls* avoids the traditional division Victorian "spacial tropes of the feminine private and masculine public, or racialized slums and classed surbub" (Olund 486). It shows quite the opposite, as danger reaches its full scale in private and secluded rooms, away from the public sphere, which is to be reassessed as a "modern place of free circulation and of social and gendered mingling" (Olund 497).

Even though unlawful behaviors and wrongdoings are to be observed in the streets, train stations, harbors and shops [20:07–33:38], the movie highlights the fact that crime is at its utmost when delinquency is safely concealed behind the walls of brothels and in secure gathering places for the underworld [8:11–9:05]. The film shows the audience what lurks behind the facades: the hidden and vicious side of the city. It seems to take on a kind of journalistic approach, as if it were to be seen as a true-to-life report despite its fictional nature, all the more so since it was released in the middle of a controversy on the status of prostitution in the U.S. and crusades by anti-vice committees (Matsubara 55–58). The attention-seeker bias of the film derives from a negotiation between the National Board of Censorship, the organ of motion picture self-regulation formed in 1909 and directed by John Collier (Stamp 43), and the production studios that had accepted that their work would be reviewed by the board (Rosenbloom 309–10). In the case of *Traffic in Souls*, it proved difficult to establish the right balance between so-called morally "good" and "bad" scenes. Indeed, it was difficult to explain that enjoyable places of respectable leisure, like dancing halls and tea rooms, could be used as seductive venues to trap young women. The studios had to juggle with preserving the reputation of those decent places and describing how they could be misused by the underworld to lure innocent victims. These places of indoor sociability could, at times, be converted into deceptive traps [39:27–43:05]. However, the depiction of entertainment sites is pitted against the representation of places far more bleak and gloomy, like the whorehouses where young women are locked up against their will, in order to confirm the wretched reality of the white slave trade as imagined by American people at the time (Olund 496) [5:56–7:40]. The movie aims to portray both accurately and imaginatively the various positive and negative spaces used to get hold of the female body. Shelley Stamp's (1999) expression "elaborate vice ring" (43) cleverly encapsulates the large-scale setup scheme designed to entrap gullible young women coming from outside the city or country.

Urban organized crime is also represented in indoor scenes; wrongdoings do not only happen outside. If "beaters" (touts) and informers run wild in the streets and other public sites, pimps and go-betweens meet in whorehouses and offices to bring the profits of their traffic to their superiors and discuss their abduction methods. The office of Trubus's righthand man is a collective room, located right above the office of the big shot, who is officially the president of the highly respected "International Purity and Reform League." By contrast, Trubus's own office, not to say his den of iniquity, is a secluded space, protected by the word "PRIVATE" written in big bold letters on the two doors, where people can only come in when allowed. This room is designed to protect Trubus's intimacy; he has set up a sophisticated tape-wiring system there, which enables him to listen to what is going on in the underground meeting room downstairs and to deliver his orders, unbeknownst to other people [8:11–13:55]. Trubus's office is highly protected and provides him with a haven of vice, where only a select few are accepted, since he holds most of his official meetings in his secretary's cabinet. His own office appears like some kind of modern fortress he believes to be impregnable, which helps him conceal his true self. The office may seem inviolable, but Trubus will corrupt the "sacredness" of the place by letting Mary in to clean some ink stains; he gives her the opportunity to break the protective wall he built. Trubus, the fearless wolf, has let Mary, a seemingly inoffensive lamb who will trick him and ruin his empire of crime, into his den.

In spite of its happy ending which insists on the heroine and her friends' power, *Traffic in Souls* highlights the threat women start to represent for their male counterparts in the new social order of the early 20th century and, therefore, illustrates how controlling female bodies is a way for men to regain some of their lost power.

Depriving Women of Their Intimacy and Controlling Their Bodies

The opening scene of *Traffic in Souls*, showing Mary as the head of the family, brings straight evidence of the advent of the "New Woman" in American society. However, even if women were not yet full citizens able to vote, the reality of recent female empowerment represented a threat to traditional male hegemony. The New Woman was defined as "a self-governing subject" (Olund 485) who did not need her father's, brother's or fiancé's approval to act; she was entitled to do whatever she wanted and go wherever she felt like going. As employees in an elegant candy shop, Mary and her sister epitomize the emancipation of American women; they are self-sufficient and do not need a man's help to take care of the household. However, Mary is not against welcoming a decent man into her well-organized and independent life, and is happy to make room for her beloved Officer Burke (Olund 490–92). Women's lives had changed in modern American society: they could choose both their occupation and the man they wanted. Contrary to Mary and her sister, Trubus's daughter is portrayed as a passive subject, dependent on the decisions of her parents who select a husband for her; she appears as a living reminder of the former system of unquestioning patriarchal command that ruled the country and the world for centuries.

Like other white slave films, *Traffic in Souls* can be considered bold because it bravely reveals men's desire to downgrade the female body in order to punish women for their newly-gained authority (Matsubara 57). The white slave trade, even if some regard it more as an urban fantasy efficiently fueling people's hostility and hatred towards immigrants, and providing an opportunity to blame foreign newcomers for social evils (Matsubara 54–55), can also be seen as a way to break women, be they American or not. The movie pinpoints that there is something rather obscene in modern society. For Estelle Bayon, "[w]hat is obscene is not the unknown sex, but the desire to break the other physically and disrupt the victim's quietude"[2] (9, my translation). The attacks committed on young women, especially when Mary's sister is held captive in the brothel and ordered to strip and put on prostitute's garments instead of her regular city clothes, show that exhibiting the female body is a way to take control of her soul. If men can impose their will and do whatever they want with the body of women, then the latter may be lost forever and subjected to an insane influence, turning them into objects. Bayon has explained that "undressing a prisoner to torture him/her affects his/her mental image and his/her representation of himself or herself"[3] (9, my translation). This statement echoes Lorna's ordeal when she refuses to expose the intimacy of her naked body in front of the procuress and give up her true identity to put on the role and attire of a whore. However, Lorna's refusal is a way of increasing eroticism and arousing the spectator, as decency and partial unveiling are often considered to be a greater source of pleasure than full exhibition, which, as Bayon has suggested, destroys desire (10). As a result, by weeping frantically and fainting, Lorna manages to keep her clothes on and, in so doing, asserts her refusal of the tyranny of the underworld, which, in effect, represents the rule of male society.

The dehumanization of women by the crime syndicate is pregnant with meaning in the movie: women are not regarded as persons by their kidnappers but as goods they can sell and exchange. The Swedish girls on the liner are no more than disposable chattel for the criminals, while the young woman coming out of the train station is a prey surrounded by predators with animal instincts [20:07–33:38]. The candy shop scenes exemplify this desire to treat women as objects: the victims are observed through the candy shop window by their captors, as if they were themselves sweets one could purchase instead of human beings [7:41–8:00; 37:45–38:40]. It seems that men can practically purchase women in the candy shop, bring them wherever they want and store them in brothels so that other men can get a taste of them. *Traffic in Souls* testifies to the attempts at reification made on women by several corrupt men, like the cadets or the go-betweens, whereas others, for instance Officer Burke, acknowledge and respect the free spirit and empowerment of the New Woman, and vow to protect her—a perplexing illustration of the limitations of her power. Making women sex slaves is a way to annihilate their influence and deprive them of the social role they want to play. The title of the film, in particular, underlines the fact that you can totally break someone's spirit by transforming the body of the person into a consumer good and refusing to recognize him/her as a human being. Human trafficking condemns women to a great vulnerability and takes away any kind of power they could aspire to. The traffic of the body and souls of young immigrants and native-born Americans restores the domination of the masculine world over women who are treated as inferior beings, unable to take part in the new social order. The movie pays special attention to the struggle for power between the different genders and the consequences linked to the outcome of that battle.

The value of a movie like *Traffic in Souls* has been debated amongst scholars because two antithetical opinions about white slave films have appeared. On the one hand, critics like Shelley Stamp (1991) explain that this form of panic narrative of rescue and capture served to criticize women's increased presence in public places of both work and amusement (90–91). Stamp (1991) has also pointed out that the film obscures the actual economic facts and social consequences of prostitution, and avoids dealing with issues such as poverty or underemployment, arguing that "[d]ramatic rescues from cruel kidnappers are proposed, instead of the comprehensive social and economic reforms necessary" (92). For her, *Traffic in Souls* by no means encourages social reforms because it focuses more on the city's perils for young women by resorting to a detective narrative meant to entertain the spectator, rather than raise awareness of social evils. On the other hand, Miriam Hansen tends to present motion pictures as a real agent of change in modern society, inciting people to rethink their role in the community and analyze the world they are living in. She considers that silent era cinema addresses the spectator as a member of a social group rather than as a passive consumer, and encourages her/him to participate in a public event by watching the movie (84–85). Motion pictures also convey a sense of distraction, while mobilizing the spectator and transforming her/his perception of society. Moreover, Hansen states that early motion pictures serve as a potential public sphere, offering new spectators, and more precisely women, an opportunity to be socialized within a developing consumer society (114–17). Hansen's vision of cinema as a new way for women to participate in the economy and gain access to information about the country is, in my opinion, extremely relevant when considering reception. I believe that a film such as *Traffic in Souls* addressed the new female audience of the time and encouraged a critical reaction and a real involvement in social problems. I disagree with Stamp's refusal to see any meaningful political discourse in the film, because white slave films provided distractions and strong sensations to the spectator, putting the movie strictly under the category of Gunning's "cinema of attractions" (Staiger 12–15).

Entertainment requirements are not necessarily opposed to educational messages. The movie may well be a drama of deception in the big city, but it also offers some critical thinking about the fact that most men felt threatened by modern women and were ready to do anything to preserve whatever power they had. Beyond the rather scandalous story about white slavery, *Traffic in Souls* offers an insight into a real problematic issue that caught the attention of progressive reformers, local authorities and police forces, among others. It also depicts some of the growing tensions between the so-called genteel middle class and the working class that was too often held responsible for urban evils (Matsubara 55–56). And yet the film debunks that hackneyed vision of who the good and decent citizens really are by convicting Trubus, the "Man Higher Up." It is interesting to see that the movie also targets the existence of prostitution networks and the risks not only for morality, but also for hygiene, as, at the time, the U.S. began to portray itself as a superior nation in many fields, including ethics and cleanliness (Matsubara 63–65). If we follow this line of argument, then, degrading the bodies of women through prostitution and those of men through extramarital intercourse would endanger the souls of American citizens both female and male. The traffic affects not only the souls of women, but also those of men, thus the souls of the nation as a whole. Consequently, the spectator could understand the movie as a plea enjoining the U.S. to recover its moral grandeur through social and political intervention in order to stand irreproachable and embrace its new international leadership.

The public success of *Traffic in Souls* was absolutely tremendous; it played simultaneously at several theaters and generated huge profits. Its triumph was, no doubt, symptomatic of the audience's interest in this controversial issue;

as Shelley Stamp (1997) has remarked, it "tells us a great deal about the new role that socially conscious films were playing in urban culture" (352). However, the craze for vice films faded almost as soon as it had appeared, and they ended up spoofed or despised by both the movie profession and moviegoers. Nevertheless, the whole fuss around *Traffic in Souls* and other white slave trade movies "signaled the arrival of motion pictures as a major cultural force" in American metropolises (Stamp 1997, 361), and introduced the debate about the social role of silent films and the dual image of cinema as both a conscious agent of change (Jacobs 37) and, on the contrary, a reckless industry pursuing a profitable economic activity (Jowett and Linton 79; Bidaud 253). By labeling moving pictures as "business pure and simple, originated and conducted for profit," the 1915 Supreme Court ruling *Mutual Film Corp v. Industrial Commission of Ohio*, 236 U.S. 230, tended to reinforce the second view.

What *Traffic in Souls* actually stresses is the ambivalent nature of motion pictures of the time, as the blunt exposure of intimacy and sexuality was a way both to attract large audiences thanks to sensational and shocking elements designed to thrill people, and at the same time, to raise awareness about social problems in modern urban America. This type of early film is double-edged, because even if it made people more familiar with contemporary issues and served as a vigilant warning, it also nurtured the critical vision of anti-movie activists who represented cinema as an uncontrollably dangerous media, helping vice to circulate around the nation, perverting the mind of the population and, ultimately, provoking demands for a more radical instrument of censorship (Grieveson and Krämer 2004a, 140). Not everything could be shown on American screens, as the U.S, even at the dawn of the 20th century, remained a nation of traditional Puritans, despite its image as a champion of modernism.

Notes

1. The expression "white slavery" refers to forced prostitution, which was one of the main concerns during the Progressive Era. In the U.S., the 1910s saw a huge outpouring of "white slavery" material (articles, pamphlets, magazines, novels, plays, movies) denouncing the sexual dangers faced by young women and serving the moral crusade of lawmakers, journalists and moral reformers to eradicate coercive prostitution. These narratives, presenting women who had been captured and held against their will, were used to condemn commercialized vice and expressed concerns over the pace and direction of social transformation in modern urban America. They used sensational devices similar to the "mysteries and miseries of the city" or capture narrative genres (Donovan 1–2; Stange 76).

2. Original text: "Ce qui est obscène ce n'est pas le sexe méconnu mais la volonté de détruire l'autre à travers le corps et l'irruption dans la paix de la victime."

3. Original text: "mettre à nu un prisonnier pour le torturer agit sur son image mentale et sa représentation de lui-même."

Works Cited

Bayon, Estelle. 2007. *Le Cinéma obscène*. Paris: L'Harmattan.
Bidaud, Anne-Marie. 1978. "Le Cinéma américain ou les ambiguïtés idéologiques d'un medium de masse." *RFEA* 6 (October): 251–68.
Brewster, Ben. 2004. "*Traffic in Souls* (1913): An Experiment in Feature Length Narrative Construction." *The Silent Cinema Reader*. Eds. Lee Grieveson and Peter Krämer. London: Routledge. 226–41.
Chevrier, Jean-François. 2001. "Walker Evans et la question du sujet." *Communications 71*: 63–103. http://www.persee.fr/web/revues/home/prescript/article/comm_0588-8018_2001_num_71_1_2080. Retrieved on 20/12/2013.
Donovan, Brian. 2005. *White Slave Crusades: Race, Gender, and Anti-vice Activism, 1887–1917*. Urbana: University of Illinois Press.
Grieveson, Lee. 2004. *Policing Cinema: Movies and Censorship in Early-Twentieth-Century America*. Berkeley: University of California Press.
Grieveson, Lee and Peter Krämer. 2004. "Cinema and Reform." *The Silent Cinema Reader*. Eds. Lee Grieveson and Peter Krämer. London, New York: Routledge. 135–44.
_____. 2004b. "Feature Films and Cinema Programmes." *The Silent Cinema Reader*. Eds. Lee Grieveson and Peter Krämer. London: Routledge. 187–96.
Gunning, Tom. 2004. "The Cinema of Attractions." *The Silent Cinema Reader*. Eds. Lee Grieveson and Paul Krämer. London: Routledge.
Hansen, Miriam. 1991. *Babel and Babylon: Spectatorship in American Silent Film*. Cambridge, MA: Harvard University Press.
Jacobs, Lewis. 1939. *The Rise of American Film*. New York: Harcourt Brace. http://www.archive.org/details/riceoftheamerica000739mbp. Retrieved on 8/12/2013.
Jowett, Garth. 1976. *Film: The Democratic Art: Social History of American Film*. Boston: Little Brown and Company.
Jowett, Garth and James Linton. 1980. *Movies as Mass Communication*. New York: Sage.
Lindsay, Vachel. 1916 [1922]. *The Art of Motion Pictures*. New York: Macmillan. http://www.archive.org/stream/cu31924074466933#page/n55/mode/2up. Retrieved on 10/22/2013.
Matsubara, Hiroyuki. 2006. "The 1910s Anti-Prostitution Movement and the Transformation of American Political Culture." *The Japanese Journal of American Studies* 17: 53–69.
Musser, Charles. 2004. "The May Irwin Kiss: Performance and the Beginnings of Cinema." *Visual Delights Two: Exhibition and Reception*. Eds. Vanessa Toulmin and Simon Popple. New Barnet, UK: John Libbey. 97–115.
_____. 2005. "A Cornucopia of Images: Comparison and Judgment across Theater, Films and the Visual Arts during the Late Nineteenth Century." *Moving Pictures: American Art and Early Film, 1880–1910*. Eds. Nancy Mowll Mathews and Charles Musser. Manchester, VT: Hudson Hills Press. 5–38.
Olund, Eric. 2009. "*Traffic in Souls*: The 'New Woman,' Whiteness and Mobile Self-Possession." *Cultural Geographies* 16.4: 485–504.
Rosenbloom, Nancy J. 1987. "Between Reform and Regulation: The Struggle Over Film Censorship." *Film History* 1.4: 307–25.
Slattery, Tom. 2001. *Immodest Proposals: Through the Pornographic Looking Glass*. Bloomington, IN: iUniverse.
Sokalski, J.A. 2005. "Performed Affection: The Spectacle of Kissing on Stage and Screen." *Allegories of Communication: Intermedial Concerns from Cinema to the Digital*. Eds. John Fullerton and Jan Olsson. New Barnet, UK: John Libbey. 299–320.
Staiger, Janet. 2000. *Perverse Spectators: The Practices of Film Reception*. New York: New York University Press.

Stamp, Shelley. 1991. "Wages and Sin: *Traffic in Souls* and the White Slavery Scare." *Persistence of Vision* 9: 90–102.
_____. 1997. "'Oil upon the Flames of Vice': The Battle over White Slave Films in New York." *Film History* 9.4: 351–64.
_____. 1999. "Moral Coercion, or the Board of Censorship Ponders the Vice Question." *Controlling Hollywood: Censorship and Regulation in the Studio Era*. Ed. Matthew Bernstein. New Brunswick, NJ: Rutgers University Press. 41–58.
Stange, Margit. 2002. *Personal Property: Wives, White Slaves, and the Market in Women*. Baltimore: Johns Hopkins University Press.

Fictions of Intimacy and the Intimacy of Fiction
"Going into people's houses" and the Remediation of 1920s Film Reception

Fabrice Lyczba

This essay proposes to situate intimacy, both the intimacy of the home and the intimacy of the body, at the heart of the encounter of 1920s audiences with cinema, via the examination of a few examples of the remediation of cinema's reception through the domestic media of radio and print. It has become fairly common in film studies today to look at cinema as a blurred, cross-border media phenomenon: as a medium deploying its fictions through several media (Jenkins 2006), scattered among a multiplicity of reception sites—the movie house, the home, but also any place where one can use a small-screen multimedia player—raising issues about the very nature of the media identity of cinema (Elsaesser 1998; Manovich 2001; Gaudreault 2008). If, as Philippe Marion has singularly proposed, each medium has "a specific 'imaginary'" ("Narratologie médiatique" 79), one of the issues of film studies today, and of cinema audience and reception studies more particularly, is to understand how such a constant crisscrossing of media borders may re-mediate cinema's imaginary. Remediation is a concept introduced by Bolter and Grusin in their 1999 breakthrough work to describe what happens when one media contains, deploys or expands on another. My analysis will focus on the paradoxical "double logic" of remediation (Bolter and Grusin 5–6)—on how one media's quest for "immediacy," which Bolter and Grusin use to designate the cultural desire "to erase all traces of mediation," "depends on hypermediacy" (6), that is, on the reliance on *other* multiple and non-transparent media.

In what follows, I take an archeological view of this question in film history by proposing to look at two examples of how 1920s American cinema explored remediation possibilities offered by emergent media (radio) or more established ones (print) that had, contrary to cinema, a decidedly *domestic* horizon of reception. I seek to understand how these two media were deployed to move film fictions *beyond* the reception sites and media-specific limits of cinema—then public, and often spectacular, in its main modes of reception— with the aim of making cinema an intimate and familiar object of reception. Thus, I contend that the use of other media to market films was not just good publicity practice—the age-old publicity impulse to "make some noise" by any means necessary (*Reel Journal*, 20 November 1926)—but impacted cinema's imaginary by allowing it to expand in a more intimate direction, by making it, so to speak, homebound. Cinema, thanks to radio and print ads, managed to project itself not just as public event, but also as private, domestic occurrence—not just as glamorous, but also as decidedly down-to-earth. The remediation of cinema through radio and print allowed audiences of the 1920s to navigate across reception spaces and reconcile conflicting expectations of where film worlds could take them.

My investigation was inspired by a curious scene in a film meant as a vehicle for Harry Houdini: *Terror Island* (James Cruze, 1920). In the film, Houdini plays an inventor whom a friend hires to salvage treasure from sunken ships. For the benefit of his friend, the inventor demonstrates one of the advanced features of his new, secret submarine: a device he calls the "electric periscope," a wired display transmitting live images to a remote observer. An early example of remediation, this filmic representation of the emergent technology of the (soon-to-be-wireless) transmission of live sound and images—namely radio and television— seemed too intriguing to ignore. What, I wondered, could have been the nature of cinema's relationship with emerging media in the 1920s, at a time when both radio and print were helping to define the media landscape of the modern world? Though movie-going in the 1920s was a very loud, public affair (Hall 1961), did those technologies, with their decidedly domestic and private horizon, have any sort of influence on the reception of films at the time? Could a model (albeit a minority, and possibly failed, model) be constructed for a horizon of reception that, even in the 1920s, would have included the intimacy of the home?

The second jolt in this inquiry came from an article published in the *Los Angeles Times* of April 23, 1929, by Irving Thalberg, then MGM Vice-President, where he expressed his thoughts on the still on-going transition to sound in Hollywood productions:

> The great quality that made motion pictures a success is realism. One has a feeling of going into people's houses, of looking into their eyes and seeing their

thoughts, of gazing into their hearts and of understanding their emotions. Now voice has been added to pictures, making them just that much more intimate, more real.

Realism, domesticity and intimacy. One would not necessarily, offhand, associate this trio of concepts with Hollywood productions of the 1920s, with their oft-studied emphasis on spectacle to be consumed in the splendor of large movie palaces. Yet Thalberg is far from the only Hollywood producer at the time to claim this realistic horizon as the legitimate, ultimate objective of Hollywood productions. Indeed, by 1929, Hollywood already had a long history of yearning for *social* legitimacy by seeking recognition for the *artistic* achievements of its products thanks to an emphasis on *realism*. This is a trick that Hollywood may have simply borrowed from older literary and theatrical traditions in which "realism" had become, during the 19th century, the ultimate test of the artistic worth of all fictional endeavors—becoming, as Peter Brooks has noted, "the norm [of] what we expected fiction to be" (5). Even more intriguingly, in 1929, Thalberg was also channeling another part of the history of realism that fixed the intimacy of the home as a hallmark of a realist style, a history that stretched back, at least, to Alain-René Le Sage's *Le Diable boîteux* (1707) and the character of Asmodée, the Devil. In a well-known passage of this novella, the Devil takes the hero (and the reader) up to the top of the highest tower in the city of Madrid, then removes all the city's rooftops to reveal what is happening in the rooms thus exposed to view. "Seeing through the roofs and facades of the real to the private lives behind and beneath," an act that Peter Brooks (from whom I borrow this reference) uses as a starting point in his discussion of literary realism (3), is what Thalberg in 1929 suggested cinema did best. It is, indeed, on the part of Hollywood producers, a diabolical effort—or, as the reference to Houdini suggests, a *diabolically magical* effort—to try and conflate realism with domestic intimacy, an effort I would like to call Hollywood's *intimacy project*. It is this project and its possible consequences on *reception* that interest me here. Whether or not we follow Thalberg in the belief that watching a Hollywood film, albeit with sound, "is like watching life"—recently, Lea Jacobs (2008) has impressively argued that a drive towards more simplicity and less sentimentality could be detected in Hollywood films throughout the 1920s—I would like to propose that Thalberg's fantasy of realism should also be understood as a form of marketing discourse, and thus equally as a horizon of reception, so that invading the *intimacy of the home* could, perhaps, be analyzed as a long-term historical trend in the reception of Hollywood films, including in the ballyhoo of the 1920s.

My object here is not to repeat the excellent research already conducted on the history of "home movies"—the history of the projection of movies at home—as part of the history of non-public, alternative sites for movie consumption. Working back from our contemporary mode of film reception as an increasingly *domestic* reception, this research has come to focus notably on "home cinema" as a particularly pregnant site for film cultures. Indeed, as Ben Singer has argued, "efforts at home cinema [...] prefigure many of the ways in which visual media would ultimately be consumed in our society" (37), with Alexandra Schneider, more recently, reminding us that "the history of home viewing began not with television but with the film reels of the 1920s and 30s" (353). The findings of such research challenge us to posit the ontology of cinema as more than a public spectacle, that is, as a *private, intimate* phenomenon more often associated with the reception of television. For Peter Kramer (2003), indeed, a "televisual imagination" (16) could be shown to animate film history from, in fact, its very "beginnings" (13), most famously via the telephonoscope, which, according to Thomas Elsaesser, provides evidence that "the late nineteenth century did not expect the cinema [but] [...] rather devices of simultaneity and instantaneity" (47). What Donald Crafton has called cinema's "electric affinities" (26–27 and *passim*) further prove, for Haidee Wasson, the inscription of cinema within emerging notions of modernity and the automation of home appliances in the 1920s (2009, 4). Cinema should, she argues, be "insert[ed] into an earlier history of the entertainment industry's domestic agenda" (2009, 4), in the hope of understanding "the conditions in which we watched, discussed, thought about, and wrote about moving images" (2009 2). The history of home viewing of Hollywood films, thus, should be an integral part in a historically-grounded search for this elusive culture of media images in our daily life, this "common sense about the place of moving images in everyday life [...] generated not just in movie theaters but also just about everywhere else" (Wasson 2007, 220).

While vital in helping us study film reception as the dynamic, plural phenomenon that it has always been, such research, however, has failed so far to link public and non-public (or alternative) consumption of movies satisfactorily, continuing to confront both film cultures rather than look for their potential synergies. Haidee Wasson, for instance, while suggesting that the answer to "what cinema means" may have been generated in a multiplicity of spaces, including the space of the home, remains within a traditional dichotomy of public vs. private, theater vs. home, as private spaces of film consumption are understood to offer the chance to "wrest mass media from its threatening populist and commercial power" (2007, 221).[1] I would like to suggest that there is no such dichotomy, that the "populist" success of cinema also depended on its capacity to project itself onto a domestic horizon in order to engage with audiences. If one looks at the other media technologies that started emerging or expanding in the 1920s (namely, the wireless and the print media) and cinema's relation with these media, one is struck, in fact, less by their opposition than by a commonality of purpose. Beyond the technologies of public film exhibition, film worlds also circulated in print and on the radio in the 1920s. These media allowed film worlds to reach an extra-theatrical, domestic horizon of film reception that in fact *expanded* the commercial reach of cinema by proposing to engage with potential viewers everywhere and merge multiple reception spaces together: the theater, of course, but also the street, and indeed the home. In its reliance on multiple media to circulate its imaginary, cinema emerges as a paradoxical phenomenon, at the same time public and intimate, industrial and domestic, glamorous and familiar.

Numerous studies have thus shown how the arrival of radio as a medium of mass entertainment in the early 1920s was seen both as dangerous competition *and* as an opportunity for film distribution. Exhibitors tended to fear radio's impact on movie attendance, with quite a few blaming the attendance slump of the 1922–1923 season on the competition from the "radio euphoria of 1922" (Butsch 175) and on radio concerts that loomed large in the accusation that radio kept entertainment-hungry people at home. A June 1922 *Photoplay* editorial thus recognizes that as "the radio rage is sweeping the nation [...] this new competition has the picture barons worried a trifle," but the editorial quickly points out that such "concern is hardly justified," since "the theatre is 'some place to go.' We like to have our thrills and laughs with the crowd. The radio is relatively a solitary pastime" (48).

Yet this seeming opposition between, on the one hand, film as a public event and, on the other, radio as private and solitary, is immediately questioned by the next sentence, which evokes "dreamers [...] at work on the problem of sending pictures broadcast by radio. There is a thought for tomorrow!" In other words, the opposition between public and private is, here, more porous than we might expect. Radio Films, or the use of radio to transmit live sound accompaniment to several movie theaters at the same time (whether music, a lecture or even, in a 1925 Norma Shearer experiment, dialogue), an obvious cost-cutting device, has been studied elsewhere (notably by Donald Crafton), yet it should be noted that such uses of radio seem more a continuation of ongoing reception practices of the 1920s than a revolutionary technological break. In a bid to put radio to any profitable potential use, MGM even experimented in 1927 with what it emphatically, if optimistically, called "telemovies." First, for a showing of *Ben-Hur* (Fred Niblo et al., 1925) in November at the Pantages, in Salt Lake City, "an announcer broadcast description of the picture as he viewed it from a box at the theatre. During this performance he also announced all subtitles as they were flashed on the screen" (*The Film Daily*,

11 November 1927, 11). Then, on December 20, 1927, for the opening of *Love* (Edmund Goulding and John Gilbert, 1927), a romantic vehicle for Greta Garbo and John Gilbert, at the Embassy theater in New York, famous radio announcer Ted Husing was on hand, delivering a running commentary on the film live from the theater. Only the massive arrival of sound films in 1928–1929 seems to have made "the idea of a movie 'announcer'—going back in concept to the narrators of nickelodeon days—[...] no longer [...] necessary" (Hilmes 79), and to have put a damper on such experiments (Fig. 6).

Yet beyond such curious and seemingly paradoxical experiments in turning silent films into radio plays, Hollywood's uses of radio for film distribution were so frequent and of such varied nature during the 1920s as to impose a reconsideration of what the industry was, in fact, looking for when using the emerging technology of radio jointly with the more established one of silent film projection. Despite technical limitations (notably in sound projection), other more successful efforts by theater managers to exploit the "radio craze" in the 1920s ranged from the utilization of radio as part of the on-stage show entertainment (for instance, at the McVickers theater, Chicago, according to the *Exhibitors' Herald* of January 23, 1924) to that of radio in order to broadcast concerts given by the theater orchestra, both extra concerts that were not part of the normal movie shows (on Sunday mornings, for instance) and the musical part of the film program itself, a tradition started by showman Roxy Rothapfel on November 19, 1922, with the Capitol Theatre Grand Orchestra, with Roxy describing the sets and costumes, and introducing the songs of pre-film entertainment (Hall 71–75).

Radio was also used for more obvious and, in this case, studio-controlled publicity purposes, for instance, to report on on-going Hollywood productions, either through a radio journalist ("Nat Rothstein will broadcast tonight over WPCH offering a graphic account of production of *Uncle Tom's Cabin*," *The Film Daily*, December 1, 1927) or on the progress of productions related by directors themselves ("Arrangements have been completed by W.W. Van Dyke, who sailed recently with Robert Flaherty for the South Seas [for the production of *White Shadows in the South Seas* (1928)], for nightly radio communication between a Culver City station and Station DAM at Tahiti," *The Film Daily* December 13, 1927). Lastly, following the 1925 recommendation of Harry Warner to have "[film] artists talk into the [radio] microphone and reach directly millions of people who have seen them on the screen, but never came in contact with them personally or heard their voices" (*The Film Daily*, April 3, 1925), United Artists in 1928 was still trying to exploit the fame of its stars by having Norma Talmadge, Charlie Chaplin, Douglas Fairbanks, D.W. Griffith, Lionel Barrymore and Dolores Del Rio come before the microphone live from the Fifth Avenue Playhouse in New York in a special broadcast of *The Dodge Brothers Hour*, for an expected audience of 50 million people (Crafton 44).

While some of these examples certainly bear out Michele Hilmes's conclusion that "the interest by the motion picture industry in experimenting with radio must be seen in the context of the industry's internal tension between producers and exhibitors" (82)—the United Artists broadcast, for instance, provoked the fury of exhibitors, as it took place during regular movie showtimes, 9 to 10 pm—they also reveal a surprising faith that there is *continuity* between the two media, and thus very little opposition. With hindsight, one may legitimately wonder whether choosing announcer Ted Husing, nicknamed "mile-a-minute Husing" for his pioneering quick-fire style of sports radio commentary, for an advertised "blow-by-blow" account of Garbo and Gilbert's steamy romance was entirely appropriate.[2] Yet I have found no such suggestion in contemporary accounts of the special screening/broadcast. Such a choice, in fact, shows that Husing was picked as a radio celebrity known to audiences around the country and for his radio identity, regardless of any potential stylistic conflict between his staccato reporting style and the more sedate and elevated tempo of the movie, and that it was this radio *media* identity which was somehow meant to fuse with the movie to create a "telemovie." Together, (silent) movies and radio, it would appear, formed a *third* medium (still to be invented: television) and existed (at least potentially) within a *media continuum* that even justified using a sports announcer for a romantic drama. The media identity of this continuum certainly has to do with the potential *intimacy* of the radio, a quality amply exploited, for instance, by "Roxy" Rothapfel in his own radio broadcasts of his Capitol theater shows with the on-the-air reading of letters from distant listeners and the immediate gratification of their wish for musical numbers performed by theater stars (Hall 75). Radio, contrary to the exoticism of film worlds, abolishes distance.

Thus, underlying Hollywood's and exhibitors' experiments with radio during the 1920s was clearly a search for an increased *illusion of presence* of film worlds, a quest for intimacy that would manage to reconcile what, at first, might seem opposite: the silent dignity of film stars and the proximity of their radio voices; distant, city, luxurious entertainment and the intimacy of the poorest of homes. By broadcasting movie worlds over the radio, such stunts suggest a *continuity between home and public theater space*, between intimate reality yet unmediated and public media worlds, making film worlds intimate, accessible and present in the home.

Apart from radio, which was still an emerging force for much of the 1920s, the other medium largely present in American homes at the time was print, notably in the form of fan and movie-themed magazines. Indeed, as several authors have already noted, fanzines are key texts to understand the interplay of cinema with contemporary cultural developments: the inscription of cinema within a broader consumption culture (Studlar 1996; Dixon 2003), within the context of rural development (Fuller 1996) or within competing notions of femininity (Studlar 1995; Morey 2002). Most research into the fan press has shown that, while fan magazines formed the core of film fan culture, they also allowed film imaginaries to branch out in surprising ways. Anne Morey, for instance, has noted how "a single issue [of a fan magazine] might contain articles that variously endorsed and criticized the modern girl," a sign that conflicted viewpoints about Hollywood glamour might appear throughout the pages the fan press (335). Adrienne McLean, in her survey of 1930s-1940s novelizations of films published in various fan magazines, has similarly been struck by "the number of different signifying systems [...] at work [...] in a typical two-page story spread" (6), and has demonstrated how the novelization of films through the pages of fan magazines often worked in ways "that seemed to exceed the capacity of the simple cause-and-effect narratives to explain" (6)—in other words, that the publication of film plots in novelized form before the release of films would often work against the plot-centric nature of Hollywood classicism. Fan magazines, it would appear, did not just follow Hollywood fashions, but shaped film spectatorship in ways that could conflict with the diktat of Hollywood classicism.

Thus, an analysis throughout the 1920s of the content of sample issues of *Photoplay Magazine*, "the most important" American fan magazine, according to Anthony Slide (383), reveals a systematic goal, pursued through a diverse range of magazine content, of offering what we could call a fiction of intimacy to its readers, often in conflict with the glamour of Hollywood worlds that other aspects of the magazine would put forward, and often displayed visually on the same pages. The July 1916 issue, for instance, contains many features that aim to take the reader/fan behind the scenes and position him or her as a Hollywood insider. This is evident in the "Beauty and Brain contest" (23), for instance, that plays on the sense that beauty will lead to Hollywood, or in the article quoting "three distinguished scenario chiefs" at Fine Arts, Famous Players and Vitagraph on how unsolicited scenarios need to be written to stand a chance of being accepted (79, 83). In other words, the transition from being part of the audience to becoming a Hollywood worker remains possible, maybe, as the ad on the back-cover suggests, just by drinking Coca-Cola like Mabel Normand. The proximity of Hollywood is further reinforced by features detailing how close film stars really are to their fans: Fannie Ward, waiting for a phone call from Cecil B. DeMille on the set of *The Cheat* (1915), talks about her house and her desire to go home every evening; Lillian Gish, though shown stepping into a luxury car, is ironically presented as "the poor working girl"; and Mabel Normand is shown "at home" (51–53), lounging in her pajamas, reading her copy of *Photoplay Magazine*, the magazine thus celebrating its penetration of American homes through reflexivity. Other features focus on educating the gaze, on taking readers behind the scenes of filmmaking and developing a critical understanding of film images, for instance how to decode such narrative stereotypes as "the crumpled note" or "our dear preparedness friend, the Gun in the Drawer" (76). In this July 1916 issue, serious reporting, such as the article on Herbert Brenon's efforts at fighting malaria while filming on location scenes for *A Daughter of the Gods* (1916) in Jamaica, contains, however, less information in this respect than fictional descriptions of Hollywood life, such as the opening of the serialized novel *The Glory Road* (1916), a story of a young budding actress kidnapped for two days while filming in the Los Angeles mountains. The story starts with a description, through the main actor's eyes, of a location shooting in the California hills, where the actor thinks he can see the California of seventy years ago before his very eyes:

> This was the picture, and there in the warm afternoon sunlight, fanned by the balmy breath of the Pacific, Romance had her way with the imagination. Other days nearer, perhaps, to the heart's desire seemed to live again! Then the "fade-out" began. One saw that every face was ghastly with yellow make-up; [....] that the California village at the water's edge was merely "backings" held by props [26].

Fiction though they may be, such novels contribute to educating the audience's gaze, as they linger on the gray zone where fiction and reality merge in Hollywood, thus foregrounding a key operation of Hollywood fictions.

The features I have underlined in this issue of *Photoplay Magazine* were common throughout the 1920s. The September 1927 issue, for instance, still plays on the sense of a proximity to film stars: Tom Mix declares after a long vacation that "there's no place like home" (33), while Terry Ramsaye continues his series of "intimate visits to the home of Famous Film Magnates" with the house of Joseph Kennedy (50–51, 102), giving the "favorite recipes of stars" (81). Behind-the-scenes information is provided in the form of a cartoon ("while the camera grinds" 84), of tidbits from the studios ("Gossip of all the studios"), or "Strange Yarns," a collection of strange anecdotes on film production (56–57), while the debunking of film hokum is provided by the column "Brickbats and Bouquets," where "the real critics, the fans, give their views."

To this consistent effort at constructing familiarity between fans/readers and film worlds should also be added the ads published in the margins of the magazine. The types of products advertised through the pages of *Photoplay* remain remarkably constant throughout the 1920s. Most ads deal quite specifically with the audience's intimate, private lives and domestic environment. A first series of ads aims to help readers transport modern entertainment into their homes: the Edison phonograph in 1916 or the Crossley radio in 1927 (Fig. 6); a piano in 1916 or a Bluescher saxophone in 1927; playing home billiards in 1916 or learning how to play jazz music in 1927. A second series of ads, dealing with health and beauty, demonstrate the oft-studied ideological nexus of youth and modernity that was a bedrock of both consumption culture and films in the 1920s (Cohen 2001), as they seem to promise familiarity with film worlds through the improvement of one's personal appearance: Palmolive soap, Vivaudou talcum, Colgate toothpaste or Pond's Two Creams, whether endorsed by stars or not—Anna Q. Nilsson wearing *Ben-Hur* perfume in 1927—are thus a natural fit with other pages of the magazine dwelling on the clothes, beauty or physical well-being of actors and actresses.

What is more surprising about this issue of *Photoplay* is how personal and intimate some of the issues raised by a third series of ads are. It is as if film worlds were offered a chance to project readers into fictions of intimacy that went beyond anything discussed in the movies themselves. Throughout the 1920s, underwear, whether male (BVD in 1916) or female (corsets by Gossard in 1927), were regularly advertised, along with books and "methods" discussing intimate issues like sex—sexology in *Photoplay*, July 1916, *Sexual Knowledge* (illustrated) in *Motion Picture Classic* of June 1920, and Elinor Glyn's *The Philosophy of Love* in *Photoplay* of February 1924. In some ads, intimate problems are discussed in frank terms: hair problems (dandruff, loss of hair), foot problems (bunions, corns), constipation, bad breath (with evocative ads showing how that problem can cost one's social position) or "woman's oldest hygienic problem" are all gleefully advertised alongside stories of Douglas Fairbanks's boundless energy or Garbo and Gilbert's kiss. These ads, and their inclusion in the pages of a mainstream fan magazine like *Photoplay*, suggest, again, a continuum between film fictions and the intimate lives of fans, as if the goal of the magazines and, by extension, of the films themselves and of film worlds, were to allow entry into joyful modernity and its world of endless self-improvement, a mission that fan magazines, through very personal advertisements, took, however, to very pragmatic, at times unglamorous, proportions. Thus, intimacy, ranging from domesticity to more embarrassing, bodily problems, emerges as a key element in the editorial policy of fan magazines, allowing potential transfers of fiction between film worlds and the fictions of advertisers. It is not just that you will be as well-dressed as Anna Q. Nilsson if you wear Olovnit garments and hosiery (*Photoplay*, September 1927), but that "you will

Fig. 6. An ad in the September 1927 *Photoplay* for radio in a film fanzine in which the new medium, though very bulky and visible, is shown to abolish all distance in an illustration of the "double logic" of remediation and immediacy achieved through opaque media (Media History Digital Library).

star in the same picture" as Mabel Normand (*Photoplay*, July 1916)—as if the only thing standing between the reader/fan and the world of film-inflected romance were, ultimately, hair tonic or cod liver oil. Ads for intimate products, when appearing in fanzines, bring film worlds, indirectly or directly, down to the most intimate level for the fans, thereby offering a fictional continuum, a mixed-up, mashed-up, imaginary universe where consumption meets film dreams to realize the fans' intimate projections of self-improvement.

What this material suggests is that, once one starts looking at the different media across which film imaginaries were deployed as early as the 1920s and through which they were encountered, however fleetingly, by audiences, two features become apparent. First, media technology does not determine the reception of cinema. As I have attempted to show, film imaginaries were deployed across competing, wildly different, and at times paradoxical media (as in the case of the "silent radio film") as early as the 1920s. The reception of cinema, thus, does not just concern the traditional sites of movie consumption (the film theater) and their requisite technologies (the projector, the presence of live music, etc.), but has *always* been a cross-media phenomenon, with different media, indeed, participating in the construction of cinema's imaginary all along, incorporating and borrowing from the imaginaries of other media. Second, cinema actively pursued technological, hypermedia solutions to complement the movie-going experience and allow film reception to branch out in directions clearly opposed to the majority model of public movie-going experience, a model long accepted to represent the experience of cinema until, that is, the gradual replacement of the public screen with private modes of film consumption that are now ubiquitous. Indeed, by utilizing other emergent media technologies of print and radio to help circulate its imaginary, the film industry of the 1920s showed a latent desire to imagine film reception as a private, domestic and intimate moment—a dream arguably unfulfilled for most of Hollywood's history in its actual reception conditions, though certainly activated by audiences that have never stopped taking Hollywood stars and worlds *home* with them. By the 1920s, cinema had dreamed itself as a particular kind of magical "electric periscope" deployed, as in the 1929 version of Irving Thalberg's dream, to invade audiences' domestic intimate spheres, even if it had to rely on other media to do so.

In a post on his research blog *Confessions of an Aca/Fan* entitled "*District 9* (Part One): Can a Bench Be a Transmedia Extension?" (2009), Henry Jenkins, tracking transmedia convergence into our present media-saturated lives, argued for the possibility that bench advertising in Los Angeles for the release of *District 9* (Neill Blomkamp, 2009) should, in effect, be considered as an extension of filmic story-telling by other means, noting that the message on the bench situated audiences "emotionally and intellectually inside the fiction" (notably in reference to America's history of segregated public spaces). In 1924, Mr. Rosenthal, theater manager of the Strand in Waterbury, Connecticut, wrote to *The Exhibitors' Herald* to offer his latest stunt as an example of good, sound exhibition policy: for the release of *The Humming Bird* (Sidney Olcott, 1924), a star vehicle for Gloria Swanson in which she plays a Paris street urchin who ends up decorated for her bravery during World War I, Rosenthal arranged a tie-in with a local shop selling Hummingbird products, in this case, stockings. It is not the practice of the tie-in that the *Herald* wished to point out to its readers as a novelty, nor the fact that the Strand manager had rather unimaginatively used the title of the film as an excuse for a campaign with a product of the same name (but with no link whatsoever to the story).[3] What caught the attention of this trade publication was, rather, the degree of possible fusion of the worlds of the cinema and domestic consumerism: for a short time, the theater lobby, decorated with the products of the shop, was turned into an actual window display full of stockings. Rosenthal would not have called it thus at the time, but his effort, in the light of the available documentation linking film worlds with intimate worlds of audiences and fans, seems to me to participate in this remediation of the reception space of Hollywood films in the 1920s, helping to situate audiences "inside the fiction," inside a space where fiction and reality may meet at intimate, private, and secret junctures. As Phil Wickham has argued (2010), the future of reception studies lies, in part, in the study of such ephemeral marginalia of film culture as experiments in silent film radio broadcasts, fictional accounts of contemporary Hollywood life or ads for intimate body problems running alongside reports on stars, film production and Hollywood life, in an effort to understand what cinema meant and how its imaginary may have circulated. If a bench can today tell a story, what stories could a pair of stockings have told audiences in the 1920s?

NOTES

1. See Miriam Hansen's "Early Cinema" for a similar distinction.
2. Unfortunate, but not unprecedented. This use of a radio commentator echoes the widespread use of live presenters during film exhibition in early cinema—and well into the 1920s for ethnic audiences. In 1908, for instance, "twelve of the twenty-one rounds in the Gans-Nelson fight were shown at Hammerstein's in New York, with the accompanying commentary of a live, professional referee," as Gwendolyn Waltz notes in her Ph.D. dissertation (4). See also *Show Biz* by Green and Laurie (55).
3. A tie-in campaign with hosiery products, on the other hand, may make more sense as a remediation of the image of the star of the film, Gloria Swanson, long identified with modern feminine fashions thanks to the Cecil B. DeMille features *Don't Change Your Husband* (1999), *Male and Female* (1919) and *The Affairs of Anatol* (1921).

Works Cited

Altman, Rick. 2004. *Silent Film Sound*. New York: Columbia University Press.
Bolter, Jay David, and Richard Grusin. 1999. *Remediation: Understanding New Media*. Cambridge: MIT Press.
Brooks, Peter. 2005. *Realist Vision*. New Haven and London: Yale University Press.
Butsch, Richard. 2000. *The Making of American Audiences: From Stage to Television, 1750–1990*. Cambridge: Cambridge University Press.
Cohen, Paula Marantz. 2001. *Silent Film and the Triumph of the American Myth*. New York: Oxford University Press.
Crafton, Donald. 1997. *The Talkies: American Cinema's Transition to Sound, 1926–1931*. New York: Charles Scriber's Sons.
Dixon, Simon. 2003. "Ambiguous Ecologies: Stardom's Domestic Mise-en-Scène." *Cinema Journal* 42.2: 81–101.
Elsaesser, Thomas. 1998. "Louis Lumière—the Cinema's First Virtualist?" *Cinema Futures: Cain, Abel or Cable?* Eds. Thomas Elsaesser and Kay Hoffmann. Amsterdam: Amsterdam University Press. 45–61.
Fuller, Kathryn H. 1996 [2001]. *At the Picture Show: Small-Town Audiences and the Creation of Movie Fan Culture*. Charlottesville: University of Virginia Press.
Gaudreault, André. 2008. *Cinéma et attraction: Pour une nouvelle histoire du cinématographe*. Paris: CNRS Éditions.
Green, Abel, and Joe Laurie, Jr. 1951. *Show Biz: From Vaude to Video*. New York: Henry Holt.
Hall, Ben M. 1961. *The Best Remaining Seats: The Story of the Golden Age of the Movie Palace*. New York: Bramhall House.
Hansen, Miriam. 1995. "Early Cinema, Late Cinema: Transformations of the Public Sphere." *Viewing Positions: Ways of Seeing Film*. Ed. Linda Williams. New Brunswick: Rutgers University Press. 134–54.
Hastie, Amelie. 2006. "The Miscellany of Film History." *Film History* 18.2: 222–30.
Hilmes, Michele. 1986. "Hollywood and Broadcasting: From Radio to Cable." PhD, Department of Cinema Studies. New York University.
Jacobs, Lea. 2008. *The Decline of Sentiment: American Film in the 1920s*. Berkeley: University of California Press.
Jenkins, Henry. 2006. *Convergence Culture: Where Old and New Media Collide*. New York: New York University Press.
———. 2009. "*District 9* (Part One): Can a Bench Be a Transmedia Extension?" *Confessions of an Aca/Fan* (Sept.). http://henryjenkins.org/2009/08/disctrict_9.html. Retrieved on 9/3/2012.
———. 2011. "Transmedia 202: Further Reflections." *Confessions of an Aca/Fan* (Aug. 2011). http://henryjenkins.org/2011/08/defining_transmedia_further_re.html. Retrieved on 6/27/2012.
Klenotic, Jeffrey F. 2007. "'Four Hours of Hootin' and Hollerin'': Moviegoing and Every Life Outside the Movie Palace." *Going to The Movies: The Social Experience of Hollywood Cinema*. Eds. Richard Maltby, Melvyn Stokes and Robert C. Allen. Exeter: University of Exeter Press. 130–55.
Kramer, Peter. 2003. "The Lure of the Big Picture: Film, Television and Hollywood." *Big Picture/Small Screen: The Relations Between Film and Television*. Eds. John Hill and Martin McLoone. Luton: University of Luton Press. 9–46.
Manovich, Lev. 2001. *The Language of New Media*. Cambridge: MIT Press.
Marion, Philippe. 1997. "Narratologie médiatique et médiagénie des récits." *Recherches en communication* 7: 61–87.
McLean, Adrienne L. 2003. "'New Films in Story Form': Movie Story Magazines and Spectatorship." *Cinema Journal* 42.3 (Spring): 3–26.

Morey, Anne. 2002. "'So Real as to Seem Like Life Itself': The *Photoplay* Fiction of Adela Rogers St. Johns." *A Feminist Reader in Early Cinema*. Eds. Jennifer M. Bean and Negra Diane. Durham: Duke University Press. 333–46.

Schneider, Alexandra. 2007. "Time Travel with Pathé Baby: The Small-Gauge Film Collection as Historical Archive." *Film History* 19.4: 353–60.

Singer, Ben. 1998. "Early Home Cinema and the Edison Home Projecting Kinetoscope." *Film History* 2.1: 37–69.

Slide, Anthony, ed. 1985. *International Film, Radio, and Television Journals*. Westport, CT: Greenwood Press.

Studlar, Gaylyn. 1995. "'Out Salomeing Salome': Dance, The New Woman, and Fan Magazine Orientalism." *Michigan Quarterly Review* 34.4: 487.

_____. 1996. "The Perils of Pleasure? Fan Magazine Discourse as Women's Commodified Culture in the 1920s." *Silent Film*. Ed. Abel Richard. New Brunswick: Rutgers University Press. 263–99.

Thalberg, Irvin. 1929. *Los Angeles Times*, 23 April, C6.

Waltz, Gwendolyn. 1991. "Projection and Performance: Early Multi-Media in the American Theatre." Ph.D., Drama, Tufts University.

Wasson, Haidee. 2007. "The Reel of the Month Club: 16mm Projectors, Home Theaters and Film Libraries in the 1920s." *Going to The Movies*. Eds. Richard Maltby, Melvyn Stokes, and Robert C. Allen. Exeter: University of Exeter Press. 217–35.

_____. 2009. "Electric Homes! Automatic Movies! Efficient Entertainment!: 16mm and Cinema's Domestication in the 1920s." *Cinema Journal* 48.4: 1–21.

Wickham, Phil. 2010. "Scrapbooks, Soap Dishes and Screen Dreams: Ephemera, Everyday Life and Cinema History." *New Review of Film and Television Studies* 8.3: 315–30.

The Impossible Sex Life of Couples in the Screwball Comedy

GRÉGOIRE HALBOUT

Intimacy, Hollywood and the Screwball Comedy

Can intimacy, or at least the representation of intimacy, serve a political agenda? This may be what the filming of private life in classical Hollywood productions managed to achieve under the Hays Code in the 1930s, when screwball comedies became one of the main comedy subgenres, thriving from 1934 to approximately 1943. Screwball comedies focus on romantic couples and their conversations about love and sex. These "conversations," as Cavell has shown, are expressed in a specific style, combining slapstick comedy and verbal sophistication based on witty dialogues (18–19). In this case, defining the genre in formal terms is not an easy task, since comedy is, by definition, an indeterminate and unstable genre, as opposed to the Western or the musical. Thus, at first glance, screwball comedy is mainly characterized by its particular style and inflection. However, its unique focus on couples (married or not), the ongoing battle of the sexes, and the overall obsession with reciprocal rights when it comes to married life help to identify the social function of this subgenre of comedy and deduce its generic identity.

The underlying identity of the films was not derived solely from aspects within the films themselves, but was also influenced by the strict censorship laws that affected the underlying message each film could depict. That is to say, these stories about sexual happiness and mutual satisfaction in marriage were box office hits at a time when Hollywood movies were severely ruled by the Provisions of the Production Code, enforced by a zealous and obsessive Production Code Administration, i.e., the "Hays Office." Under its Particular Applications, the Code stipulated that "the sanctity of the institution of marriage and the home shall be upheld" (paragraph 2: "Sex"). Surely, it is no accident that the first screwball films were released in 1934, the year the Production Code was reinforced by the studios, as a self-protecting measure against the increasing number of boycotts across the country, often called for by the Catholic Church. The representation of intimacy swept into film scripts just when censorship hit the *talkies*. Thus, addressing the intimacy of Hollywood cinema in the classical era means questioning how censorship or self-regulation influenced screen representations of intimacy, particularly where screwball comedies are concerned.

For the last twenty-five years, studies of Hollywood have been revisiting censorship as a key element in the institutional context of the American movie industry. In the 1980s, film scholars (Bordwell, Staiger and Thomson 1985; Schatz 1988) started to look differently at Hollywood, now considering it more as an industry and a system, with its specific modes of production. This accounts for the importance of censorship in the studio system approach, as opposed to auteur theory. Intimacy on the screen is intrinsically linked to a subtle compromise between the expectations of public opinion and a particular institutional context in 1930s Hollywood. Considered in terms of reception, mainstream movies have always been included in a general conversation with their audience. From the time talking pictures became the number one medium (ahead of radio) in the 1930s and the 1940s, Hollywood cinema was in a position of dialogue with movie-goers. It never was a "top to bottom" creative process, but a constant compromise between filmmaking and the audience's expectations (Handel 3–11). The question was, therefore, how to set up a proper dialogue between the audience, which was now identified as the rising middle class, and the movie industry. This conversation focused on personal life (the private sphere) and how to manage amorous feelings together with marriage as a key social structure. Screwball comedy took part in this political and cultural debate by presenting scripts that reflected the public discourse of movie-goers, pertaining to their wedded and private life. The three main themes of this public discourse were sex, equal status and divorce. This is the reason why intimacy and film genre are so closely related in classical Hollywood screwball comedy, a genre meant to represent a new understanding of marital status and sex in order to meet the expectations of modern society.

Screwball plots deal with nothing but intimacy: "cute meetings" and marriage proposals, brides eloping on their wedding days, unfaithful husbands, spouses leaving one another because of sexual dissatisfaction and miraculously returning a few years later, husbands pretending to be insane, dressing up like a woman to win their wives back or even considering bigamy as an option, to mention only a few. In a genre that deals mainly with matrimonial issues, the comedy largely relies on intimate matters. So from a filmographic and political perspective, how do private matters and aspirations become public, in the boy-meets-girl, the "Why don't we make love anymore?," the "Why don't we make love just right now?" or the "Let's remarry" scenarios?

My analysis of how the representation of intimacy is consubstantial to classical Hollywood comedy involves a threefold approach. First, it is necessary to give an account of the fierce ideological battle between liberal reformers and conservatives in the 1930s, and how it led to a coded representation of desire, sex and married life. This roundabout discourse went public, so to speak, through the mainstream theatrical releases of these films, thus raising the question of intimacy versus publicity. I will then argue that screwball comedies endorse, to this end, a social function and stand, in the words of Thomas Schatz, as "a way of cultural collective expression" (1981, 12–13).

Happy Sex and Marriage vs. The World of the Censors

With talking pictures upgraded to include more sophisticated content, middle-class individuals now a fundamental economic and social component, and theatrical attendance down by 50 percent because of the Depression, economic issues turned into a major ideological confrontation. To prevent business decline and avoid bankruptcy, Hollywood producers came up with tough, sexy and shocking stories that were immediately successful. Movies like *Hot Stuff* (Mervyn LeRoy, 1929), *Dishonored* (Josef von Sternberg, 1931), *A Free Soul* (Clarence Brown, 1931), *Night Nurse* (William Wellman, 1931) and *Tarnished Lady* (George Cukor, 1931) were meant to attract audiences and keep shareholders happy. These "preCode movies" were based on stories dealing with illicit love, adultery, crime, gangsters and more. The scheme was highly successful until 1933, when Hollywood had to face a countrywide opposition led by religious groups and the Legion of Decency, as well as ideological and social groups such as women's clubs, and politicians from various allegiances, and by federal and state governments.

Because talkies had become such a powerful medium, it was generally agreed that the content of films needed to be cleansed and controlled. Interestingly enough, Eleanor Roosevelt herself welcomed the new Hollywood regulations in her first radio broadcast in 1934:

> The matter of moving pictures is very important to the whole country. I am extremely happy the film industry has appointed a censor within its own ranks.

Mr. Joseph Breen, assistant to Will H. Hays, will act as censor in their ranks. It has long been a question of great interest to women's organizations, particularly of course, because of the fact that moving pictures are so popular with children. [...] This new announcement should do much to make these organizations feel that the film industry as a whole desires to cooperate and use its tremendous power for the improvement of the country.[1]

In doing so, Hollywood subscribed to an ideological scheme: the building of a moralistic and social vision of America. Struggling with definitions of cinema ranging from "entertainment" (that ought to be "clean") and "art," the Code writers, in the Reasons Supporting Preamble of Code, stated that "motion pictures are very important as ART" and immediately related cinema with the world of emotions and intimacy: "Though a new art [...], it has the same object as the other arts, the presentation of human thoughts, emotion [...], in terms of an appeal to the soul through the senses. [...] Art enters intimately into the lives of human beings."

Owing to the purportedly dangerous consequences on the audience's minds, any representation of intimacy—including cuddling, kisses, sexual intercourse and even suggestive clothing—was banned by the Code, which cited a surprising blend of themes and motifs: "sin," "evil," "scenes of passion," "lust," "the effect of nudity or semi-nudity upon the normal man or woman," and "impure love [that] must not be detailed in method or manner." It was the elite's conviction that the audience would not have enough free will to resist the lure of this "imitation of life." Therein lies the paradox of the Hollywood industry: censoring themselves in order not to be censored by any official board. On the one hand, the Hollywood industry was considered by the New Deal administration (National Industry Recovery Act) as an economic laboratory and a partner on the grounds of its vertical integration and best business practices, while on the other, it was subject to suspicion and put under strict observation.

At the same time, a vast public discussion on marriage had been going on since the 1890s in "Advice Literature," as a consequence of a drastic change in private habits (Seidman 65–91). In fact, by the time censors and conservative groups started to focus on the contents of films, American society had already undergone a profound evolution. The number of employed married white women increased by 300 percent between 1900 and 1940, and women represented 50 percent of the professional work force by 1930. More specifically, by 1920, 50 percent of college-educated women chose not to marry (versus 10 percent for the national average). The first Kinsey report published in 1953 revealed that 14 percent of women born after 1900 had premarital sex, which suggested an uncoupling of sex and marriage, not to speak of the use of contraceptives (92 percent of men and 87 percent of women in 1932). "Advice manuals," providing guidance for better sex in marriage and improved marital relationships, reflected this evolution in private life. These best-selling handbooks (which usually sold over one million copies) sought to redefine marriage by reconsidering the importance of sex: a happy marriage was based on sex, and sex education needed to become a public responsibility, and one that was openly discussed. Liberal reformers had their say in this and did their best to enhance and give support to social progress. Alice Stockham in *Karezza* (1896), Ben Lindsey in *The Companionate Marriage* (1927), Theodore Van de Velde in *Ideal Marriage* (1930), and newspaper-syndicated columnists like Dorothy Dix endeavored to spread this new approach to private life.

So how was a muzzled medium like cinema to account for a major social turnaround and come up with an "acceptable" representation of modern life at a time when these issues were becoming highly publicized? And how did censorship influence scripts and filmmaking in key scenes dealing with intimacy?

The Representation of Attraction, Desire and Sex

Hollywood studios kept in mind that sex and love themes had been successful in the early 1930s. Only now, things had to be said in a different way. If romantic comedy was to become the new winning formula, it had to comply with censorship affecting language, bodies and the representation of sexuality. These institutional limitations generated narrative techniques that allowed the intimacy of the couple to be disguised and represented as marital familiarity. The only way to achieve this was to create a very elaborate form of "indirect discourse."

Screwball comedy could be defined as the art of innuendo. It uses puns and gags as a specific cinematic language. Critics and scholars often mention the "bone" sequence in *Bringing Up Baby* (Hawks, 1938). The whole movie metaphorically revolves around a lost bone and an empty box. In this woman-chases-man story, the bold young heiress is pestering a somewhat uptight scientist more concerned about his future museum and its brontosaurus skeleton than courting his fiancée. The climax of the bone and box plot comes when the partners are desperately looking for a stolen intercostal clavicle apparently taken by the dog from the box it was mailed in. It offers a delightful excuse to express the sexual intensity of the characters' relationship and mutual frustration. The word "bone" is uttered twenty times throughout the sequences located in Connecticut, and not less than ten times within the central sequence dedicated to the bone hunt [36:11–48:43]. David's "precious bone" was in a box. Susan opened the box, played with the bone and put it back. Then the dog stole the bone. Deprived of his bone, David is upset; he yells at Susan who keeps claiming she put it back in the box. Through such repetition, the scene appears highly provocative, and there is no doubt as to the *double entendre* based on the slang connotation of these words: *bone* (penis) and *box* (vagina). The sexual subtext in the series of scenes builds up tension and prepares the ground for the final running gag when David and Susan chase the dog to have him show them where he buried the bone. Significantly, the narratives of classical Hollywood comedies frequently include a series of symbolic objects that are touched and manipulated by the romantic pair. For example, in *The Good Fairy* (Wyler, 1935), the lawyer and mentor shows his "benefactor" a cherished pencil, asking her to touch and feel how its head is well and efficiently sharpened [45:33]; Dr. Sporum says to Luisa: "Glorious! Like a needle! Feel! Did you ever see such a point?" They sharpen pencils together, and the intensity of their privacy comes forth in this dubious (and symbolically phallic) activity.

The efficacy of these instances of word play is often enhanced by elliptical editing. This is notably the case in the dining car scene in *The Palm Beach Story* (Sturges, 1942) [44:00–44:40]. Gerry has run away from her husband and boarded a train to Florida with a view to finding a millionaire. During the eventful first part of the train ride, the gold-digger loses her clothes, but manages to meet a rich young man. When she has to show up the following morning for breakfast, she imaginatively arranges an outfit with pajamas, sheets and towels. In this scene, the viewer never really knows what is going on. Gerry enters the restaurant car with a haughty expression. While she moves towards her new (boy)friend offscreen, she is filmed in a backward tracking shot. In the background, another gentleman sitting at a table sticks his neck out with bulging eyes, looking at Gerry's buttocks. The audience still sees nothing and cannot make out the look on this man's face. When Gerry is about to sit at the table, there is a cut to a closeup of her buttocks wrapped in a towel and one can read "Pullman." She has improvised a skirt with a towel taken from the sleeping car. The pun here is salacious and provocative. It emphasizes the purpose and narrative status of this lady who is looking for big money, evoking expressions such as "pullman," "pull a man" or "pull me." This visual and textual double entendre relies on an interesting visual construction, starting with the use of the offscreen to hide the object of curiosity (the "labeled" bottom), until the final revelation on the branded towel. In accordance with the momentum building gag technique of slapstick in silent cinema, Preston Sturges appeals to the audience's intelligence to add it all up and figure out the real meaning of the scene and the gag. It is a way of involving the audience in the forbidden representation. Hiding the offensive image before showing a pun on a lady's buttocks ends up being even more provocative due to the shared connivance, thereby establishing an intimate, though highly coded relationship between the viewer and the film.

More generally, finding ways to suggest sexual intercourse was a necessity for any representation of love and intimacy. It implied challenges in screenwriting and camerawork, and possible trouble with the Hays Office, since neither nudity nor sexual relationships—be it "pure" or "impure," "licit" or "illicit" love—were acceptable. Arguing and fighting to suggest sexual tension and attraction, feeling hungry and being vocal about it, were not enough to express desire and its satisfaction. That's what *The Palm Beach Story*, with its sexually happy couple that breaks up because the wife wants more money, is about. The only way for the husband (Tom) to retrieve his wife (Gerry) is to have her back in the name of wonderful sex, even if "this is going to cost us 200,000 dollars," the price Gerry's millionaire suitor is willing to invest in her current husband's airport project in order to marry her. For such pivotal scenes, it is mandatory to steer narration toward other grounds where sexual intercourse must be filmed in a metaphorical or metonymical manner. Matrimonial intimacy is represented in a suggestive way, so that it seems like mere conjugal familiarity. The argument is built on two symmetrical scenes: the first occurs in New York the day before Gerry runs away [18:10–20:05], the second in Florida where Tom has managed to track down his wife [73:44–78:48]. Both scenes deal with a dress that cannot be unzipped. In the second scene, Tom is put up in a separate suite. After dinner, her new suitor is singing with a band outside her room window. Trapped in a dress she cannot unzip, Gerry has to ask Tom to help her. Obviously, only her husband would hold the key to open this symbolic entrance to his wife's body. She has to sit on his lap, so that he can maneuver more easily, and it all ends in a kiss and a very telling fade-out. Filming Gerry struggling in her dress, as if it were a sort of elegant peepshow, has prepared viewers for what's to come. Her evening gown both hides and displays the details of her anatomy; she is filmed in a medium closeup that underlines her bosom, the high-key lighting making her skin glow under the transparent fabric covering her shoulders and upper chest. This sets the tone before showing serious action. The audience is able to interpret this as a sex scene because they mentally refer to the previous similar scene that took place at the beginning. Again, connivance between narration and viewers is established by appealing to their intelligence and their ability to link the two scenes together. The zipper has become a metonymy of sexual foreplay and imminent intimate intercourse. This masterpiece of "adroit indirection," which the Production Code Administration would call duplicitous narration, nonetheless requires a final punctuation mark: the usage of the fade-out/fade-in that closes on the embraced couple and opens up on a canary singing in its cage in the morning sunlight, both an understatement and a metaphor for the happy outcome of the previous scene.

From a textual perspective, the encoded representation of intimacy in screwball comedies, easily decoded by a savvy audience, helps define a film genre with its "particular cinematographic codes" (Metz 49–52). Understatements, puns, visual metaphors, symbolic objects, recurring editing techniques and the use of gags—all create a world of familiarity and a common style that not only define the genre aesthetically, but also provide the audience with convenient mental landmarks. As Rick Altman has argued, "the interpretation of generic films depends directly on the audience's generic expectations," based on "predictable development" (13–22). With the creation of this specific discourse, the Hollywood comedies of the 1930s managed to make private matters into successful film material. In this "remaking of intimacy," through "sexualizing love" and "eroticizing sex" (Seidman 65), mass fictions established intimacy as a public topic.

Happiness and Intimacy are Public Matters[2]

Over one hundred comedies were produced in ten years for some eighty-three million moviegoers and a weekly average of three movies per adult in the 1930s: something beyond the mere entertaining of the masses was going on. Clearly, Hollywood studios knew how to represent contemporary issues and manage audience expectations. *The Palm Beach Story*'s working title, *Is Marriage Necessary?*, was, not unexpectedly, rejected by the Hays Office. My contention is that portraying couples' issues and claims onscreen is, in effect, a social statement and appears as a visual and fictional translation of the public debate on modern marriage. Screwball comedies developed an elaborate plea for the defense of new aspirations, with husbands and wives demanding a marriage based on sexual contentment. In *The Philadelphia Story* (Cukor, 1940), Dexter Haven explicitly describes his ex-wife, Tracy Lord, as a frigid goddess. *The Awful Truth* (McCarey, 1937) opens on a matrimonial fight over the mutual right to extra-marital flings. The characters of *Libeled Lady* (Conway, 1936) and *Too Many Husbands* (Ruggles, 1940) even consider bigamy, deeming that society's laws are no longer in tune with their personal longings. Marriage is no longer a public affair to be ruled by public law. Screwball couples go down an alternative route based on a private set of regulations that precedes public rules, e.g., *Mr. and Mrs. Smith* (Hitchcock, 1941).

Simultaneously, these private matters need to be taken into the public sphere. Making intimacy public is the only way new aspirations can become official and acknowledged. Cavell has emphasized this recurrent motif of taking one's marriage to court, regardless of what is at stake: a dog's custody in *The Awful Truth* (1937) (242–43) or sex equality in *Adam's Rib* (Cukor, 1949) (194). Intimate issues need be fixed publicly. Even declarations of love must happen in public, preferably in front of a judge, e.g., *Midnight* (Leisen, 1939). But whatever the configuration of the conflict, divorce is recognized as a guarantee of freedom, which is exactly what the advice manuals of the time preached. The right to terminate an unsatisfactory relationship is the guarantee of free citizenship. Happily married citizens are the basis of a democratic state, in the tradition of thinkers like Milton, also referred to by Cavell (193).

And this is precisely the reason why this debate between loving couples and older generations takes place in public venues. The romantic couple takes possession of the entire city when they chase one another across New York and stroll in Central Park—e.g., *5th Avenue Girl* (LaCava, 1939)—wandering frantically by car, bicycle, train and any means of public transportation (Halbout 359-77). Their romances end or blossom in courthouses, prisons and police precincts, e.g., *Love Is News* (Garnett, 1937). Love at first sight, breaking up and making up are public stories; for instance, in *Theodora Goes Wild* (Boleslawski, 1936), Theodora triggers a scandal at her beau's father's party and reconciles with him when she triumphantly returns to her provincial hometown.

What more efficient amplifier of this intimate, albeit public conversation than the press, which stands as the most symbolic image of free and democratic speech? Through the recurring front page shots, as Cavell has explained (103–4), private scandals (e.g., *Too Many Husbands*), broken marriages, betrayals (e.g., *The Awful Truth*) and reconciliations are recognized as prominent public questions. The discussion on marriage becomes a public debate (e.g., *Love Is News*). The press stages and advertises intimacy. Newspapers echo the rise of the sphere of intimacy in western societies. In showcasing this debate on marriage and love, the press points to a model of contractual agreement for a society, here the United States of America, historically and constitutionally based on negotiation and mutual consent.

Making intimacy a public issue in Classical Hollywood comedy establishes the bond of love as a reinterpretation of the democratic bond. The screwball genre is one of Hollywood's expressions of participation in the democratic debate and the defense of democracy. But its originality lies in its providing a meditation on democratic dialogue through the representation of the relationships of love and marriage, hence intimacy. This is conveyed by means of conversation, which is all the more significant in screwball comedies given that steamy and sexual acts and gestures have been placed under Hollywood's own self-regulation. It is by filming this amorous discourse, with its questions about sex and marriage, that democracy is discussed and a democratic debate takes place. This amorous discourse had its place in the evolution of American democracy at a moment when representative democracy started running out of breath (participation in elections was in decline) and, as a deliberative aspect of democracy, it became all the more significant and especially important, since cinema was not protected by the First Amendment and was, like advertising, considered "business pure and simple" until 1952 (*Joseph Burstyn Inc. vs. Wilson*). Ironically, freedom of speech was being promoted by a medium that was very much controlled.

Screwball comedy performs a public recognition of the place of speech in a democracy in two complementary ways. On the one hand, this amorous, erotic and social discussion dares make demands concerning the terms of a relationship and marital agreement: leaving a spouse for financial reasons—e.g., *The Palm Beach Story*—or because of sexual dissatisfaction—e.g., *My Favorite Wife* (Kanin, 1940). Always open for discussion, the marital pact becomes, then, a metaphor for a social contract that is freely entered into. As a result, this "sonorous and collective thinking" (Iacub 18) makes issues of private life public and political, precisely because it is the place where all values and rules are experienced and risked: divorce, bigamy, the refusal to consummate a marriage or the expression of sexual dissatisfaction. Intimacy and sexual expression are part of the democratic debate.

Conclusion: Narrative Mediation of Social Modernization

Mainstream fiction, be it "advice literature" or Hollywood screwball comedy, acts as a mediator for new social expectations regarding sex, marriage and marital sex. It heralds a new definition of intimacy. Previously considered as a border between family and marriage versus exterior social relationships, intimacy becomes a criterion and a value that defines marriage *per se* through the notion of harmony between spouses. However, this alliance resides in a complex dialectic that assumes that individual happiness is a condition of social well-being: "Lovers were expected to find in marriage a social unit that promoted individual growth while providing social integration. Modern companionate love was to make self-fufillment possible within a framework of social and moral solidarity" (Seidman 98). This opposition between public and private spheres, individuals and society, depends on fictional representations to become real. In this sense, screwball comedies provided audiences of the 1930s and early 1940s with symbolic and/or temporary solutions and definitions of intimacy and marriage.

Notes

1. "Movies Discussed by Mrs. Eleanor Roosevelt (9th July 1934). In Debut as Radio News Commentator, She Praises Action for Self-Censorship," *The New York Times*, July 10, 1934.
2. I have developed the question of intimacy becoming a public matter in screwball comedies in the third part of my book, "La fête screwball et la discussion démocratique" (The Screwball Party and the Democratic Debate).

Works Cited

Adam's Rib. 1949. Dir. George Cukor. With Spencer Tracy (Adam Bonner), Katharine Hepburn (Amanda Bonner), Judy Holliday (Doris Attinger) and Tom Ewell (Warren Attinger). MGM. DVD. *Tracy & Hepburn: The Signature Collection*, Turner Entertainment, 2004.
Altman, Rick. 1999 [2002]. *Film/Genre*. London: BFI.
The Awful Truth. 1937. Dir. Leo McCarey. With Irene Dunne (Lucy Warriner), Cary Grant (Jerry Warriner) and Ralph Bellamy (Daniel Leeson). Columbia. DVD. Columbia Classics, 2003.
Bordwell, David, Janet Staiger and Kristin Thompson. 1985. *The Classical Hollywood Cinema: Film Style and Mode of Production to 1960*. New York: Columbia University Press.
Bringing Up Baby. 1938. Dir. Howard Hawks. With Katharine Hepburn (Susan), Cary Grant (David) and Charles Ruggles (Major Applegate). RKO. DVD. Turner Home Entertainment, 2005.
Cavell, Stanley. 1981. *Pursuits of Happiness: The Hollywood Comedy of Remarriage*. Cambridge: Harvard University Press.
Fifth Avenue Girl. 1939. Dir. Gregory LaCava. With Ginger Rogers (Mary Grey) and Walter Connolly (Mr. Borden). RKO. DVD. Warner Archives, 2010.
The Good Fairy. 1935. Dir. William Wyler. With Margaret Sullavan (Luisa "Lu" Ginglebuscher), Herbert Marshall (Dr. Max Sporum) and Frank Morgan (Konrad). Universal.
Halbout, Grégoire. 2013. *La Comédie screwball hollywoodienne (1934–1945): Sexe, amour et idéaux démocratiques*. Arras: Artois PU.
Handel, Leo. 1950. *Hollywood Looks at Its Audience: A Report of Film Audience Research*. Urbana: University of Illinois Press.
Iacub, Marcela. 2010. *De la pornographie en Amérique: La liberté d'expression à l'âge de la démocratie délibérative*. Paris: Fayard.
It Happened One Night. 1934. Dir. Frank Capra. With Clark Gable (Peter), Claudette Colbert (Ellie) and Walter Connolly (Andrews). Columbia. DVD. Columbia Tristar Studios, 1999.
Leff, Leonard, and Jerold Simmons. 2001. *The Dame in the Kimono: Hollywood, Censorship and the Production Code*. Lexington: University Press of Kentucky.

Libeled Lady. 1936. Dir. Jack Conway. With Jean Harlow (Gladys), William Powell (Bill Chandler), Myrna Loy (Connie Allenbury) and Spencer Tracy (Haggerty). MGM. DVD. Warner Home Video, 2005.

Love Is News. 1937. Dir. Tay Garnett. With Tyrone Power (Steve Leyton), Loretta Young (Tony Gateson) and Don Ameche (Martin J. Canavan). Fox. DVD. 20th Century–Fox, 2008.

Metz, Christian. 1971 [1974]. *Language and Cinema*. The Hague: De Gruyter.

Midnight. 1939. Dir. Mitchell Leisen. With Claudette Colbert (Eva Peabody), Don Ameche (Tibor Czerny), John Barrymore (Georges Flammarion), Francis Lederer (Jacques Picot) and Mary Astor (Helene Flammarion). Paramount. DVD. Universal Studios, 2008.

Mr. and Mrs. Smith. 1941. Dir. Alfred Hitchcock. With Carole Lombard (Ann Smith), Robert Montgomery (Dave Smith), Gene Raymond (Jeff Custer) and Jack Carson (Chuck Benson). RKO. DVD. Universal Pictures, 2005.

My Favorite Wife. 1940. Dir. Garson Kanin. With Irene Dunne (Ellen), Cary Grant (Nick), Randolph Scott (Burkett) and Gail Patrick (Bianca). RKO. DVD. Éditions Montparnasse, 2003.

The Palm Beach Story. 1942. Dir. Preston Sturges. With Claudette Colbert (Gerry Jeffers), Joel McCrea (Tom Jeffers), Mary Astor (The Princess Centimillia) and Rudy Vallee (J.D. Hackensacker III). Paramount. DVD. Universal Studios, 2005.

The Philadelphia Story. 1940. Dir. George Cukor. With Cary Grant (C.K. Dexter Haven), Katharine Hepburn (Tracy Lord), James Stewart (Macaulay Connor) and Ruth Hussey (Elizabeth Imbrie). MGM. DVD. Columbia Tristar Studios, 1999.

Schatz, Thomas. 1981. *Hollywood Genres: Formulas, Filmmaking, and the Studio System*. New York: Random House.

—-. 1988 [1996]. *The Genius of the System: Hollywood Filmmaking in the Studio Era*. New York: Henry Holt.

Seidman, Steven. 1991. *Romantic Longings: Love in America, 1830–1980*. New York: Routledge.

Theodora Goes Wild. 1936. Dir. Richard Boleslawski. With Irene Dunne (Theodora Lynn) and Melvyn Douglas (Michael Grant). Columbia. DVD. *Icons of Screwball Comedy* vol. 2, Sony Pictures, 2009.

Too Many Husbands. 1940. Dir. Wesley Ruggles. With Jean Arthur (Vicky Lowndes), Fred MacMurray (Bill Cardew) and Melvyn Douglas (Henry Lowndes). Columbia. DVD. Sony Pictures, 2009.

Intimacy Shared in Laughter and Tears
Brief Encounter *and* The Seven Year Itch

RAPHAËLLE COSTA DE BEAUREGARD

In terms of intimacy, *Brief Encounter* (Lean, 1945) and *The Seven Year Itch* (Wilder, 1955) address the viewer within a range of ten years in oddly similar ways. Intimacy is, of course, a major literary topic in poems, letters, soliloquies or dialogues. It has also attracted painters attempting to depict the inner life of subjects with visual metaphors, resorting notably to synesthesia, as in musical performances (Laurent 2008–2009), landscape contemplation (Baridon 2008–2009) or devotion (Raguin 2008–2009). The distant gaze of the sitter, his/her gestures suggesting touch and hearing, have correlatives in sound, distant space or religious ecstasy, and express emotions like joy, contemplation and elation. In *Brief Encounter*, strategies that recall such rhetorical devices are used to convey Laura's inner life and represent an intimate relationship between herself and her lover Alec. Wilder's comedy *The Seven Year Itch* is rife with references to the earlier melodrama (Starfield 2009), in particular the citation of the musical arrangement score of Rachmaninov's *Second Piano Concerto*. This piece of music has been widely performed ever since the year it was created (1900–1901), particularly in the U.S. This essay will examine the soliloquies, dreams and the use of Rachmaninov's concerto, which, in both films, convey Laura's and Sherman's intimate feelings, as they (and we the viewers) experience them.

A general overview of the two plots reveals undeniable echoes, our knowledge of *Brief Encounter*, no doubt, adding to our enjoyment of *The Seven Year*

Itch. To start, both films open with the cliché of love-at-first sight, a narrative motif which foregrounds that intimacy between two protagonists is the dominant theme. A fortunate (or unfortunate) accident causes a disturbance in the characters' marital relations. Whether under the guise of a piece of grit, not altogether uncommon in a train station, as Alec, in his role as Dr. Harvey, explains to Laura Jesson [18:00], in *Brief Encounter*, or, in *The Seven Year Itch*, of a tomato plant in a flower pot [22:46], which is not at all uncommon on balconies in two-story high buildings, Cupid's disguises only make his bow and arrow all the more potent. However, the tone of Wilder's film is mainly ironical, that of Lean's film sentimental. The pain in Laura's right eye makes her close and open them again to meet Alec's attentive gaze [17:48]. The cliché of eye contact as a traditional expression of romantic love at first sight may have caused some members of the audience to titter during the film's preview, as David Lean recalls[1]; the director explains that he had been afraid of having gotten "the mood of England wrong" and that "they [would] never like it." As for the crashing flower pot and the narrow miss of the victim (Sherman), followed by the "heavenly" appearance of the creature's head and shoulders above yet more flower pots (the character is never named and Sherman even calls her Marilyn Monroe with a giggle), the cliché of the "sun stroke" inevitably provokes laughter in the audience [23:09]. However, in both films, the initial intimacy and emotion, which the accident gives birth to, are soon repressed by both protagonists, who are overcome by shyness and a reluctance to confess their secret emotions. Thus, the shock of mutual recognition is relegated to the realm of the elusive, secret and silent inner life of the characters, and their brief glimpse of intimacy and love is conveyed through embedded narratives of memories and dreams, and more generally the ambiguities of their imagination.

On the other hand, the two protagonists, Laura and Sherman are frustrated by a cruel lack of intimacy in their married lives. Laura's husband is busy with crossword puzzles, as she silently confesses to him the story of her affair with Alec, and only after a long time does he actually look at her and express dismay at her melancholy face [12:51]. As for Sherman's wife, she is busy with her knitting and shows an inability to respond with anything other than disbelief at her husband's tales. The function of these domestic scenes is twofold: they depict (1) the frustration of romantic characters struggling against the weight of everyday chores which have grown unbearably tiresome, and (2) their love stories within the deformed perspective of a reminiscence. The similitude of the device in both films is striking: the infatuated lovers are shown recalling their love affairs by means of an imaginary confession. We hear Laura's confession in voiceover throughout the film, but it turns out that, instead of addressing the viewer directly, she is actually addressing her husband. Unlike the utilization of voiceovers in film noir, the voiceover in Lean's film (and in Noel Coward's script) bridges the gap between the diegetic and non-diegetic worlds. There are many scenes with Laura and Alec together, but all of them are flashbacks. In Wilder's film, Sherman's three confessions are also flashbacks. To a present but thoroughly absent-minded husband in the melodrama is symmetrically opposed an absent but (in her husband's imagination) clear-sighted wife in the comedy. In the melodrama, Laura eventually breaks into sobs and seeks comfort in her husband's slightly reluctant arms [82:16], suggesting that the truth is at last heard and their shared intimacy is finally restored. In the comedy, Sherman imagines that his wife comes home to shoot him, and he actually knocks down his visitor, Tom MacKenzie, whom he mistakes for his wife's lover [97:40]. The burlesque tone is maintained throughout, thanks to the large and ubiquitous paddle which Sherman's son has forgotten and must be sent to him.

The two films therefore conclude that intimacy is an elusive object: it quickly evaporates in the boredom of marital life, cannot be shared with someone else by telling him/her about it, and can only be enjoyed in memory, as if, ironically, close friendships and relationships could only exist in the intimacy of utter solitude.

Such is the paradox that subsumes both films. Its most telling expression is the *mise en abyme* of romance that occurs when we see the lovers going to the movies. In the two sequences, the protagonists' shared intimacy is represented on two different levels: in the shots from the films we see and in the characters' reactions to these shots. In *Brief Encounter*, a feature film called *Flames of Passion*[2] is screened twice. The first time Laura and Alec go to the movies together, the lovers watch the film's trailer before confessing their love for each other [24:46]. The following week, they sit down in the movie theater to "abandon laughter and experience tears," as Alec puts it before *Flames of Passion* starts [40:45]. In *The Seven Year Itch*, the lovers also go to the movies to watch a horror movie, *Creature from the Black Lagoon* (Jack Arnold, 1954) [71:55], the theme of animal love recalling the three flashbacks. Both films also underline the symbolic significance of sharing a movie together as a cliché of "intimacy in the dark." A similar shot of the lovers strolling on the sidewalk after viewing the film suggests this intimate moment [40:30]. However, the topical references are also significant as they qualify the idea of intimacy at the time. Alec and Laura agree that the film's romance is excessive and ridiculous as they come out of the theater, reflecting the British spectators' inhibitions in regards to the open expression of sentiments, as Richard Dyer has suggested when speaking of "the heartbreakingly touching awkwardness of its characters, what Laura describes as the English being so 'shy and difficult'" (65). A similar disregard for melodrama and romance was the fashion in the U.S. in the 1950s, in keeping with the development of consumer society (Sklar 1999). The topicality of the embedded film is visible when Sherman and Marilyn come out of the theater, but the star soon stops to enjoy a breath of fresh air from the subway under her skirts. This incident was a quote from a recently retrieved 1901 film, which made it topical to movie fans, but also caused a scandal because of its direct reference to the star's private life (Grieveson 46).

In both films, these movie theater scenes foreground the experience of intimacy in an illicit love affair by drawing attention to the clichés of Hollywood cinema. The latter is seen as fake intimacy in Lean's film, while Sherman's neighbor, who is quite impervious to emotions such as terror (provoked by the film) or guilt (when the wind lifts her skirts), impersonates the naïve spectator for whom intimacy is a source of neither tension nor frustration.

Having suggested that the situations in which intimacy in the two films is rendered, i.e., either by its absence or its excess, act as foils to scenes of genuine intimacy, I would now like to draw attention to the fact the language used in both films is just as ambivalent when it comes to intimacy. Key words used by Laura are repeated in the Wilder/Axelrod film in monologues and dialogues. For instance, Laura's statement: "I am a happily married woman, or was until a few weeks ago" [15:18], is later repeated by Sherman: "I am a happily married man" [27:17], while Miss Finch's saying to Sherman: "we have so little time, I'll have lost you forever" [16:37], recalls the words spoken by Alec when leading Laura into a friend's apartment with a similar plan in mind [57:27]. Moreover, in both films, dialogues are subverted by lies and fake confessions in a similar manner, sometimes using similar words.

While, quite ironically, looking at herself in the mirror, Laura lies to Fred whose silhouette we can notice at the back of the room. The confession, a paradigmatic form of intimate address, turns out to be a fake one. Laura never allows Fred to hear her story, and yet, ironically, she pretends to address him by telling him a story. She also uses references to dates and moments of the day, as if she were writing a fake diary. This fake confession might even stand for an imaginary love affair, as if she had only had a glimpse of Alec in the station (Dyer 18–19). In *The Seven Year Itch*, the confessions Sherman makes to his wife are also fake, since he just imagines her in the empty deckchair in front of him. However, unlike Laura, who, from time to time, voices her sense of guilt in her confession, Sherman is quite free from remorse and even tells about his encounters with so much glee that we are equally uncertain about their ever having taken place otherwise than in his imagination.

Thus, it seems that the confession form remains a purely imaginary icon of intimacy in both films and actually serves to depict the psychology of the characters by giving us an intimate knowledge of their inner life and personality. For Dyer, "[n]o film is more of a melodrama than *Brief Encounter*. Yet the film itself asks not to be treated as melodrama but as realism" (49). Though Dyer is referring to its realistic portrait of the English middle class, yet there is also great realism in the contradictions of the two storytellers telling fibs which betray their frustration. In Laura's "diary," we realize that she is flattered by the stranger's admiration for her, while also made to feel secure in the company of a man who cares for her [47:12]. Her family life is deprived of any sense of warmth or any concern for her feelings. Worse still, she sees her son's accident as a punishment she deserved. In Wilder's parody, psychological realism is also at the core of the protagonist's confessions, that dramatize male hypocrisy by showing the infatuation to have been only on the women's side.

The literary trope of the fake confession that connotes imaginary intimacy is always filmed with an obstacle of some kind between the speakers. This leads to much irony during the highly ambiguous dialogues. For instance, when Fred is doing crossword puzzles, Laura is requested to find a missing word in seven letters in a line by Keats: "Huge cloudy symbols of a high..." [12:51]. She suggests "romance," a word which, in this film, is practically a synonym for "intimacy"; her husband then comments that the word fits between "delirium" and "Baluchistan." The audience, who is in the know, realizes that her secret romance is cruelly ridiculed. Wilder's film also contains similar puns on key words referring to intimacy. Sherman's wife merely raises her eyebrows and declares sarcastically that such tales about "the beast in him" are but the product of his "imagination" [16:08], thus demeaning his virility, and, ironically, we not only laugh at Sherman's inflated ego, but also at his helpless body, which connotes a comic lack of virility, whether hunched at his desk [15:05] in a hospital bed [16:35] or lying on a beach [18:38].

So in both films, the dialogues and monologues subvert the alleged intimacy of married life. Moreover, dialogues between the lovers only superficially express intimate understanding. For example, the lovers' small talk expresses a mutual interest in Alec's work, until they come to realize that they are sharing something else: the pleasure of being together. Nor can Sherman avoid the erotic power Marilyn's body exerts on him, despite his effort at commonplace small talk; the pair achieves some degree of intimacy in the burlesque mode when they play *Chopsticks* together on the piano and topple over as the bench collapses under them [51:12]. If intimacy, understood as close friendships and relationships, only exists in both films as repressed experiences, thoughts, emotions, usually kept secret, the truth of such intimate moments is, nevertheless, enjoyed by the characters. But it is largely thanks to the music that we capture these moments.

Lean's film is usually remembered for the unity it achieves between images and music. This is testified by at least two of the people who are interviewed in the documentary "A Profile of *Brief Encounter*," both declaring that the film and the concerto cannot be separated. The fact that the well-known pianist Eileen Joyce is announced in the credits as the soloist adds to the association between the piano soloist and a female inner voice [1:05]. As Dyer has noted, the concerto evokes Laura's own voice for several reasons, an effect the editing greatly contributes to: "it is first heard during her and Dolly's train journey home; it seeps in as the camera moves very slowly into an extreme closeup of her and we hear her voiceover for the first time. When Dolly interrupts her thoughts, the music stops" (17).

As in classical Hollywood cinema, music, here, expresses the characters' mood—both Laura and Sherman are deeply upset. To Sherman, the empty apartment looks uncanny, and he sees Marilyn's sudden presence or the doorkeeper's calls to take away Mrs. Sherman's carpets as weird intrusions by some extraterrestrial beings. Laura is also distraught, so much so that only romantic music can express her inner crisis; for Dyer, she is actually suffering from a hysterical fit, as she speaks of being "hysterical inside" when she gets home from an afternoon with Alec to find out her son has had an accident (20).

According to Michel Chion, there are three ways of relating to sound in a film: it is heard as a cause (diegesis); it conveys a semantic or narrative meaning (leitmotivs); and music can also be "acousmatic" for the audience who reacts directly to the musical performance for its own sake (*Audiovision* 25–30). Ironically, such distinctions are embedded in Wilder's film, namely when Sherman is dismayed because Marilyn has no emotional reaction to Rachmaninov's music [47:47]. What he hoped would trigger her emotion (Chion's "causal listening") fails, and he explains what it is all about ("semantic listening") and tells her how to experience pure acousmatic pleasure ("reduced listening") by lying down on the floor. In both films, the concerto weaves its way in and out of the diegetic and the non-diegetic.

The concerto is diegetic when Laura turns the radio on and Fred complains that the sound is too loud [46:14]. In Wilder's parody, Sherman turns the record on in order to set fire to his beautiful visitor's imagination, but he soon finds himself shifting in and out of an imaginary world where she is dressed in silk, looks like a femme fatale and confesses that the concerto thrills her [29:13]. Rachmaninov's concerto, therefore, has a diegetic function: the characters play his music in order to infuse some romantic music in an everyday world of boredom and solitude. In *Brief Encounter*, it is contrasted with other types of instruments, including a barrel organ, a quartet and an organ. It also relates to sounds like the train whistle. In Wilder's film, it is also related in several ways to sounds, mostly when people knock at Sherman's door [30:10]. In such moments, the concerto connotes intimacy as a part of the protagonists' present life.

Due to its presence in the real world of sounds, the concerto is "naturalized," since we assume that it is heard by the protagonists, even when it is not, and that it only accompanies their changing moods. The choice of Russian romantic music to express Laura's inner suffering and joy seems to be particularly appropriate in view of the several references to Greta Garbo in *Anna Karenina* (Clarence Brown 1935), for instance, when the camera focuses on Laura's face and on her suicide attempt at the train station [80:08]. Besides, the Russian novel is also about a love triangle. Moreover, the form of the concerto endows the piano solo with a "human" voice, and we hear the musician's mute voice as a subtext to Laura's own. The *Second Concerto*, which was written while Rachmaninov was recovering from a depression, is divided into three parts that have an autobiographical meaning: *Moderato, Adagio sostenuto* and *Allegro scherzando*. The opening bars express the musician's awakening to real life. He first reminisces about the causes of his depression. His past suffering is told in deep tones and loud chords. With the *Adagio*, the musician recovers hope in life, even though his melancholy is still present. Finally, in the *Allegro Scherzando*, music is reinstated as the superior joy of the musician (Bertensson 67–96).

As Mike Cormack explains in his discussion of the music in the film (19–30), a timing sheet would show that the duration of the three movements—11'06" for the *Moderato*, 11'53" for the *Adagio sostenuto*, 11'34" for the *Allegro scherzando*, for a total of 33'93"—does not coincide with the length of the film which is eighty-six minutes long. The excerpts are arranged and repeated in the musical soundtrack to create leitmotifs. The repetitions are necessary for the audience to identify separate signifiers, such as the urgency theme when they race through the station [39:52], a recurring mood which pervades Laura's conscience and spoils her happiness [50:12], or the love theme, for instance, when Laura tells Alec that he suddenly looks much younger [28:59]. Leitmotifs convey information lacking in the dialogues, as the examples of implicit intimacy show.

The transmutation of the concerto into a cue sheet, if unbearably tiresome to music lovers, is the chief means of expressing intimacy in the film. As soon as the opening credits, the opening bars can be heard accompanying a shot of a dimly lit station at night, while a thundering express train charges from the left foreground into the distant right background, its white steam invading the black sky towards us to conclude the credits and introduce the platform and the refreshment room [1:30].

However, when Laura turns on the radio at home, we do not hear the opening bars comprised of low piano chords, but rather a "streaming" effect, with the flow of strings alternately shifting between the foreground and background of the soundtrack [30:40]. The concerto itself, of course, already employs strong contrasts between accelerating or decelerating tempos, and these changes in rhythm are organized to match the heroine's changing feelings. The music is also used to indicate her awakening memory, sounding softly in a distant place, as it were, and progressively drawing nearer as the volume increases. The variety of arrangements in the music actually serves as a gradient to various degrees of intimacy which could be listed as follows: expressions of solitude in solo pieces or irresistible gushes of feeling with the full orchestra, or intimacy and happiness when piano and orchestra merge within a single musical harmony.

Like the excerpts from the concerto, the modalities of Laura's voiceover are similarly divided between moments of self-awareness and analysis akin to a soliloquy—for instance, when she fantasizes a happy Hollywood romance, the sound of a waltz briefly introduces the fantasy before the concerto is resumed [48:05]—and moments of direct address in which she talks to the absent-present Fred. During the train episode when her imagination actually runs wild, she is shown looking at (or through) her own reflection in the train window, her shadowy face superimposed over the imaginary scenes, and the concerto music matches her dreamy expression on the somewhat opaque glass [47:12]. Sound and image are welded together in this dream of perfect intimacy with Alec, at a ball, then in a restaurant, her soliloquy imitating the mode of the piano solo so that the spectator shares her dreams and desire.

It is striking that the music in this sequence achieves empathy with spectators, even though it is not diegetic but underscores the heroine's mood. The repetition of Laura's theme addresses the viewer's memory, not of the concerto, but of the fragments we have already overheard, which become symbolic for us. For example, the horn piece occurs several times as a counterpoint in the distance to the shrill stationmaster's whistle [75:50]. Comprised of only one note, it hovers between sound and signal. The piano solos in lyrical parts, where every note is clearcut and rings separately, are opposed to the loud chords rising like soaring passion. Just as the two railway lines meeting at the junction become metaphors of the protagonists' destiny, as the two trains are repeatedly announced by the loudspeaker, metaphors of intimacy are found in the repetition of excerpts borrowed from the concerto.

The depiction of Sherman's infatuation with Marilyn also relies on the concerto and repetition. He plays the record and listens to it as if he were at a concert [28:18]. He then begins performing on his own piano, exhibiting typical empathy with the performer (Gorbman 24), while the orchestra can be overheard as if it were absent, until we realize it actually comes from the record that is still playing (Fig. 7). The playing of the record shows that Sherman is moved by the music, and his appropriation of the piano part expresses his belief in its power over his guest. In the ensuing fantasy sequence, his female visitor, who enters as if summoned by the concerto, speaks of the loss of control over her emotions which the concerto triggers in her, and, indeed, uses words that recall Tolstoy's male character hearing Beethoven's *Kreutzer sonata*. In this respect, *Kreutzer Sonata* is just as much of a subtext for Wilder's film as *Anna Karenina* is for Lean's film.

Chopsticks then successfully replaces the concerto in Sherman and Marilyn's intimate moments, to the point of imposing repetition as being, once and for all, and ironically enough, the only music which succeeds in giving her the coveted "goose-pimples." Their mutual frenzy in the mechanical performance ends in a hilarious collapse, a comic visual metaphor of falling "head over heels" in love. But this is only the first half of the film, and the concerto reappears more than ever as a new plot is introduced, i.e., Sherman's sudden fear that Marilyn's commercial for Dazzledent might arouse his wife's suspicion [64:50].

The TV screen, here, replaces the earlier musical instruments, landscapes or heavenly visions, as a visual metaphor, albeit a comic one, of intimacy.

With the imaginary appearance of Marilyn on his TV set, Rachmaninov's

Fig. 7. In Billy Wilder's *The Seven Year Itch* (1955), Richard Sherman (Tom Ewell) pretends to play Rachmaninov's *Second Concerto* while his neighbor (Marilyn Monroe) listens.

concerto now conveys his fear [66:32]. We first see Marilyn performing on a set, framed by the two cameras on either side of the shot framing the commercial. Wilder's camera slowly tracks forward on Marilyn, as she leans forward to whisper her secret in the middle of her Dazzledent commercial. Sherman's hallucination now shifts to another TV on a table by a lakeshore where his wife and son are watching Marilyn's performance. The concerto, which is heard throughout the sequence, is used now to express Sherman's rising hysteria. Hysteria has already been introduced, and thus naturalized, in the film earlier on, as a common feature of the three women who assault him, so we recognize the motif here when it reappears within Sherman himself (André 2011). While Laura fights her "secret" hysteria in *Brief Encounter*, in Wilder's comedy, hysteria induces comic mechanical automatisms on the character's living body (Bergson 22). Sherman's shoulder twitches spasmodically, as do his head and neck, as if he were being strangled by some invisible assailant.

The repetition of characteristic fragments from the concerto then underlines the automatic behavior of Sherman's wife, as she suddenly intrudes on his apartment to shoot him, using honeyed clichés about justice and women, and he subsequently yields to a weird pantomime as he knocks down his rival, Tom MacKenzie, who has only come to fetch the child's paddle [97:59]. The actual "mickey-mousing" of the record player [97:59], which collapses at the same time, writes off the concerto's emotional power once and for all from the world of the film. In parallel to this elimination of Russian romanticism, the reference to Tolstoi's *Kreutzer sonata* reminds us that the hero of that novel is driven to murderous jealousy by hearing Beethoven's romantic piece. In the end, Wilder's comedy seems to indulge in what Frédéric Sounac calls "melophobia" (7–29).

In both the melodrama and the comedy, the audience is made to share the inner consciousness of the two main protagonists, who are a prey to the "flames of passion" and their struggling emotions, mainly through the nondiegetic soundtrack. We are never allowed any insight into the other characters' emotions, whether it be Alec or Marilyn. What is common to the two films, and makes the parody entertaining by showing the female "ur-text" in an inverted mirror through the prism of male fantasies, is the topos of intimacy and its deformed simulacra. If both films emphasize that intimacy is a figment of one's imagination, then it is imagination, and the power that Rachmaninov's concerto has over our imaginations, that are at the core of our interest in these films. It seems as if imagination, the "madwoman of the household" ("La Folle du Logis"), as the French would say, had displaced the madwoman in the attic by establishing its empire over the intimacy of the sitting room as a substitute for the intimacy of the bedroom.

NOTES

1. In the DVD extra: "A Profile of *Brief Encounter*."
2. Although there are several films of the same name, this film remains untraceable to this day. I have not been able to ascertain whether it is not, in fact, a fictitious film.

WORKS CITED

Altman, Rick. 2007. "Early Film Themes: Roxy, Adorno and the problem of Cultural Capital." *Beyond the Soundtrack: Representing Music in Cinema*. Ed. Daniel Goldmark. Berkeley: University of California Press. 205–24.
André, Emmanuelle. 2011. *Le Choc du sujet : De l'hystérie au cinéma (XIXe- XXIe siècle)*. Rennes: PUR.
Baridon, Michel. 2008–2009. "The Emergence of the Landscape and the Expression of Intimacy." *Interfaces* 28: 127–36.
Bergson, Henri. 1899 [1958]. *Le Rire: Essai sur la signification du comique*. Paris: PUF.
Bertensson, Sergei, and Jay Leyda. 1956. *Sergei Rachmaninoff: A Lifetime in Music*. New York: New York University Press.
Brief Encounter. 1945 [2000]. Dir. David Lean. Based on the play *Still Life* by Noel Coward. Music by Sergei Rachmaninov. With Celia Johnson (Laura Jesson) and Trevor Howard (Alec). Cineguild. DVD. Carlton Visual Entertainment.
Chion, Michel. 1985. *Le Son au cinema*. Paris: Cahiers du cinema/Edts de l'Etoile.
———. 1990. *L'Audio-vision: Son et image au cinéma*. Paris: Nathan.
Cormack, Mike. 2007. "The Pleasures of Ambiguity: Using Classical Music in Film." *Changing Tunes: The Use of Pre-Existing Music in Film*. Eds. Phil Powrie and Robyn Stilwell. Burlington, VT: Ashgate. 19–30.
Gorbman, Claudia. 1987. *Unheard Melodies: Narrative Film Music*. Bloomington: Indiana University Press.
Laurent, Beatrice. 2008–2009. "The Bower's Secret: Intimacy in the Art of D.G. Rossetti." *Interfaces* 28: 13–29.
Raguin, Virginia. 2008–2009. "Intimacy Through Visual Touch: The World Before Gothic Art." *Interfaces* 28: 83–94.
The Seven Year Itch. 1955 [2002]. Director Billy Wilder. Based on a play by George Axelrod. Music by Alfred Newman. With Tom Ewell (Richard Sherman), Marilyn Monroe (The Girl), Evelyn Keyes (Helen Sherman) and Sonny Tufts (Tom MacKenzie). Twentieth Century–Fox, 1955. DVD. Studio Fox-Pathé Europa.
Sklar, Robert. 1999. "The Lost Audience: 1950s Spectatorship and Historical Reception Studies." *Identifying Hollywood's Audiences*. Eds. Melvyn Stokes and Richard Maltby. London: BFI. 81–92.
Sounac, Frédéric. 2012. "Avant-propos." *Littératures*: 66 "La Mélophobie littéraire": 7–29.
Starfield, Penny. 2009. "Couleur et musique dans *I've Always Loved You/Je vous ai toujours aimé* de Frank Borzage." *Cinéma et Couleur/Film and Colour*. Ed. Raphaëlle Costa de Beauregard. Paris: Michel Houdiard. 370–84.

The Intimate Gaze
(Deviant) Uses of the Subjective Camera in Lady in the Lake *and* La Femme défendue

CHRISTOPHE GELLY

Film history is partly the history of famous experiments. A technical experiment designed as an attraction or a spectacle rather than an "art"—whatever this vague term may refer to—film was, first and foremost, an elusive practice that could lend itself as easily to the realism of the Lumière brothers' sequence shot (an anachronistic name, of course) of *Workers Leaving the Lumière Factory in Lyon* (1895) or to the illusions of a Georges Méliès, for instance. Hovering between realism and expressionism has always been, it seems, the fate of cinema, and in order to explain this, much has been made of the "newness" of the art, i.e., the fact that, as a fledgling artistic practice, cinema needed experiment more than other arts to establish its own language (although the notion of a cinematic language was also much disputed, especially in the 1970s, by Christian Metz among others). Another argument might explain why experiments took place noticeably at a period and in a place—Hollywood in the 1940s—when American films were dominating the world market and setting the tone for mainstream production: because of the dominance of Hollywood productions, it might have been easier, less daring and implied less of a financial commitment to try and innovate with new techniques. Another, albeit opposite argument towards explaining the rise of experimentation in these years lies in the fact that, despite the general dominance of Hollywood in the 1940s, the economic pressure during and after World War II—a favorite factor to account for the emergence of film noir for critics like Andrew Spicer (19–20)—made it necessary to look for innovating aesthetic devices that were not costly in themselves, but could nonetheless renew the cinematic experience for spectators. This may be one of the reasons why Hollywood turned to the subjective camera in those years, especially in some film noirs like *Dark Passage* (Delmer Daves, 1947), whose opening scene includes a famous sequence in which a man escaped from a jail, played by Bogart, enters a wooden barrel and rolls down a slope, so that the viewer "experiences" his journey in the barrel and, perhaps, the queasiness that goes with it. In the 1940s, this device—the subjective camera—was thought to be a token of proximity between the spectator and the character, an argument that Robert Montgomery made explicit when Phillip Marlowe, in the first, non-subjective sequence in the film, explains the point of following his investigation: "You'll see it just as I saw it, you'll meet the people, you'll find the clues.… And maybe you'll solve it quick, and maybe you won't" [3:13–3:19]. Of course, there was an element of challenge and competition involved in this address to the spectator, but the gist of the matter was precisely to (pretend to) put the spectator in the P.I.'s shoes, so as to play fair with him in this competition to find the truth.

My aim will be to evaluate exactly how this subjective device came to be presented as a token of truthfulness and unbiased communication between film and spectator in 1947, and compare its usage to that in *La Femme défendue* (Philippe Harel, 1997), where it serves the opposite purpose of exposing deceit in an adulterous affair and revealing the full extent of the male character's double-dealing with others and even himself. Although both films are very different, they do relate essentially to the issue of intimacy in ways that are connected. Montgomery's adaptation of Raymond Chandler's novel takes for its main aesthetic tenet the idea that the subjective camera device enables the spectator to share the intimacy of the focal character's perceptions, hence, to work from these perceptions towards the solving of the criminal case on an equal footing with the fictional detective, whose psychological and physical apprehension of the diegetic world, including clues and interviews with suspects, is supposed to be reflected on the screen through that device. In Harel's film, though the terms are not stated as explicitly as in *Lady in the Lake*, we enter the story of the adulterous couple from the inside through the subjective device that is supposed to mirror the subjective reality of the cheating husband, his lies and sometimes his self-hatred—in short the complete range of his secret, intimate feelings during his affair. In both films, proximity with the focal characters through the precise reproduction of their point of view is considered (explicitly or tacitly) as a means of understanding their reaction in the story and conveying "the" truth about the characters: in one case, the detective's "live" experience of his own investigation, in the other, the unfaithful husband's "true" feelings about his mistress. Both cases will serve to highlight the peculiar relationship of this device to intimacy, whether it be the detective's supposed psyche in Montgomery's film, or the "inside" of the affair which we, as spectators, are supposed to witness directly as it unfolds in *La Femme défendue*.

1947: A Time for (Some) Formal Experimentation

From a classical critical perspective, based notably on Laura Mulvey's psychoanalytical tenets, the utilization of the subjective camera in *Lady in the Lake* can be interpreted as a deviation from the mainstream position attributed in the cinematographic apparatus to the spectator—a position that is characterized as voyeuristic. Catherine Williamson has shown that, because the film sticks to the male voyeuristic gaze, it conveys a feeling of anguish and uneasiness connected to the voyeuristic activity which appears here just *too obvious* to be fully enjoyed by the spectator, though this activity is at the basis of the spectator's activity in Hollywood classicism:

> Montgomery's experiment, a misguided attempt to replace voyeuristic pleasure with the more visceral pleasure of "action," fails as classical cinema for the simple reason that the pleasure of that cinema *is* voyeurism and the denial of that pleasure, through interruptions, disruptions, and limitations, is enormously frustrating to the viewer [21].

Williamson argues that, by sticking almost constantly to the detective's perspective, the film denies the spectator any visual freedom, and it especially denies him/her a *place* from which s/he could "safely" enter the fiction and enjoy the narrative in a classical voyeuristic fashion. For instance, Williamson notices that the device precludes the utilization of the shot/reverse shot technique, which would signal to the spectator his/her own freedom *outside* the realm of the characters, i.e., his/her freedom to gaze at them without their knowing it (19). Instead, the subjective camera constantly confronts the spectator with his/her own participation in the story as an active, but threatened agency, not as a passive voyeur.

A good example of this occurs in the scene where Marlowe gets punched by Chris Lavery, a suspect he came to cross-examine [18:03–18:15], or in the scene where he is kissed by Adrienne Fromsett, the woman who hired him to locate her boss's missing wife [76:40–77:18]. These two sequences operate, of course, quite differently, but reveal the full extent of the film's dependence on devices other than the subjective camera to evoke the character's feelings. In the first scene, the fact that the detective is taken by surprise by his opponent can only be suggested when the camera pans toward the clock on the fireplace mantelpiece (which Marlowe is thus looking at), suggesting his surprise that

Lavery should be asking him what time it is; in so doing, Lavery's reflection is shown in the mirror above the mantelpiece, whereas we had been following his face (from Marlowe's point of view) from the time Marlowe entered the house. It seems that the film *requires* this spatial disorientation, this turn away from Lavery's face, to convey Marlowe's surprise. The effect for Marlowe (and the viewer) would not have been the same, had he kept his eyes on Lavery. In other words, the subjective camera *is not enough*; it does not really express the character's feelings, but only replicates a part of his visual field. The same could be said of the kissing scene that obviously does not work without the sentimental backdrop: the non-diegetic music used to signify that this *is* a love scene. This is especially true if we compare this scene to an earlier scene where Marlowe had only pretended he was going to kiss Adrienne Fromsett and where, without any music, the full extent of his insensitiveness appeared (14:55).

It should come as no surprise that, as a device, the subjective camera fails to express the intimate feelings of the characters, since it is a commonplace in film theory that feelings on screen are mostly expressed by the faces and looks of characters: if we cannot get access to Marlowe's face, then we are locked out of his psyche. What is more interesting to me is the peculiar use Montgomery made of it. By eluding the voyeuristic apparatus of classical Hollywood productions, although this may have been unconscious on his part, Montgomery also defamiliarized the scenes that were meant to depict the female character as the typical object of the male gaze. In the previously mentioned scene, for instance, Adrienne Fromsett comes to represent a threat insofar as she obscures Marlowe's field of vision, thus constituting an objective obstacle to the male voyeuristic gaze. Williamson construes this as the representation of castration anxiety (23), which places the male spectator in a passive situation that deconstructs, once again, classical subjective positions in Hollywood cinema. Outside of this theoretical framework, which may appear a bit rigid, it may be argued that the device in this film works at debunking mainstream gender roles in terms of the gaze without making debunking conspicuous, because Montgomery was not concerned with such subversive aims. To put it bluntly, it was a "side effect" of the technical experiment that was neither taken into account, nor even welcome from his perspective.

An example of the way Montgomery tries to return to a more classical form of spectatorship in spite of his experimentation with subjectivity, is the way he handles his main character. As J.P. Simon has noted (162–63), Marlowe is in control of everything: he introduces the narrative with a preliminary sequence in his office, shot in a classical way, like an interview; he is the one who tells the story, sees it and even provides explanations (in the form of analepses), when episodes from the story are not shot "subjectively"—for instance, he tells us how he got to Little Fawn Lake to meet potential witnesses [26:40–27:35]. In other words, the way Marlowe takes on narrative, visual and enunciative authority is quite intriguing. It may point to his paranoid desire for control, *especially if we remember that the subjective camera device deprives him of an important part of this control* (keep in mind that the kissing scene puts him in a passive position). Other diegetic elements that point to his (thwarted) desire for "authority" would tend to confirm this: when he meets Adrienne Fromsett for the first time, it is because he has sent a crime short story he wants her to consider for publication—another sign of his desire for authority, especially since, as a P.I., he should be vested with ideal credentials for writing this type of text. Unfortunately, this desire for authority is sadly disappointed, since Fromsett uses his text as a mere excuse to get in touch with him and hire him as a detective, so that his quality as a writer is not even considered. Similarly, the title he gave to his text—"If I Should Die Before I Live"—voices a specific type of anxiety that has much to do with effacement, oblivion and passivity: it is as if, in spite of the numerous signs of Montgomery/Marlowe's excessive presence in the narrative as enunciator, actor and director, the subjective camera had ultimately destabilized and undermined the status of the male character and spectator. What is expressed through the device is, then, not the "interiority" of a character's psyche—as one might naively have thought in 1947—but rather the frailty of a male identity *devoid of any definite content owing to the subjective camera*. Although this was certainly not the film's aim, it nevertheless accounts for the enduring appeal of the film to modern viewers, since it comes to fit a vision of male frailty that is more in keeping with the spirit of our times.

To conclude on Montgomery's film, and to illustrate the way the device produces meaning, I wish to briefly compare two sequences. The first depicts Marlowe and Fromsett's first meeting [10:00–10:50]; in the second, he calls her for help after getting into a car accident, provoked by a corrupt policeman named DeGarmot [70:25–73:10].

What is striking in the scene where Marlowe misleads Adrienne Fromsett on purpose, notably by claiming that her "lipstick is on crooked" in order to mock her vanity, is that his voice never changes, whether he is offending her on purpose when he understands she had him come for other reasons than to buy his story, or telling a downright lie to check out what a "vain female" she is. In other words, the voice does not suffice to express his feelings. If he had been shown uttering this sentence about her lipstick in a classical medium closeup, we may have perceived some elements of irony in his face, but again POV shots do not allow for this. This explains why both characters go to stand in front of the mirror, so that we may at last see the smirk on Marlowe's face

Fig. 8. Phillip Marlowe (Robert Montgomery) looking at himself and at Adrienne Fromsett (Audrey Totter) in a mirror in Robert Montgomery's *Lady in the Lake* (1947).

once he has played his trick (Fig. 8). By contrast, the second scene is supposed to express that Marlowe is *not* lying and truly desperate in his call for help ... but it fails all the same, due to the very static shot on the phone which is strangely inexpressive, despite the anguished, breathless way Marlowe speaks to Adrienne at the other end of the line. The reason why this scene remains interesting for us today has much to do with the way it *actualizes* and *literalizes* the destabilization of the male gaze and authority. This destabilization may explain some of the pleasure we derive from watching the film today.

1997: Adultery and Subjectivity

Can we find the same elements of destabilization in Philippe Harel's film, which uses the subjective camera even more consistently, since Harel never swerves away from this device, whereas Montgomery inserted three "interview" scenes in Marlowe's office shot in a classical way? Of course, the production context is quite different from that of *Lady in the Lake*. When Harel set out on his project—filming the adulterous relationship between an unfaithful husband and his mistress from the point of view of the husband—he did not specifically refer to Montgomery's experiment. His intentions were, in fact, quite different. Whereas in *Lady in the Lake* the aim of the device is to encourage a form of competition between the spectator and the (fictional) detective on a seemingly fair cognitive basis, here the object is more openly "subjectivist." Harel's project has to do with the restitution not of "reality," but of the true feelings of the couple as they experienced a "forbidden" love affair. The intimacy that is supposed to be conveyed has nothing to do with murder, but everything to do with affect. Significantly, though, the very same effects, produced by the device, that are challenging and unexpected in a crime film like *Lady in the Lake*, are somehow welcome in *La Femme défendue*. Indeed, focusing the male gaze on Muriel as she is courted and seduced by François results in the same feeling of unreality and danger that can be very well integrated in the scenario insofar as the mistress is an objective danger to the unfaithful husband. The defamiliarization of the female "object" (the mistress) is also perfectly understandable, as the male voyeuristic gaze is deeply destabilized by this woman who comes to shatter his previous emotional certainties. In other words, the effect of the subjective camera seems to have been integrated and taken into account in the script in a more knowledgeable way by Harel. The historical distance between both films, no doubt, helped him to do so.

This destabilization is presented very differently in Harel's film than in Montgomery's. For instance, in the second sequence, right after the two characters have met in the previous sequence, the subjective camera quickly glances at the café where François offers to buy Muriel a drink, before returning to her face [3:03–4:15]. This quick movement points to the male character's restlessness, which can be related to his sexual desire, a type of movement that would not appear so suddenly in *Lady in the Lake* (although Montgomery also suggests Marlowe's sexual interest through pans that follow Fromsett's female secretary, rather than through such a sudden shift of vision).

Likewise, when he calls her from his cell phone, François is so anxious to meet Muriel that he does a U-turn in the middle of the road and gets insulted by another driver. The hectic shifts in perspective are, here, related directly to the male character's feelings, and more explicitly to his dependence on a female character whom he wishes to control for his exclusive enjoyment. The explicitness of the discourse on male loss is also to be found in the very last sequence of the film, which involves a voiceover reading the letter François sends to Muriel after their final separation. The following extract from the letter is read over a visual background of slow pans over the country house where François had once taken Muriel:

> Before we met, I did not know if I loved women too much or if I hated them. Today I know. They have that elusive kind of magic we believe we can capture

when we take them. That deadly vanity that is a challenge to us. The mystery of these bodies that we unveil, but which reappears as soon as they get dressed again. In fact, I wish I had had enough time to get tired of you, to exhaust desire. I still had a lot to give you[1] [94:20–94:54, my translation].

There is no doubt here that Harel has constructed a very different discourse from Montgomery/Marlowe's desire for control, that is, an elegiac discourse that integrates the loss of the object and the failure of the voyeuristic gaze within the subjective perspective of the male character. This discourse fits the formal qualities of the POV shot more efficiently, it seems, even if comparisons can still be made between both films, e.g., the identity between director and actor that accounts for a specific connection between autobiography and the utilization of the subjective camera, as Nadja Gernalzick (2006) has pointed out.

To conclude on this comparison between two revealingly different uses of the same techniques, I would like to highlight one last significant difference between the two films. In *Lady in the Lake*, mirrors are typically utilized to *objectify* Marlowe's body, for instance, when he looks at himself in the mirror after lying to Adrienne about her "crooked" makeup. This is what Jean Châteauvert and André Gaudreault have to say about that scene, and also about the later scene when Marlowe is crawling on all fours towards the public phone booth:

> Furthermore, when Marlowe and Fromsett talk in front of the mirror and she addresses the (subjective) camera while looking into the mirror, we are surprised to realize that back in the reflected image (thus in the background), Marlowe's face swerves away from her just when the camera eye (whose viewpoint is supposed to represent what he is seeing just then) gives us a stable point of view on Fromsett. Unlike what happens in visual self-examination, the use of the subjective camera technique in front of a mirror necessarily involves a spatial gap, a departure between the location of the onlooker and the location of the character who is being looked at.
>
> In fact, whenever the shot is taken subjectively, any representation on the screen of the body of the onlooker is bound to be conveyed with some measure of unrealism and implausibility. Laurent Benoit (1992) emphasizes on that score that hands, feet and the whole body in the shots from *Lady in the Lake* are answerable to the representation of a body whose size is unrealistic, and that appears through its mechanical gestures. Everything happens, in fact, as if subjective shots absolutely precluded the representation of the character's body as whole, when that character is the focal point of the shots[2] [99–100, my translation].

Châteauvert and Gaudreault's interpretation would confirm that this objectification of the body endows the male gaze with very little subjectivity. By contrast, this scene can be compared to the scene in *La Femme défendue*, where François looks at his own reflection in a mirror while phoning Muriel for the first time [5:05], or when he wakes up in the middle of the night because he is too restless to sleep [83:10] (Fig. 9).

Fig. 9. François (Philippe Harel) looking at his reflection while talking on the phone with his mistress Muriel in Philippe Harel's *La Femme défendue* (1997).

These scenes focus, first, on the insecurity of François, who needs to "check" his own image (so that he can see the face of a liar?) when embarking on this adulterous affair, and secondly, on his helplessness when he has been jilted, once again, by Muriel. There is an element of surprise and shock in these two shots, especially the second one. Indeed, both reintegrate the character of François in a passive position, almost a feminized position in Mulvey's terms, which, in the film, is explicitly dealt with as the source of a nostalgic discourse on loss and sexual frustration.

This explicitness—and the higher awareness of what the subjective camera implies—is surely what accounts for the contrasted handling of it in both films. The issue of intimacy, as it is dealt with and expressed (quite differently in both films) through the usage of the subjective camera, should, then, be understood in connection with our cultural position as spectators. In Montgomery's film, this device creates a feeling of thwarted voyeurism, which, in the context of Hollywood classicism, works at redefining our experience of cinema as apparatus. In Harel's film, this uneasy, voyeuristic position has become integrated as the very topic of the film, and not, as often seems to be the case in *Lady in the Lake*, as pure experiment. Thus, the two films' distinct authorial projects result in the very different perspectives on intimacy presented to the spectator.

Notes

1. Original text: "Avant de te connaître je ne savais pas si j'aimais trop les femmes ou si je les détestais. Aujourd'hui je le sais. Il y a cette magie insaisissable qu'on croit capturer au moment où on les possède. Cette arrogance vénéneuse qui nous défie. Le mystère de ces corps qu'on dévoile mais qui réapparaît aussitôt qu'elles se sont rhabillées. Au fond, j'aurais voulu avoir le temps de me fatiguer de toi, d'épuiser le désir. J'avais encore beaucoup à te donner."

2. Original text: "Qui plus est, lors des conversations entre Marlowe et Fromsett par miroir interposé, et au cours desquelles cette dernière, tournée vers le miroir, interpelle la caméra (subjective), on se surprend à découvrir, dans la profondeur du miroir (dans l'arrière-plan donc), le visage de Marlowe dont le regard *s'écarte* de son interlocutrice alors même que la caméra (qui représente censément ce qu'il est en train de voir à l'instant) livre un *point de vue stable* sur Fromsett. Au contraire de la situation qui prévaut dans le cas de l'autoscopie, la mise en scène d'une caméra subjective aux prises avec un miroir implique de façon obligée une discordance spatiale, un écart entre la position du personnage regardant et celle du personnage regardé.

"En fait, dès lors que le plan se conjugue sur le mode de la subjectivité, toute représentation, à l'image, du corps du sujet du regard est condamnée à une certaine forme d'irréalisme et d'invraisemblance. Laurent Benoît (1992) souligne à ce propos que les mains, les pieds, le corps tout entier que révèlent les plans de *The Lady in the Lake* [sic] constituent un corps aux dimensions improbables que trahissent des mouvements mécaniques. C'est un peu, au fond, comme si la subjectivité du plan excluait de façon impérative que l'on montrât de façon intègre le corps du personnage dans lequel s'ancre le regard mis en film..."

Works Cited

Benoit, Laurent. 1992. "Le Corps et la caméra subjective." *Les Cahiers du CIRCAV* 1.2: 101–15.
Chateauvert, Jean, and André Gaudreault. 1996. "Le Corps, le Regard et le Miroir." *Semiotica* 112.1–2: 93–107.
La Femme défendue. 1997 [2006]. Dir. Philippe Harel. Written by Éric Assous and Philippe Harel. With Isabelle Carré (Elle, Muriel), Philippe Harel (Moi), Nathalie Conio (Ma secrétaire) and Sophie Niedergang (Ma femme). Les Productions Lazennec. DVD. Arte editions.
Gernalzick, Nadja. 2006. "To Act or to Perform: Distinguishing Filmic Autobiography." *Biography: An Interdisciplinary Quarterly* 29.1 (Winter): 1–13.
Lady in the Lake. 1947 [2007]. Dir. Robert Montgomery. Written by Steve Fisher. With Robert Montgomery (Phillip Marlowe), Audrey Totter (Adrienne Fromsett), Lloyd Nolan (Lt. DeGarmot), Leon Ames (Derace Kingsby), Jayne Meadows (Mildred Havelend) and Dick Simmons (Chris Lavery). MGM. DVD. Warner.
Mulvey, Laura. 1975. "Visual Pleasure and Narrative Cinema." *Screen* 16.3: 6–18.
Simon, J.-P. 1983. "Énonciation et narration : Gnarus, auctor et Protée." *Communications* 38: 155–91.
Spicer, Andrew. 2002. *Film Noir*. London, Routledge.
Telotte, J.P. 1984. "The Detective as Dreamer: The Case of *The Lady in the Lake*." *Journal of Popular Film and Television* 12.1 (Spring): 4–15.
Williamson, Catherine. 1996. "'You'll see it just as I saw it': Voyeurism, Fetishism, and the Female Spectator in *Lady in the Lake*." *Journal of Film and Video* 48.3 (Fall): 17–29

Shooting Stars and Poet Friends in My Bedroom
Domestic and Poetic Intimacy in Pull My Daisy

Céline Murillo

> Tranquil bird in inverted flight bird
> Nesting in air
> —Guillaume Apollinaire

If cinema is an art of spectacle and movement that often involves telling a story to unknown people, while intimacy is about what happens among people who are very close, or even about what happens inside oneself, then representing intimacy on the silver screen is, no doubt, a feat. It takes a rare bird, a "bird in inverted flight" (Apollinaire 75), to do so. I aim to show that *Pull My Daisy* is just that. Even if it has not been shown much, the film has been praised as the emblem of Jonas Mekas's New American Cinema Group and is a landmark in the history of underground and experimental cinema. It opens the way to a new kind of avant-garde, one less given to formalism and more focused on documenting the everyday, the commonplace and its intimacies. Shot in 1959 by painter Alfred Leslie and photographer Robert Frank, it is one of the rare films that was made by and about the Beat Generation poets who are the stars of the film. Jack Kerouac, a "shooting star" who was already very famous in 1959 and died less than a decade later, adlibs all the voices in the film, while his poet friends, Gregory Corso, Allen Ginsberg and Peter Orlovski, play their own roles. The room, which is actually a bedroom, where the scenes take place is Alfred Leslie's loft. The film's plot is based on an event that took place at Neal and Carolyn Cassady's home in California when they had invited a bishop interested in Buddhism, with all their poet friends attending, including Kerouac and Ginsberg.

My contention is that this film offers viewers three degrees of intimacy, progressing from the widest to the narrowest and from the most accessible to the most hidden. Accordingly, attention will be paid, first, to a shared or social intimacy that corresponds to the intimate circle of the Beats, which the film portrays as a family, then to the poetical intimacy which involves only two people (Corso and Ginsberg), but requires, above all, poetry as a special vehicle for the intimate relationship, and finally to the specific stance vis-à-vis intimacy created by Kerouac's voiceover.

The Intimate Sphere of the Beat Poets: Pull My Daisy *as Home Movie*

Spectators watch, and hopefully enjoy, *Pull My Daisy* as an experimental, underground or avant-garde film, because of its beautiful grainy photography and/or Kerouac's poetic and unrealistic voiceover. Yet I would suggest that it is also a home movie that enables the viewer to share in the group intimacy of the Beat poets.

Leslie's studio is the first element that makes the film similar to a home movie and favors the representation of a form of family or social intimacy— an intimacy shared by a reduced number of people in a sheltered place. In the one-room apartment, we can see all the little things and daily mess that evoke the intimate zone a family lives in. The film depicts some very mundane actions, for example when a young woman opens the blinds [1:26], a little boy has breakfast [2:16] or a man washes his face [7:52]. In the meantime, Kerouac's voiceover talks about the daily life of this woman who tidies her husband's clothes. The place is thus defined, both visually and orally, as a home that proves welcoming for all the friends that either drop by or are invited there.

As in a home movie, our perception of this social intimacy is enhanced by the lack of a dense and gripping narrative. We are left to focus on a rather boring event: a dinner among friends. In a collection of articles about intimacy, Lila Ibrahim-Lamrous says there is nothing more intimate than "enjoying the simple pleasures of a family meal or a festive evening among friends" (9, my translation). In other words, the viewer can only enjoy these sequences if s/he believes, through secondary identification, that s/he is really an intimate member of this group. Indeed, for Eric De Kuyper, "those onscreen and those in the room belong to the extended family of the underground cinema and the beat movement, and may experience a feeling of intimacy watching the movie" (20–21, my translation). For spectators familiar with the Beat poets, the film offers a unique occasion for closeness with them. We are admitted to witness their attacks on bourgeois values: first, there is no food at this family dinner, and second, the small talk typical of a commonplace evening among friends is replaced by "strange and interesting" discussions, as stated by the bishop [12:28].

The somewhat tenuous story line relates an evening among the Beat poets, so that the poets who are in the film (Corso, Ginsberg, Orlovski, Larry Rivers and a few others) did not have to play a character part, just their own role. Since no direct sound was recorded on the set, the text of the play did not have to be recited. This freed the participants from the need to use acting techniques linked to reciting a text. In the same way, their movements did not have to meet the requirements of stage acting. In other words, the poets were at a friend's place and just had to follow a screenplay that was not very different from what they would have done without any screenplay at all. Technical constraints were reduced to a bare minimum. The apparatus remains visible for the spectator, notably due to Kerouac's dubbing all the voices. The lack of technique and the running commentary makes the film even more like a home movie.

On its release, the film aroused heated debate as to whether it was a "vérité" film (Sargeant 23): the question was to find out whether the film had been improvised or rehearsed. However, by looking at it as a home movie, the binary rehearsal/improvisation becomes irrelevant, since, if it had been rehearsed, then it would provide an opportunity to see the Beat poets playing rehearsed parts. As Jack Sargeant has noted, "if part of Jack Kerouac's literature was to live and document life as poetry then this may also be viewed as part of a *weltanshauung* behind the production of the film, which appears to be a joyful cinematic affirmations of the Beat way of life" (23).

The spectatorial contract that enables us to watch the film as a home movie is not the only element that facilitates the perception of group intimacy: the aesthetics of the film also concur to the portrayal of a sheltered, well-bound place that favors shared intimacy. The homely depiction of the loft, and the fact that the film was mostly shot indoors in a way reminiscent of *Kammerspiel* films, contributes to this impression. Out of four outdoor sequences, three are shot from the inside, through a window of the apartment, causing the lighting and the texture to change. The only outdoor sequence shows the bishop preaching [14:10–15:02]: its narrative motivation is so scant that it could easily be considered as a mental image, representing the meditative bishop's reverie. Moreover, this scene, which shows people chanting and preaching, is deprived of any voiceover and feels strangely silent: this stylistic variation, together with the lack of clear motivation, gives the impression of a "collage," as if it did not really belong to the narrative and, as a result, did not open up the diegetic space.

The film also depicts the flow of time. Unlike most films, there are no ellipses marking clearcut divisions in time. Nor does the film rely on "real time." Instead, time is contracted: the story takes place between about eight a.m. and eleven p.m., that is, fifteen diegetic hours reduced to twenty minutes of screen time. Time goes on steadily to show us a small-scale model of this party. This approach endows the film with a fluidity similar to Kerouac's voiceover. Indeed,

> Kerouac appears to have regarded the stream of images in cinema as a dematerialized and hence ungraspable phenomenon that constitutes a natural analogue for three other phenomena in which he was deeply interested: the flow of human mental processes, the flow of spontaneous prose that captures and represents those processes, and the flow of change and "becoming" [Sterrit 51].

This management of story time can be seen as an attempt to make group intimacy more intense and perceptible. The spectator is immersed in it, with very few outlets to escape either mentally or visually, thereby reinforcing her/his identification with the members of the group with whom s/he shares a form of seclusion. Watching the film as a home movie and immersing her/himself into a flowing and protective narrative, a metaphorical "nesting place" (Lamrous 9), the viewer is presented with what is ambiguously both a presentation and a representation of a group's social intimacy.

Poetry and Intimacy

At this point, the film appears as a private zone where no intruders are allowed and intimate relationships can further develop. This is especially true when it comes to Corso and Ginsberg's poetic duet. However, this duet between two people present onscreen could also be understood either as a monologue since the only voice we hear is Kerouac's, or even as a trio if we add Kerouac's aural performance to Corso and Ginsberg's visual performances.

The two men's poetic intimacy appears through the closeness of their bodies: sitting side by side, they share a joint [4:58] (Fig. 10). The close shot of the joint and their lips turns smoking into a metaphorical kiss. This obliquity is not only due to the camera's shying away from direct representation of

Fig. 10. Gregory Corso and Allen Ginsberg sharing a joint in Robert Frank and Alfred Leslie's *Pull My Daisy* (1959).

homosexuality, but it also suggests a means of leaving a mental space between the idea and its visual representation in order to preserve intimacy from the immediacy of filmic images. The poets' faces appear very close to the spectator; thanks to the rather conventional utilization of the shot/reverse-shot technique, space seems unified and easy to apprehend. The closeups may be interpreted as a form of physical, emotional and intellectual closeness between the two friends. This sense of proximity also comes from the dynamic and centripetal composition of a two-shot that winds upon itself: there is a void at the center, while we can see the characters' hands at the bottom of the shot and half of their faces at the top, causing our eyes to circulate around the central emptiness. This shot foregrounds the characters' closeness: the movement of the viewer's eyes induced by this peculiar composition suggests the characters are engaging in closeness and intimacy.

Some of the extreme close shots used in this film create a form of "haptic visuality," a term used by Laura Marks to describe "the way vision itself can be tactile, as though one were touching the film with one's eyes" (xi). According to Gilles Deleuze, images can "allow the eye to function like the sense of touch" (85). In other words, through synesthesia, our sense of sight provides information that is more relevant to our sense of touch. Here, the viewer can feel the woolly fabric of Ginsberg's shirt, the rough skin of his finger, the more delicate skin of his face or the slight moisture on his lips.

Nearness and intimacy make way for "extimacy" when the slightly transparent pages of Ginsberg's notebook appear [4:38]. Speaking for Ginsberg, Kerouac's voice mentions "the purple moonlight pages, where the sacred naked doodlings do show." The auxiliary "do" is used to emphasize this unique occasion to see this most desirable vision, while the phrase "purple moonlight" evokes a romantic and nocturnal atmosphere, as well as the difficulty to see in the dark or doing something forbidden, like "moonlighting," for instance. Yet all we can see are "doodlings," a derogatory word referring to a form of mock-writing, something childish and infraverbal, whose meaning is not accessible. As such, they are like the visible trace of the person who made them—of her/his body. If we pursue this metaphor, these doodlings are clothed in neither meaning nor style and are, as such, "naked." Doodlings are not engrossing like a novel or informative like a newspaper; the only interest they can arouse is voyeuristic. Describing the iconic image of handwritten pages as "secret naked doodlings" is a way for Kerouac to reinstate words back where cinema had removed them by visually transforming poetry into illegible graffiti. Both written and infraverbal (when they are onscreen), these doodlings are the visible trace of the person who formed them; they are a sign of their hands and body. Consequently, there is a voyeuristic interest in looking at them in all their "nakedness."

The "doodlings" we get to see and hear, if neither quite "secret" nor "naked," are nonetheless born from the intimate and commonplace, a space from which an improvised poetic voice emerges. For example, the two men who are drinking beer comment on what happens around them: "Look at those cars out there. Out there, a million screaming 19-year-old men being run over by gasoline trucks: so I'll throw the match on it" [3:00]. First, the voice announces the situation—the cars in the street; then it gives way to a lyrical evocation, drifting away from reality into metaphors, when we hear about young men screaming and the oil business, an utterance that might refer both to the incipient Vietnam war and the opposition to capitalist oil mining industries. Corso acts out these deprecating comments by mimicking the gesture of setting fire to the outside world, here the heavy New York traffic we can see in a reverse shot [3:02]. The effect is rather striking since the evocation starts with what the characters and viewers can actually see, links it to loftier considerations about world politics, and returns to the character's position by synchronizing a sentence—"I'll throw a match on it"—and a gesture. In the shelter of the apartment, the two men are free to enjoy their own company. They comment on the outside world in very negative terms. It is difficult to say if they are voicing political discontent or if they are just snugly defending their intimacy by rejecting what is not part of it, since there is not, strictly speaking, a binary between intimacy and political life; indeed, political thoughts could also be constitutive of an intimate relationship.

As the sequence wears on, poetic diction becomes omnipresent. The film announces from the start that the poets are "bursting with poetry," leading the viewer to expect a poetic outpouring. The disclosure of intimacy depends, here, on the poets' talent and ability to produce a lyrical voice. Poetry regains its original meaning of production. The lyrical voice functions as a chiseled form of inner life made to be cautiously revealed. We are no longer, here, in the scope of a public reading, but rather in the Lacanian framework of what Serge Tisseron calls a movement toward "extimacy" where what is intimate is shared in a safe social zone in order to receive an empathetic response and be reworked interiorly:

> I will call "extimacy," the movement that drives everyone to expose part of their inner life, both psychological and physical. This tendency has remained unnoticed even if it is essential for human beings. It consists of the wish to communicate about one's inner world. This movement would be impossible to understand if it only entailed "expression." If people want to expose certain parts of their life, it is to better appropriate them afterwards, by inwardly reworking them in another way thanks to the reaction they elicit from their kinship. The desire for extimacy is actually geared towards creating a deeper intimacy [Tisseron 52–53, my translation].

In *Pull My Daisy*, onscreen oral poetry coincides with all sorts of facial expressions and small gestures. These expressions and kinetics are so many restrained emotions. We understand from Ginsberg's smile that he is in wonderment when he mentions "all the strange gum-chewing geniuses" [5:57], or from Corso's gestures that he becomes angry when he tells his friend to "stop jumping up and down like a hipster cat" [5:38]. In these two examples, gestures are outer signs of ordinary inner life, as opposed to the poetry reading that was an exceptional demonstration of a different kind of inner life. To confirm this, small expressions and suppressed gestures, evoking the emergence of the characters' inner lives, continue after the poetic duet turns into a larger party, affecting all characters including the bishop, whose tightly interlocked hands might express in a non verbal way his suppressed anxiety [13:48]. If the film enables us to perceive the characters' inner lives, is it possible, as Tisseron's understanding of "extimacy" seems to suggest, to do so without destroying the film's own interiority?

Voice and the Danger of an Open Body

The previously discussed poetic overflow is an expression of inner life, but it is by no means certain that the viewer witnesses the second moment of extimacy where the characters are supposed to take back what they have exposed and rework it into further intimacy. Kerouac's voice, the most important medium of the poetic voice in the film, plays an ambivalent role in the representation of intimacy. The voiceover ushers us into the Beat poets' circle, stating everything the characters are supposed to say in a manner similar to the barker of early silent films, or more recently, to the person screening a home movie who identifies people and cues saying: "here on the screen this is your father, he was saying..." (De Kuyper 213).

This voice addresses the spectators alone. Surprisingly enough, Kerouac's voice was added onto the already edited film (Sargeant 20). As a result, there is a two-way process of adaptation (Murillo 2012) between Kerouac's 1957 play, entitled *The Beat Generation*—which was never produced (Sargeant 20) and was not published in book form until 2005—and the silent images of *Pull My Daisy*. Thus, Kerouac's play has inspired the images that his voiceover then reacts to. Indeed, Leslie and Frank deliberately kept Kerouac off the set for fear of his disruptive behavior (Sargeant 37, 42).[1] As a result, his voiceover works as a spectatorial response to the images or as a second enunciative source added to the one that relies on the spectators' identification with the camera. More often than not in cinema, the voice and other aural elements are synchronized to the images; thus, even if the filmic enunciation depends on several channels, it cannot be separated into various independent sources, contrary to what happens here. In *Pull My Daisy*, the discrepancy between what is seen and what is heard becomes blatant. There is no make believe, no pretence that sound and images were recorded together. For example, when we see a pensive Delphine Seyrig with her mouth shut, we hear the thoughts of her character in voiceover: "If [...] we could have made an impression to the bishop" [16:23]. When the voice verbally expresses a feeling, the image conveys something else, not only because it is a different medium, but also because the speaker does not have access to the emotion the actor feels or tries to represent. So as spectators, we see two different, and somehow parallel, attempts at conveying an emotion. In the previously analyzed sequence, we can see Corso's snarling lips and shiny eyes, while the voiceover says: "I could tell you poems that would make you weep with long hair, goodbye, goodbye" in a surprisingly angry tone [6:06]. This line plays with the modal "could" that suggests impeded will, and is therefore consistent with the exasperated grin, but it also includes a sense of melancholy thanks to the word "weep," which is at odds with what is visible onscreen. Throughout the film, we are constantly reminded of this gap between what we can see and hear. I would argue that it creates, for the spectator, an interstitial space that can be invested with the character's inner life: we are revealed certain things through the voice, but the image (and especially the facial expressions) do not reveal the same things, as if this inconsistency were the sign we were missing clues that are left untold as they belong exclusively to the characters' inner life.

Kerouac's voice addresses the spectators alone. The voice is, then, direct insofar as it is not mediated by an actor's body visible onscreen. Kerouac's voice is "acousmatic" (Chion 65), i.e., it is not localized relative to the diegetic world onscreen. It comes from nowhere and is present everywhere, enveloping the spectators. At the same time, it retains a voice's ability to connect the interior and exterior of the body. According to Paul Zumthor,

> The voice lodges in the silence of the body, as did the body in the womb, but contrary to the body, it may return to this shelter at any time, annihilating itself as speech or sound. Should it speak from within, it resonates with the echo of this desert dating back from before separation, out of which life and peace, death and madness oozed [11, my translation].

To put it differently, when Kerouac's voice is heard, it emerges from the "silence in his body," the innermost part of himself that is hidden and unspeakable: it refers to the body as matter. This brings to mind Roland Barthes's notion of the "voice's grain," according to which a voice, even deprived of virtuoso qualities, still attracts our attention as it denotes a unique human being (236, my translation). In this case, the voice's "grain" or texture functions as a powerful synecdoche of the entire body's materiality, since the body is left entirely to the spectator's imagination. Hearing Kerouac's voice is like feeling his breath touching our ears. From this angle, Kerouac's voiceover increases our intimacy with him and our closeness with the film in general.

Yet for Kerouac and the Beats, the body is often something to be exhibited, to the point that it becomes deprived of interiority. Its sexual life or excremental functions can be shown without restraint. Here, Kerouac associates the "sacred naked doodlings" with the "secret scatological thoughts" [4:38]. Orally, we cannot distinguish between "scatological" and "eschatological," which creates a comical confusion between a religious or philosophical paradigm centered on the end of time, and bawdy play dwelling on excrements that is reminiscent of Bakhtin's conception of "the grotesque image [which] ignores the closed, smooth and impenetrable surface of the body and retains only its ex-crescences (sprouts, buds) and orifices" (318). This pun marks Kerouac's specific conception of life and of his body: for him, the body is not a sanctuary, as opposed to the apartment in the film, it is not completely closed, which puts to the test the Christian ideal of salvation, as confirmed by the following quote from *The Vanity of Duluoz*: "How can you be redeemed when you have to pass food in and out of your body's bag day in and day out, how can you be 'saved' in a situation so sottish and flesh-hagged as that?" (265).

So on the one hand, Kerouac's nearly uninterrupted vocal flow of description and thoughts may be obscene and expose too much, as it is connected to his body. Yet, on the other, the content of what is said prevents this: the presence of hidden thoughts, that are mentioned but not stated, leaves a layer of secrecy. Altogether we may experience the slight obscenity of the voice's flowing exhibition of thoughts with the intense, nearly physical closeness the acousmatic voice creates. I would argue that this is, in effect, a true movement of extimacy, where the voice "extimates" what the haptic image, with its autonomy and its insistence on surface and obliquity, returns to the inner self of the characters. This movement is only for the spectators, as it relies entirely on our various perceptions of the voice and images.

Casting, narrative and stylistic choices tend to center *Pull My Daisy* on an ambivalently strange and commonplace event: a dinner among the Beats the movie invites us to. A private apartment, lack of professionalism and flowing narrative time endow the film with an impression of captured intimacy. The film also succeeds in giving us access to the intimate because it uses a poetic voice (Kerouac's) that is at once famous and very much physical thanks to the voiceover. The utilization of the voice is reminiscent of a public poetry reading, whereas onscreen the poets dwell in their private zone, confiding in each other. A poetic voice, be it Kerouac's or another poet's, obviously contains a contradiction between public and private. *Pull My Daisy* manages to play with this contradiction so skillfully that we ceaselessly marvel at hearing Kerouac's voice, touching Ginsberg's shirt and feeling at home with the Beat poets. Thanks to a one-off configuration of aesthetic values and talents, cinema exercises, here, its power as magic lantern, continuously shedding its surprising light on intimacy.

Notes

1. Frank was afraid of "the destructiveness he could bring about" (Sargeant 42), while Leslie was only worried that he would "bring drunks up" (Sargeant 37).

Works Cited

Apollinaire, Guillaume. 1971. *Selected Writings*. Trans. Roger Shattuck. New York: New Directions.
Bakhtin, Mikhail. 1941 [1993]. *Rabelais and His World*. Trans. Hélène Iswolsky. Bloomington: Indiana University Press.
Barthes, Rolland. 1990. "Le grain de la voix." *L'Obvie et l'obtus*. Paris: Seuil, 1982. 236–45.
Chion, Michel. 1990. *L'Audio-vision: Son et image au cinéma*. Paris: Nathan.
Deleuze, Gilles. 1981. *Francis Bacon: Logique de la sensation*. Paris: Editions de la Différence.

_____. *The Logic of Sensation: Francis Bacon*. 2003. Trans. Daniel W. Smith. London: Continuum Press.
De Kuyper, Eric. 1995. "Aux origines du cinéma: le film de famille." *Le Film de Famille*. Ed. Roger Odin. Paris: Meridiens Klincksieck. 11–26.
Ibrahim-Lamrous, Lila, and Severine Muller, eds. 2005. *L'Intimité*. Clermont-Ferrand: PU Blaise Pascal.
Kerouac, Jack. 2005. 1967 [1994]. *Vanity of Duluoz*. New York: Penguin.
_____. *The Beat Generation*. Oxford: Oneword Classics.
Marks, Laura U. 2000. *The Skin of the Film: Intercultural Cinema, Embodiment, and the Senses*. Durham: Duke University Press.
Pull My Daisy. 2012. Dir. Robert Frank and Alfred Leslie. Written by Jack Kerouac. With Gregory Corso, Allen Ginsberg, Peter Orlovsky and Larry Rivers. 1959. DVD. Steidl.
Sargeant, Jack. 1997 [2009]. *The Naked Lens: Beat Cinema*. Berkeley: Soft Skull Press.
Sterritt, David. 2004. *Screening the Beats*. Carbondale: Southern Illinois University Press.
Tisseron, Serge. 2002. *L'Intimité exposée*. Paris: Hachette.
Zumthor, Paul. 1985. *Introduction à la poésie orale*. Paris: Seuil.

Public Confessions in *American Revolution 2*

Zachary Baqué

Documentary Filmmaking in the 1960s and American Revolution 2

The 1960s are most often remembered today through the media images these "exciting and turbulent years" produced and which have, in turn, shaped our understanding of the decade (Kallen 10). These "images of the 1960s [that] still haunt us, still anger us, still entrance us, still puzzle" are precisely images that have become part of "the collective memories," such as massive demonstrations, urban violence and large music festivals (Farber 3). Some historians even claim that the relative lack of success of some of the Sixties' most active members of society is due in part to the way the media distorted their ideals and the methods used to try and build a better society.[1] Among the most famous political slogans that defined the decade was "the personal is political." Greater awareness that the social and individual problems encountered by citizens could be addressed as political questions led to a greater visibility of these problems. Activists thus focused on making visible and collective what were so far understood as individual and intimate issues. The politics of 1960s counterculture, at the grassroots level, was meant, in part, to turn the personal into the political and publicize the helplessness and loneliness of the individual inside a community. Virtually every minority group used the same method of presenting their issues visibly before attempting to find solutions to better society. What, then, were the devices and strategies deployed to bring about the transformation of an intimate personal problem into a political issue that could be tackled collectively? A newfound focus on consciousness was supposed to bring about the "unraveling [of] the lessons learned from birth—the very socialization process—so that the individual could see how the system operated to mold one's social self, and in doing so, envision alternatives"[2] (Michals 42). What became the most important factor in bringing about that change or that alternative was a sudden moral realization that there was a major discrepancy between the ideals of various individuals, as well as those of the nation, and the reality at hand. This transformation can be encapsulated in the following manner: a moral realization that individual problems could also be seen as collective led to a greater visibility of those issues before finally triggering an attempt at defining solutions.

This pragmatic question about the means to include individuals in a larger political community obviously had vivid repercussions in the world of film. The main question became: how is it possible to represent what so far had remained invisible, the intimacy of individuals in a homogenized (or so it was claimed) society? How was one to cinematically account for this questioning of the status quo? Hollywood's main answer was to allow for a more explicit representation of sexuality, of course (the end of the Hays Code in 1968[3]), but also of explicit politics. Beyond works of fiction, this was treated mostly within the emergence of a new style of documentary filmmaking. These documentaries dealt directly with politics, understood as either the electoral and legislative processes or the attempts by individuals to change society on the local level. Documentaries and cinema more generally became, then, modes of political expression, whose aim was not simply to represent society, but also to be part of the solution. These works are, in the words of David E. James (2002), "simultaneously documentations of radical political activities and themselves political interventions that aimed to generate changes in the structure of American society" (294). Film could, therefore, be both a representation and an act.

Technological changes can partly explain this newfound focus on intimate subjects. Easily portable cameras and the possibility to record sound simultaneously with image, even on location, made the entire production of films easier and more accessible. According to James McEnteer, "[t]hese expanded abilities endowed nonfiction films with new levels of intimacy and power" (xvi). The intimacy he mentions is at the very least twofold: first, the intimacy of the topic tackled and, second, the intimacy of the relationship between filmmaker and filmic subject. The first level of intimacy includes aesthetic issues such as the representation of the raising of the political awareness that one's intimacy can be included in a wider collective struggle: how can the filmmaker make visible something that is largely intimate (the personal decision-making process)? Concurrently, the second level of intimacy has to do with the relationship between filmmaker and filmic subject: what type of filmic strategy should be used by the filmmaker to reach that representation of the political process on the intimate level of the individual? This question is an integral part of the study of intimacy in documentaries, because, as Calvin Pryluck has noted, "ultimately, we are all outsiders in the lives of others" (197). Indeed, as one of the filmic subjects in *American Revolution 2* explains in an intimate closeup that works as a segue between the first and the second parts: "You think you know what we have. You don't know what we have" [21:43]. In short, can the powers of cinema be used to know what others possess?

This essay focuses on one specific genre of documentary that can be called "films about political dissidents" (McEnteer xv), and more specifically on *American Revolution 2*, which came out in a small number of theaters in 1969. The movie was the product of The Film Group, Inc, a group of filmmakers who mostly directed commercials and promotional films.[4] They understood film as a collective effort, which explains the absence of credits. The most important filmmakers of *American Revolution 2* were Mike Gray[5] and Howard Alk who worked as an editor and—as one of the founders of Second City, an improvisational theater troupe in Chicago—can be considered as a cultural activist.

In August 1968, the Film Group was shooting a commercial for KFC with Colonel Sanders, and then found themselves in the streets of Chicago right when the police brutally assaulted demonstrators protesting against the Democratic National Convention that ultimately nominated Hubert Humphrey as the Democratic candidate for the forthcoming presidential election. Mike Gray and his crew recorded the mayhem surrounding them. Gray then called Alk, who felt that the footage could be used in a documentary that would deal not simply with the events of Chicago, but with the current state of America. Their aim may have been partly to show what was largely hidden from view by the media coverage of the convention due to the networks' need for sensational material at the expense of clarity and balance.[6] Under the influence of Alk, the movie became much more than an insider's coverage of the convention and the violence it triggered in Chicago. In one of the very few reviews of the film after its release, Roger Ebert (1969) writes that "the film is about how a neighborhood had its idea of Chicago permanently altered by the events of convention week." In other words, the film describes how history changes the intimacy of its witnesses.

The film is composed of three parts:

(1) the title "A few honkies get their heads beat" [00:00–21:51] appears at the end of the first part: it begins with the demonstrations surrounding

the Democratic National Convention in Chicago, one of the most famous media events of the 1960s, the coverage of which may have influenced the later victory of Nixon, and its immediate aftermath (Dick Gregory and Pierre Salinger discuss the situation with the crowd). This part concludes with another police intervention and the arrest of Gregory.

(2) "What we have" [21:52–45:43] includes various meetings with African Americans, who express different positions (the Black Panthers' ideology or thoughts from members of an older generation), and the Young Patriots, mostly poor white southerners who have just moved to Chicago. The film suggests that these seemingly opposite groups suddenly realize that they share a common problem, that of poverty, and that no help is to be expected from the liberals.

(3) "Right on" [45:44–75:07] describes the attempt by the two groups to get the community of Uptown organized: they disrupt a Model Cities meeting and speak directly with the local chief of police. The last segment of the film has a very ambiguous ending: the voiceovers of militants discussing the validity of the use of violence in a political struggle are heard over images of a cemetery and a final aerial shot very similar to the one used at the end of *Easy Rider* (Hopper, 1969).

In terms of film form, *American Revolution 2* is in between direct cinema, in which the "cinema documentarist" "aspired to invisibility" and "played the role of uninvolved bystander" to the profilmic "situation of tension," and more traditional interviews to the camera that can sometimes be likened to the practices of *cinéma vérité* that "tried to precipitate" "a crisis" (Barnouw 254–55). The film can be described much as David E. James (1989) characterizes two other films of the period:

> [a] successful attempt[] by White radicals to make themselves, their skills, and their access to the apparatus the vehicle for a discourse that is essentially the Panthers' own. [...] Thus their speeches—at rallies, in conversation among themselves, and also in direct address to the camera—make up the bulk of the films, supplying both their ideological stance and their formal organization[7] [183].

One is thus to understand that the film is a political act that includes not only the speeches of white radicals, but also, more directly, incorporates the speech of black activists. However, both Gray and Alk being white radicals themselves, James's analysis reveals its full potential in raising the question as to whether the discourse of the Black Panthers of Chicago, filtered through the white radical point of view of the two filmmakers, reaches the spectator without losing its intimate and personal conviction. Furthermore, one could wonder who the intended spectator of such a film is supposed to be. As early as 1970, Rosenthal asked: "Is one to assume, therefore, that the crusading film accomplishes little except salving one's own conscience and influencing a small section of the open-minded who have bothered to watch such a program at off-peak hours?" (17). What was true in the late 1960s and early 1970s is even more relevant today: how can contemporary viewers appreciate this film today, beyond its status as document of and from a bygone era? I will contend that the interest of the film lies in the aesthetic and ethical rapport between filmmakers and their filmic subjects who are granted, by the very process of filmmaking, the right to express their intimate point of view of the world and society at large. If the utterance of speech can be described as the public revelation of something personally intimate (Daney 167–75), then it becomes necessary to analyze the formal and ideological representation of speech in the film.

Framing as a Revelation of Intimacy

In one of the very few reviews published when the film came out, Roger Ebert (1969) claimed that, as spectators, "we see and hear only the people the film is about; they speak for themselves," thus seemingly denying the mediating role of the filmmakers. As mentioned before, the voice can be understood as the public emanation of the intimate. Framing that utterance of speech requires aesthetic and political decisions. In a striking scene, a young African American vividly describes a brutal encounter with the local police [22:51]. The camera first zooms out from the eye of the speaker, then concentrates at length on his face, before zooming back in on his eye. The young man speaks in front of a dark background. It may appear that this aesthetic choice (the blurring of the background) contradicts the political force of the voice. Indeed, as the speaker is denied his immediate context, his testimony tends to lose its specificity, i.e., the way it is highly determined by the social conditions that produced it. Despite the clear reference to a specific street, this voice and its intimate content become abstract, strangely depoliticized, as if it had come from out of nowhere. The voice becomes a pure cinematic device in the production of the film. In Ebert's words, "[t]he rhythm of the film is the rhythm of the words they're saying." From this perspective, it seems that the filmmakers used a filmic subject entirely for the visual benefit of the film.

The speaker first addresses the camera on his own behalf when we see his face entirely. Then, thanks to the slight pan to the left combined with a zoom-in, the man becomes an organic representative of the community, as emphasized by the ghostly apparition of another face in the background: the utilization of cast shadows makes these two faces blur, coalesce and become one (Fig. 11). The original speaker also speaks for others and is literally a spokesperson for his entire community. Framing also has as a political significance. In his 1969 *New York Times* review, Roger Greenspun praises the film's "willingness to push involvement to such an extent that ultimately form follows function." Zooming in is, thus, not simply a purely aesthetic decision, as in Bergman's *Persona* (1966). In *American Revolution 2*, the extreme closeup and the melting faces do not emphasize the potential schizophrenia of the character or his growing madness, but the fact that he is the last in a long line of people who have been abused by the police. He contains not only his past, but that of his community. His personal knowledge of police violence can no longer be contained; it becomes urgent for it to be uttered and made public because the intimacy of this knowledge is too much to bear.

In his study of documentary aesthetics, John Corner distinguishes between two different ways of appreciating the pictorial quality of a docu-

Fig. 11. The politics of framing: the individual as a spokesperson for his community, as shown in Howard Alk and Mike Gray's *American Revolution 2* (1969).

mentary film. First, what is called "looking through," described by Corner as "a relative transparency in the depiction" where the spectator focuses on the "referential integrity" of the film. The second mode of looking is called "looking at": it points to the act of looking at the film as an autonomous work of art, partially devoid of its referential function, the spectator thus focusing on its "aesthetic value" (Corner 53). In the long take analyzed here, these two modes of looking are neither opposed nor mutually exclusive: they both operate at exactly the same time and somehow strengthen each other. It is precisely because the image, by maintaining its aesthetic autonomy, never pretends to be an index of reality that it displays its political force as an icon.

In this respect, direct cinema ceases to be a theoretical fantasy aiming at an objective representation of reality and becomes a personal visual and aural interpretation of that same reality. Direct cinema works when the director takes responsibility for her/his take on the world and does not try to erase her/his own position in it. Direct cinema is thus the product of a distinct relationship, that of the director and his filmic subjects, as Calvin Pryluck has stated: "[i]t would not exist without the uniquely personal speech and lines made available by the people being depicted. A direct-cinema film is irreducibly the product of the personalities of the subjects as refracted through the personality of the filmmaker" (204–5). This raises ethical questions about the filmmakers' position and relation to their subjects.

Intimacy in a Collective Context

In the last part of the film, a long scene describes a public forum organized by the Black Panthers in order to hear the local inhabitants talk about their daily problems and try to instigate a collective effort to tackle these issues directly. Based on the precepts of direct cinema, it seems that the long take would be the ideal form for the representation of a public forum. In this scene, the filmmakers do, in effect, use long pans on the audience, so as to suggest that the scene's interest lies in the free circulation of voices, but it is also highly edited, even if the cuts are partially hidden by the hectic changes of point of view [46:00]. Once again, we are faced with one of the contradictions of direct cinema: the scene aims at recording reality as it is, the camera movement describing the flow of voices and the bubbling energy of the emerging community, but it also reveals that it is highly staged for the dramatic benefit of the film by the almost seamless editing. This conundrum or this inherent tension between recording and editing is partly resolved when reality itself becomes highly dramatic. In a previous scene, the camera lingers on a poster reading: "Is life an act?" [36:30]. Indeed, many 1960s protesters used the notion of life actors, first coined by the San Francisco Mime Troupe and then the Diggers (Doyle 80). If life is an act, then it is quite normal that real-life people appear as actors in a documentary, as is the case of Bobby Lee whose incredible persona is described as "remarkably Jeffersonian" in Richard Brody's 2007 review.

One could also claim that it is precisely the presence of the camera that hinders people's capacity to act as if it were not there. In that case, the entire theoretical background of direct cinema, i.e., that the filmmakers and their cameras should progressively be forgotten by the people, is put at a loss. In other words, this raises the question of whether or not it is even possible to film people's intimacy, even the little they would allow to be expressed publicly. Does direct cinema work only when dramatic events are present? During the public forum, a young white woman is asked by Lee to testify about her own perspective on police violence. Lee teases her, points at her baby, then soothes her into voicing aloud her intimate opinion. Very slowly, the woman, visibly ill at ease, opens up and tells another story of police abuse that affected her family. If it is quite certain that "the film gear serves to intimidate the wary" (Pryluck 196), it might also be possible to contend that the larger-than-life presence of Lee was a deterrent to the young woman's expressing herself. This scene highlights the ultimate ambivalence of the camera in the entire film when it comes to recording intimate experiences: it can serve as a catalyst, as in the scene in the pool hall, where many people talk at the same time in front of the camera [12:06], or on the contrary, as an element of restraint. What is certain, however, is that the previously mentioned scene with the woman is filmed as a victory, not only for the woman who has controlled her fears and accepted to share, but also for the entire community who has gained another individual ready to fight.

Concerning the problems linked to the presence of the camera, another scene is worth mentioning [76:12]. During the meeting with the local chief of police, a good example of politics on the local level where the decision-makers are directly held accountable by the community, a young man explains that he has been beaten up by the police. Pressed by the commissioner to explain the context of that violence, he reveals that he was waiting for his friend at the house of a homosexual. He has no problem, relatively speaking given the context of the public hearing, mentioning his friend's homosexuality, which means that the revelation of intimacy is not seen as an issue when it is made willingly. However, when he explains that the police forced him to say that he, too, was a homosexual, he uses a derogatory term, "fag," as if, suddenly aware of the presence of the camera, he felt the need to distance himself from what was then still widely seen as a perversion. Nevertheless, far from putting a barrier between the young boy and the rest of the community, his public voice serves as a link between citizens who appear to have no political connection whatsoever.

Very early on, the film makes it clear that the problem in Chicago has nothing to do with race relations, as the camera focuses several times on African-American soldiers during the first scenes of public demonstrations [9:11]. The film's central question is thereby put forth: how can poverty link people together despite differences? This is done through parallel editing to emphasize that, beyond obvious visible differences (the ongoing question as to whether the problems at hand are of a racial nature), all these people are fighting for a common cause. Poverty may have been partly hidden from view, but, as one cabdriver explains, if you stick around in Chicago, "you're bound to run into it" [12:04]. The task is, once again, to make something that is invisible appear in full view so that people can eventually realize that action is necessary. The film thus endeavors to show poverty as it is, potentially to raise the consciousness of the spectator who is then included in the collective effort, even if this potential spectator is probably already convinced of the necessity to build a political community of social outcasts. Clearly, making intimacy visible entails questions of power and ethics in the context of documentaries.

A Question of Ethics

In *American Revolution 2*, the ultimate intimacy of all political decisions depends on the personal realization, or belief at least, that one's problems are shared by others. Aesthetically, this implies that all individual utterances have to be represented in the same way, mostly with medium closeups of people talking. The requisite reverse shot does not separate speaker from addressee, despite the brutal cut that temporarily severs two intimacies, but, on the contrary, makes them equal in a common struggle. In instances where one speaker is obviously more advanced on his political path toward empowerment, the directors often cut to closeup on faces experiencing an opening up of their political awareness. Once again, offscreen diegetic voices connect the inherent solitude of all human beings. This aesthetic, and thus ethical, equality between profilmic people is paralleled by an attempt to establish a similar equality between filmmakers and subjects.

It seems that all of the filmic subjects included in the film consented to being filmed, although this cannot be entirely ascertained.[8] Even if it is impossible to clearly determine the motivations of these people in accepting to be in a documentary, one might surmise that they felt that the directors treated them as subjects rather than objects in a filmic experiment. The directors of *American Revolution 2* filmed both with and for their subjects. For example, in the second half of the film, a previous interviewee becomes a part of the film experience: with a microphone, he probes his fellow citizens to know if their personal problems could also be included in his general cause [20:47]. Another potential explanation for the free vocal expression of intimacy could be that the cinematic apparatus tends to empower filmic subjects, even when they have had little to no access to it. The distinction between those who feel that the camera itself may turn them into movie stars, and those who believe the recording camera may help them in their political opposition, is difficult to establish. What ultimately matters is that the voice of the people and that of the filmmakers are virtually superimposed. Indeed, it is possible to feel the collective contempt, expressed through pans over some distraught faces, for the "enemies" of this newly-gained consciousness. In the scene at the Model Cities[9] meeting, the camera is clearly on the side of the protesters, as it obviously mocks the shocked attitudes of the upper middle-class making decisions that will not affect them [58:24].

In terms of ethics, a final question needs to be addressed: What exactly makes an intimate body a filmic subject? Most of the people represented in the film are nameless, while some are briefly identified by their function (through a caption) linked to a place. For example, the only two people that are more or less identified are a "Pfc Illinois National Guard" [5:57] and later the "Executive director Chicago Convention Bureau" [11:00]. Even in the case of these two subjects that somehow represent the mainstream, the filmmakers have decided to let them retain the privacy of their name. What seems significant, here, is that the spectator can identify all filmic subjects as political bodies who retain their free will, despite their explicit belonging to a social class devoid of a voice. This is precisely what they claim the right to: having a part to play in the collective making of decisions that directly affect their lives, as in the previously described scene at the Model Cities meeting. The presence of cameras may have helped the protesters gain a voice and become both political and filmic subjects in their own right. However, the question remains: what distinguishes these people from those included in the contemporary epigones of direct cinema?

Brian Saunders contends that, taken out of their political and aesthetic context, the conclusions of direct cinema can be morally problematic:

> Inevitably, what was once a manifesto for a new artistic attitude in documentary has, since its brief domination of the genre, been vitiated. Hand-held footage

now serves as a shorthand cipher for candid honesty, appearing in television "docu-soaps" and dramas, "reality" shows, feature films and advertisements to lend a semblance of Robert Drew's avid vision [191].

If, from a formal point of view, direct cinema may be hard to distinguish from reality TV, their difference lies in the consideration of the adequate distance that can allow the person in front of the camera to express his intimacy as an exchange with the director. As Brian Winston (1998) aptly demonstrates,

> these films all involve relationships between the film-maker and the participants that add a dimension to the normal contractual bargain. The participant does not agree to allow the film-maker to document his or her life but rather joins the film-maker to document situations of the film-maker's creation [1988, 189].

The filmmaking process itself becomes a collective effort. What makes *American Revolution 2* rather unique is the filmmakers' willingness never to tamper with the experience of the participants and to somehow become participants themselves. The ultimate proof of their involvement in the lives of their filmic subjects is the brief shot of a policeman pointing at the camera and the cameraman running for his life [2:37].[10] Filming has become a political act that upsets the establishment.

Conclusion: How to Build a Community

American Revolution 2 relates the creation of a political community, albeit temporary, between the Black Panthers and the Young Patriots of Chicago. It also shows that the search for political allies is complex, as suggested by the ambivalence expressed by the local liberals when meeting this strange group of protesters. The building of a community was also fully realized on the level of production as a collaboration between Panthers and "radical White filmmakers" (James 1989, 183). However, if we accept the view that a political film should raise the political consciousness of its intended audience, *American Revolution 2* suffers from problems specifically related to its inclusion of the spectator. The absence of a clear naming strategy prevents the spectator from closely identifying with the politics of the protesters. At the beginning of the film, one policeman asks his colleague: "Do you know what Dick Gregory looks like?" [5:45]. The spectator of the film is in the same position as this policeman insomuch as both have a hard time deciphering exactly who the filmic subjects are. The film also somehow fails to account for the discrepancy in both groups' political potential and their true absence of means. But, in the end, the film's truth may well be that expressed by one of the first voices overheard through a speaker, which suggests that "mak[ing] your voice heard might possibly have some effect" [0:21].

If we adhere to "Godard's distinction between radical filmmaking and the filming of radical politics" (James 1989, 187), then *American Revolution 2* clearly falls into the second category. At the same time the film was released, other film collectives tried to practice cinema as a radical political act of intervention (James 1989, 213–31; James 2002, 290–98), with an approach that differed from Gray and Alk's rather observational strategy. The film's conclusion nevertheless points to a possible union of these political and cinematic strategies. As mentioned before, the film features harsh vocal exchanges on the values of violence and death as political devices over images of a cemetery. In his review for the *New York Times*, Greenspun (1969) wrote:

> The movie ends with a minor cinematic coup. As the voices continue in claim and counter claim, the images suddenly cut from angry people to graceful statuary, from a protest meeting to a cemetery, from indoors to outdoors, from feverish close-up to studied perspective, from the living to the dead. The juxtaposition is made quite without comment, and with only the largest, most humane kind of irony. The point is that if the film can push forward, it can also draw back, and from the pressures of our miseries it can shock us into calmness by no more than a change in scene.

I would offer an alternative reading of this scene. The film's pessimistic or, at least, ambiguous conclusion does not "shock us into calmness." Rather, it takes the original meaning of the world revolution quite literally: coming back to where one started as the title is superimposed on the very last image. The film's ending may shock the viewers into revolt and action, awakening what so many films have tended to ignore: our dormant intimate belief that there is such a thing as a world beyond the limits of the screen.

Notes

1. Gitlin, for example, lists the various "framing devices" used by the media in their covering of the movement's actions: he mentions "trivialization," "marginalization" and "disparagement of the movement's effectiveness" as the most powerful devices that favored the distortion of the movement's general message (27–28). However, Gitlin specifies that his book should not be read as "a simple blast at the media machine for lying about dissenters and crippling the movement." He includes other factors that could have led to the demise of the movement, such as its "ambivalence about authority and violence, its dependency on popular culture" and "its fascination with celebrity" (Gitlin xxi).

2. It should be noted that the chapter this quotation is taken from describes the link between the counterculture's consciousness expansion and radical feminism's consciousness raising, and, by no means, the wide spectrum of political activism in the 1960s. However, the strategy of consciousness raising, meant to "encourag[e] women to discuss matters of their private lives as part of their common condition," is very similar, albeit within a nonfeminist framework, to what the Black Panthers do in the film under study (Brick 166). The emphasis here is on the personal vocalization of private matters so that they become a collective political issue.

3. The Hays Code had already been on the wane before it was replaced by Valenti's rating system (Sklar 296-97).
4. See Chicago Film Archive website. Chicago Film Archives, "The Urban Crisis and the New Militants Series," http://www.chicagofilmarchives.org/pres-projects/the-filmgroups-urban-crisis-series. Retrieved on 9/1/2012.
5. See *Drug Crazy* website for more on Mike Gray, http://www.drugcrazy.com/mikegray.htm. Retrieved on 9/1/2012.
6. Gitlin evokes some of the framing devices used by the news media in their reports of the 1965 SDS March on Washington (27). He further contends that the devices were virtually the same during the coverage of the Chicago events (187).
7. This quotation, in fact, describes Agnès Varda's *Black Panthers: A Report* (1968) and *The Murder of Fred Hampton* (1971), also directed by Mike Gray's Film Group.
8. Brian Winston discusses the "consent defense" in "Ethics" (186-92).
9. For more on Model Cities, see D. Bradord Hunt, "Model Cities," *Encyclopedia of Chicago*, http://www.encyclopedia.chicagohistory.org/pages/832.html. Retrieved on 9/1/2012.
10. This shot is reminiscent of "footage taken by the Detroit WFPL [Workers Film and Photo League] of a 1932 strike" in which "there are shots of a panicking crowd taken by a panicking camera operator" (Winston, 1995).

Works Cited

Barnouw, Erik. 1973 [1993]. *Documentary: A History of the Non-Fiction Film*. 2d rev. ed. New York: Oxford University Press.
Brick, Howard. 1998. *Age of Contradiction: American Thought & Culture in the 1960s*. Ithaca: Cornell University Press.
Brody, Richard. 2007. "In Black and White." *The New Yorker*, June 4. http://www.newyorker.com/arts/events/revivals/2007/06/04/070604gomo_GOAT_movies_brody. Retrieved on 9/1/2012.
Corner, John. 1988 [2005]. "Television, Documentary and the Category of the Aesthetic." *New Challenges for Documentary*. Eds. Alan Rosenthal and John Corner. Manchester: Manchester University Press. 48-58.
Daney, Serge. 1983 [1996]. *La Rampe : Cahier critique 1970-1982*. Paris: Cahiers du Cinéma/Gallimard.
Doyle, Michael William. 2002. "Staging the Revolution: Guerilla Theater as a Countercultural Practice, 1965-1968." *Imagine Nation: The American Counterculture of the 1960s and '70s*. Eds. Peter Braunstein and Michael William Doyle. New York: Routledge. 71-97.
Ebert, Roger. 1969. "American Revolution Two (Review)." *Chicago Sun-Times* May 25. http://rogerebert.suntimes.com/apps/pbcs.dll/article?AID=/19690525/REVIEWS/905250301/1023. Retrieved on 9/1/2012.
Farber, David. 1994. *The Age of Great Dreams: America in the 1960s*. New York: Hill and Wang.
Gitlin, Todd. 1980 [2003]. *The Whole World is Watching: Mass Media in the Making and Unmaking of the New Left*. With a New Preface. Berkeley: University of California Press.
Greenspun, Roger. 1969. "The Screen: 'American Revolution 2,' Story of Chicago '68." *The New York Times*, October 21. http://movies.nytimes.com/movie/review?_r=1&res=9A06EED9113FE63ABC4951DFB6678382679EDE. Retrieved on 9/1/2012.
James, David E. 1989. *Allegories of Cinema: American Film in the Sixties*. Princeton: Princeton University Press.
_____. 2002. "'The Movies are a Revolution': Film and the Counterculture." *Imagine*

Nation: The American Counterculture of the 1960s and '70s. Eds. Peter Braunstein and Michael William Doyle. New York: Routledge. 275–303.

Kallen, Stuart A., ed. 2001. *Sixties Counterculture*. San Diego, CA: Greenhaven.

McEnteer, James. 2006. *Shooting the Truth: The Rise of American Political Documentaries*. Westport, CT: Praeger.

Michals, Debra. 2002. "From 'Consciousness Expansion' to 'Consciousness Raising': Feminism and the Countercultural Politics of the Self." *Imagine Nation: The American Counterculture of the 1960s & 70s*. Eds. Peter Braunstein and Michael William Doyle. New York and London: Routledge, 2002. 41–68.

Pryluck, Calvin. 1988 [2005]. "Ultimately We Are All Outsiders: The Ethics of Documentary Filming." *New Challenges for Documentary*. Eds. Alan Rosenthal and John Corner. Manchester: Manchester University Press. 194–208.

Rosenthal, Alan. 1971. *The New Documentary in Action: A Casebook in Film Making*. Berkeley: University of California Press.

Saunders, Dave. 2007. *Direct Cinema: Observational Documentary and the Politics of the Sixties*. London: Wallflower Press.

Sklar, Robert. 1975 [1994]. *Movie-Made America: A Cultural History of American Movies*. New York: Vintage.

Winston, Brian. 1988 [2005]. "Ethics." *New Challenges for Documentary*. Eds. Alan Rosenthal and John Corner. Manchester: Manchester University Press. 181–93.

_____. 1995. *Claiming the Real: The Documentary Film Revisited*. London: BFI.

The Limits of Hypermasculinity
*Intimacy in American Science
Fiction Films of the 1980s*

MARIANNE KAC-VERGNE

The successful science fiction franchises of the 1980s have often been criticized as masculinist because of their emphasis on male strength and invulnerability: while Claudia Springer denounces science fiction's "invincible armored cyborgs" as "protofascist masculine imagery" (97), Susan Jeffords analyzes RoboCop and the Terminator as "hard bodies" embodying Reagan's masculine tough stance against internal enemies (52). Although these films do showcase strong, muscular and thus "hard" bodies, I find it more productive to analyze *The Terminator* (James Cameron, 1984), *RoboCop* (Paul Verhoeven, 1987), *RoboCop 2* (Irvin Kershner, 1990), and even *The Fly* (David Cronenberg, 1986) in terms of hypermasculinity, a concept which allows to see both the glorification of masculine attributes with an emphasis on "enactments of masculinity where aggression and physical strength are accentuated" (Levy 2007) and the negative connotations of the "macho personality" defined by Mosher and Sirkin (1984) in their Hypermasculinity Inventory, which include "Calloused Sex Attitudes" and "Violence as Manly." In the words of Erica Scharrer,

> the hyper-masculine male eschews and even ridicules "soft-hearted" emotions, celebrates and views as inevitable male physical aggression, blocks attempts by women or others to appeal to emotions by belittling sexual relations or women in general, and exhibits sensation-seeking behaviors that bring a welcome sense of vigor and thrill [616].

Analyzing science fiction films through the lens of hypermasculinity allows, then, to see the limits of this masculine ideal. Indeed, it would seem from both

Levy's and Scharrer's definitions that hypermasculinity is squarely on the side of exhibition and display. However, the films mentioned above tend to counterbalance scenes of bodily display with intimate scenes in which the hero's hybrid nature is revealed, underlining the vulnerability of a male hero penetrated by an Other, be it machine or fly. This essay seeks to explore how scenes of intimacy can reveal the vulnerability of the hypermasculine subject and the limits of hypermasculinity. I will show how, at first sight, the films seem to celebrate hypermasculinity as a public exhibition of the invulnerable male body. Focusing on scenes of self-reflexive intimacy, especially mirror scenes, will, however, enable me to underline the inherent vulnerability of a constructed hypermasculinity. Finally, I will examine moments of shared intimacy, which raise the question as to whether intimacy with others, especially women, may not be the true limit of hypermasculinity.

Exhibition

Many 1980s science fiction films tend to highlight the protagonists' virility through an emphasis on the male body and manly fashion attributes. Muscles are constantly underlined, especially biceps and pectorals, thanks to repeated low-angle medium shots on naked torsos, for instance, right after the Terminator's first appearance [4:11] or when Seth Brundle comes out of the telepod holding a baboon in *The Fly* [35:10]. RoboCop's body armor is a clear example of this hypermasculine glorification and even exaggeration of the male body, since the pectorals of the metal torso are clearly delineated. In the absence of body armor, the leather jacket functions as a fetishistic expression of virility, both in *The Terminator* where the Terminator "mans up," i.e., puts on a leather jacket and sunglasses to attack the police station [56:45], and in *The Fly* where it is thematized and repeatedly associated with virile sexual performance. Ronnie buys the jacket for Seth after their first night together; her ex-boyfriend Stathis Borans, who has followed her into the shop, snatches it from her in a jealous rage and comments sarcastically on Seth's "big cock" [27:14]. After his transformation into a hypermasculine hero, Seth always wears the jacket to go out, most visibly when he leaves Ronnie in search of a new female partner, ranting about "penetration beyond the veil of the flesh" while putting on the jacket over his naked torso [46:54].

Indeed, this is the only time Seth is seen in public without Ronnie in the entire film. The scene in the sports bar underlines his peaking hypermasculinity through a public exhibition of his physical strength [47:26–49:30]. As he enters the bar, Seth is contrasted with a short beer-bellied white-bearded old man and a skinny bespectacled pool player, while all the other customers are seated, so that Seth appears bigger and taller than everyone else, towering over Tawny, the woman he has set his sights on, perhaps because she is very short. His confident stride and direct pickup lines exude an exhilarated sense of superiority, as demonstrated when he challenges to an arm-wrestling match the strongest-looking man in the bar, played by Canadian former heavy-weight boxer George Chuvalo, an allusion to Cronenberg's nationality, but also an ironical comment on stereotypical masculine competitiveness in public. In this hypermasculine phase, Seth needs to display his strength as power over others, an exhibition of invulnerability that is grotesquely pushed to the extreme, as the crowd recoils in horror when Seth breaks his opponent's wrist in two.

Hypermasculinity is thus grounded in exhibition, a connection highlighted in *RoboCop* by the contrast between Murphy's first appearance in the police station at the beginning of the film, which goes largely unnoticed [2:48–4:30], and RoboCop's dramatic entrance in the same station later on. Murphy is indeed presented as an ordinary police officer, whose mildness and slightness do not attract a lot of attention on the part of coworkers more concerned with the general problems of the Detroit police than about the insignificant transfer of a noteless officer. The police as a group institution overshadows his individuality; tellingly, his arrival is preceded by a news flash announcing the death of three police officers and an establishing shot on the police station. The first person to appear in the station is the police captain who, while trying to keep his station under control, shows his strength and determination by manhandling a lawyer and his client out of the building. Murphy is shown in the background entering the station as they are thrown out, appearing in the frame as if by accident, and then constantly surrounded by other people, officers and criminals, who move noisily around him, crowding the shot and the soundtrack so that Murphy has little room to assert himself. In any case, he is immediately directed by the captain to the changing rooms, stepping out of the shot that stays on the captain, while the next shot cuts to a group of police officers discussing the fate of one of their colleagues. Again, Murphy is not given any space or time, as a lengthy tracking shot focuses on one officer after another. The sequence portrays the officers as a group from which Murphy is not singled out: he appears only briefly onscreen, greeted by a fellow officer in a two-shot. Dressed in the same uniform as the others, he is hardly ever shown alone in a shot, and the few medium closeups of him tend to emphasize his gentle features, slim build and medium height (he is slimmer and shorter than many of his colleagues, including the officer who greeted him). The unimposing and mild-mannered Murphy is of little consequence in this chaotic world, so that we learn very little of him before he is killed off twenty-two minutes into the film.

Transformed into an impressive titanium-clad cyborg, Murphy's reappearance in the police station as RoboCop is, on the contrary, all pomp and circumstance [28:10–30:09]. Like a dignitary, his entry is preceded by a fleet of vehicles and an army of technicians in lab coats, who march through a near empty police station without paying any attention to the police captain. The latter is pushed aside slightingly by the head of the team, and his protests are suddenly interrupted by RoboCop's delayed and star-like appearance, silhouetted behind thick glass. His stately advance in a heavy gait silences the station, as all eyes turn towards him and the astounded police officers rush to have a closer look at this object of wonder. RoboCop is, in effect, on display, his exhibition foregrounded by the cage-like wire-netting that functions as a second screen behind which the public stands, while a team of professionals bustle around him. Unlike Murphy, RoboCop is the center of attention in the narration and in the frame, shot in an extreme low-angle medium closeup that magnifies his colossal metallic body as it glistens in the neon light. RoboCop's spectacular nature is further underlined by his popularity with the media, who rush toward RoboCop as soon as he arrives on the site of a hostage crisis, abandoning a tough-looking but mundanely human lieutenant [35:13]. The media are portrayed as feeding on the hallmarks of hypermasculinity displayed by RoboCop, that is to say conspicuous invulnerability—a journalist asks him, "Are you invincible?"—and an imposing, even slightly threatening physical presence, emphasized by the repeated low-angle shots of RoboCop as he gets out of his car, which contrast with the overhead shot of the miniaturized crowd of journalists filming from the ground as RoboCop throws the terrorist out the third floor window of City Hall. The television news report on RoboCop that follows starts with a reprisal of the shot on the terrorist being thrown out the window, highlighting the general fascination aroused by public displays of strength resulting in the subjugation of others [37:10]. RoboCop always appears taller and bigger than everyone else, a physical superiority enhanced by the diminutive children surrounding him in the news report or his utter destruction of a cardboard target in front of his bemused fellow officers, impressed by the weapons skills of this new "supercop," as a policewoman calls him [30:02].

Indeed, hypermasculinity thrives on physical one-upmanship, that is to say masculine bodily superiority made public. The ideal of hypermasculinity is fully realized when the hypermasculine male confronts other men and subjugates them physically, allowing the display of physical domination and the consequent enhancement of the male body. Thus, the Terminator's incredible strength and invulnerability is only revealed in his confrontation with tough and aggressive punks [5:10–6:05]. He resists their knife attack by neatly hurling two of them back with his left hand, while he bores through and lifts up the third punk with his right arm. The exhibition of hypermasculinity's fearsome power is enhanced by the ease of his victory and underlined by a gory closeup of the Terminator's bloody arm, followed by a reaction shot of the terrified face of a once-mocking opponent, an effect reprised by *The Fly* with the closeup of the broken wrist spurting blood at the end of the arm-wrestling match. Indeed, hypermasculine science fiction films of the 1980s repeatedly feature challenges to the male bodies that are met with defeat: knives that do not penetrate the flesh, blows that hurt the aggressor, bullets ricocheting off their target, fires from which male bodies emerge unscathed. The enhanced bodies stay whole, while their opponents' are pierced through and through, as evidenced by the Terminator's punching through the punk's body, the broken wrist in *The Fly* or the bullet RoboCop fires through a woman's skirt to reach her rapist's groin in the first installment [33:57].

Vulnerability

However, by exhibiting the male body, the films also highlight the vulnerability of the hypermasculine subject, turned into an object on display, while the specific focus on hybrid, transformed bodies in *The Fly* and *RoboCop* entails a fragmentation of identity most visibly revealed in scenes of self-reflexive intimacy. The body's vulnerability is expressed, first, by its "to-be-looked-at-ness." Though this concept was initially applied by Laura Mulvey to describe the status of women in classical narrative film, it has become a defining characteristic of male characters in contemporary action and science fiction films: male characters have become objects of the gaze. However, as Pat Kirkham and Janet Thumim have pointed out, the objectification of male characters is usually linked to suffering and endurance rather than desirability (5). Men can be eroticized and made desirable by the gaze, as in the scene in *The Fly* when Seth's acrobatic feats are watched admiringly by Ronnie; indeed, the whole scene is seen through her eyes, the camera mediated by the female gaze in this instance [39:29–41:30]. The eroticization of the male body is further enhanced by the camerawork and the soundtrack: the camera alternates between long shots of the whole body performing acrobatic feats and medium closeups, often low-angle, of the chest and head to highlight bulging muscles and glistening sweat, while the general silence, broken only by Seth's heavy breathing, focuses our attention on the body at work. The scene ends on a beautiful still shot outlining Seth's torso with shafts of soft light on his gleaming and well-delineated muscles. The erotic appeal of the male body is finally confirmed by a reaction shot of Ronnie's smile and the return of music.

However, male to-be-looked-at-ness generally connotes suffering. The prolonged gaze on the suffering male body is central to the RoboCop films, where the camera repeatedly lingers on the body in pain, reworking again and again the seminal scene of Murphy's execution. The body is constantly exposed, penetrated, its inner workings revealed, as in the hospital scene where Murphy is intubated in extreme closeup and his bloody torso bared for defibrillation and the insertion of needles [22:46]. Even after Murphy dons the RoboCop armor, his body is continuously assaulted, exposed and dismembered, no longer bounded and contained by his armor. In *RoboCop 2*, Murphy's execution is replayed as a brutal attack on the now metallic body of RoboCop [34:44–39:19]. When a criminal gang traps him in a factory, they first blow off his hand and his inner circuits are revealed, with electric wires coming out of his maimed arm and his severed hand, while his body goes into spasm, spouting electric sparks. He is then methodically broken down with hammers, stakes and drills piercing through his body, his limbs falling to the ground, his electrical wires pulled out of his body like entrails, with oil (in place of blood) spurting out onto his face. Now a man without limbs, his body parts are dumped in front of the police station, revealing the insides of his body, as cables stick out of his chest and unrecognizable parts lay scattered across the floor like discarded organs. His armor having been "stripped," as one policeman exclaims, and his helmet removed, his body appears exposed and vulnerable, his torso suspended and fed by tubes, wires coming out where his legs used to be, his contorted face expressing pain through uncontrollable twitches and groans, his eyes rolled upward. The film insists at great length on the protagonist's agony, since the scene lasts over four minutes and is characterized by medium closeups, zoom-ins and closeups of the body, fragmented by the camera, while the soundtrack offers no relief, dominated as it is by unpleasant noises, such as the sound of drilling, hammering, electric shocks and electronic interference.

The male body's to-be-loked-at-ness in scenes of suffering thus represents the flip side of hypermasculine exhibition, a physical vulnerability further explored in scenes of intimacy where the protagonists' hypermasculine identity is radically challenged. Indeed, by insisting on the transformation of the male hero into a hypermasculine subject, films like *RoboCop*, *RoboCop 2* and *The Fly* display the constructedness of this identity, its fragmentation revealed by the male bodies' hybridity. This is especially visible in intimate scenes of self-discovery where the protagonists inspect their transformed bodies, recognizing them as radically Other. As David Roche has argued in his article on Cronenberg, such scenes play and develop on Freud's insight that the body is always seen as a foreign body, visually displaying and transferring the dichotomy between body and soul onto a hybrid or fragmented body as locus of a fragmented identity (147). The examination of the transformed body leads to the realization that the self has become Other, especially in mirror scenes which can be read as a canceling of the Lacanian mirror stage, where the self fails to be perceived as a whole but is seen, on the contrary, as irretrievably fragmented (Lacan 453). In *RoboCop*, for instance, the mirror scene highlights the fragmentation of the male body: when RoboCop takes off his helmet for the first time, the camera reveals a divided head—a mechanical skull made of metal casing, wires and earpieces surprisingly attached to a human face [77:34–78:50] (Fig. 12). The incongruous juxtaposition of shiny blue metal with the texture of his skin emphasizes the instability of RoboCop's bodily nature as well as his identity. Furthermore, the camerawork underlines the strangeness and artificiality of the human face, which is subsequently shown *after* the metal skull as a small, distanced and hazy reflection in the mirror. The well-delineated face looks like a cut-out, a human mask covering an electronic brain, so that it is now the human elements of RoboCop's body which seem fake. Rather than celebrating a successful hybrid creature or positive "mulatto cyborg," as LeiLani Nishime argues (45), it seems to me that this scene underlines the vulnerability of the fractured cyborg, with an emphasis on pathos conveyed through the music (soft strings in a minor scale), setting (an abandoned warehouse), acting, dialogue and camerawork, the scene ending, pointedly, with RoboCop asking Lewis in a sorrowful voice to leave him alone, the camera zooming out to a long shot of the lone figure. Moreover, another mirror scene in *RoboCop 2* confirms the fracture of the protagonist's identity, again in a scene loaded with pathos. RoboCop is spying on his former wife and child when memories of his former life as the human Murphy come rushing back: the camera adopts Murphy's point of view in subjective shots of his wife, until he follows her in the bathroom and appears onscreen as a reflection in the mirror. As soon as Murphy sees his reflection, he gives a start, his smile fades, and the camera cuts back to RoboCop [14:38]. The mirror thereby emphasizes the identity split, since the eyeline match is not confirmed by the shot of the smooth-faced human Murphy we expect, but by one of a helmeted RoboCop sitting in his police car. RoboCop's dual identity in the first film has become split in two distinct identities separated by a mirror that presents his former self as an entirely different person. The scene creates a jarring and disheartening effect, as the camera switches from POV shots from Murphy's perspective of himself in soft lighting and fleshy pastel colors, to a medium closeup of Robo-

Fig. 12. In Paul Verhoeven's *RoboCop* (1987), RoboCop/Murphy (Peter Weller) looks at it/himself in the mirror.

Cop framed and distanced by the car window, his metallic blue armor shining in the bright light, while the only visible portion of his face, his mouth and jaw, is left in the shadow.

However, when the boundary between the different bodies and identities disappears, pathos turns into horror, more specifically body horror, as human bodies are scrutinized and brutalized into revealing a hidden inhuman core. Contrary to the mirror scene in *RoboCop*, where RoboCop's fragmented body is distanced and delineated by the camera so that the spectator can see and understand, the mirror scene in *The Fly* utilizes extreme closeups to collapse the line between human and fly, provoking the spectator's disgust at the disintegration of the body and its inhuman reactions, for example when Seth loses his fingernails and spurts pus from his fingers onto the mirror [55:01–55:50]. Hybridity as blending rather than juxtaposition provokes, in effect, fear and horror at the collapse of a body that has been contaminated by an Other and is no longer contained and predictable. In fact, mirror scenes are particularly arresting since they are moments both of diegetic self-awareness for the protagonist and of distance for the spectator when identification is broken by distanced monstration or disgusting proximity.

It is interesting in this regard to compare the mirror scenes analyzed above, all featured in what could be called "transformation films," that is films focusing on the transformation of the masculine subject, with an apparently similar scene in *The Terminator*, a film where the making of the Terminator occurs offscreen and is not thematized. Indeed, halfway through the film, the Terminator also looks at his face in a mirror in order to repair himself [52:21–53:18]. However, the reflection of his face in the mirror as he gouges out his fake human eye appears clearly artificial: we do not see Arnold Schwarzenegger's face but a mask. Indeed, to show the mechanical eye beneath the human one, the film resorts to a puppet that resembles Schwarzenegger but is also a visible simulacrum, a break in conventional Hollywood seamlessness and our suspension of disbelief, which leads to an interesting *mise en abyme* of the machine behind the man. The visibility of the special effects emphasizes the absence of any pre-existing human identity so that intimacy is, in fact, impossible. Intimacy is, in effect, bound to an awareness of self which is "essentially" human, so that the Terminator cannot see anything else than an automaton in the mirror, while Seth and RoboCop desperately search the mirror for a disappearing human identity.

All these mirror scenes insist, then, on the unnaturalness of the protagonists' bodies, but *The Fly* and *RoboCop* mourn the loss of a whole and "natural" male body as the repository of an equally "natural" male identity, while at the same time highlighting the falsity of this concept. Indeed, science fiction films tend to present several versions of their protagonists, which embody different versions of masculinity, foregrounding the fact that masculinity is not an unchangeable essence, but a construction that can change with time and circumstance. *The Fly* opposes the new incredible Seth to the old introverted and gentle Seth; *RoboCop* constantly underlines what separates RoboCop from his previous human identity as Murphy; *RoboCop 2* centers on the possibility of programming men and cyborgs at will, reprogramming RoboCop to be a more sociable but ineffective public servant, while casting a criminal drug addict to be the next RoboCop; finally, even the *Terminator* series famously refashions the first film's brutal Terminator into an attentive protector in the second installment (James Cameron, 1991). The films thus acknowledge that there is not one single type of masculinity, but a whole range of masculinities, and even suggest that hypermasculinity is not the best version: Ronnie comments negatively on the new Seth who "look[s] bad" and "smell[s] bad," while ordinary citizens complain about RoboCop's "destructive behavior" in the sequel.

The Impossibility of Shared Intimacy

In fact, it seems to me that these American science fiction films of the 1980s offer a critical perspective on hypermasculinity, especially from the standpoint of an impossible intimacy with others, in particular women. The films all underline the fact that the hypermasculine protagonists cannot form or maintain emotionally and sexually intimate relationships with women. In *RoboCop* and *RoboCop 2*, for instance, shared intimacy is lost forever once Murphy has been transformed into RoboCop. It is present only in flashbacks showing moments of irretrievable happiness intrinsically linked to Murphy's human identity as a gentle and attentive family man. The flashbacks are all set at home, depicting an idyllic family life with loving wife and son, that contrasts starkly with a painful present. In *RoboCop*, the first flashbacks occur as Murphy is dying on a hospital bed and underline his severance from all human connections, as his son's question—"Can you do that Dad?"—and his wife's exclamation—"I really have to tell you something!"—remain open or inconclusive. The bond is definitely cut in the last image, which shows them waving a final farewell while the camera zooms out at great speed, signifying Murphy's imminent death [23:49–24:10]. The second series of flashbacks, when RoboCop visits his former home, amplify the pathos of the first by insisting on what the hero has lost [52:05–53:54]. Indeed, the editing juxtaposes past images of a joyful and animated home where his wife and son rush towards him, expressing love and admiration, and a lonely and sorrowful present in a now-deserted house where wife and son have been replaced by a computerized real estate agent. Furthermore, the scene contrasts the metal-armored and helmeted RoboCop with reverse shots of his wife, dressed in an open-neck pink bathrobe, declaring her love for him, thus emphasizing the human warmth and intimacy of the marital bedroom, to which the hefty cyborg reacts with frustration and anger, punching through the computer as he walks out of the house. The flashbacks highlight the emotional alienation of the hypermasculine hero, opposing RoboCop's loneliness and sorrow as he is faced with the computer's cold, inhuman and materialistic palaver, to Murphy's gentle smile and twinkling eyes in the crowded opening scenes and lively flashbacks all dominated by social interaction.

RoboCop 2 further develops the theme of impossible emotional intimacy, staging early on a painful meeting between RoboCop and his former wife where he is forced by OCP to renounce his humanity and his memories of her [16:58–19:14]. RoboCop is forever denied any intimacy; indeed, the seemingly considerate remark his wife's lawyer makes before the meeting, "Let's be decent about this, give them some privacy," is given an ironical flavor as RoboCop is locked up in a fenced-in laboratory full of computers and monitors, and can only talk to his wife from inside a cage. The scene therefore insists on the distance separating RoboCop from his wife, underscored by the wire netting which fills the whole frame and symbolizes their impossible connection. When

RoboCop asks her to touch him, she can only slip one finger through the netting and gives a start: his face is cold and metallic, devoid of any human warmth, as underlined by the composition of the shot in which RoboCop's metallic blue shoulders and back of the head fill half of the frame, contrasting with her small rosy face criss-crossed by the netting. The soundtrack further emphasizes their irreconcilable difference and the unbridgeable distance that has come between them, as her voice, choked with emotion, is interrupted by his unfeeling remarks uttered in an icy electronic monotone: "Your husband is dead. I don't know you." Thus, the transformation into a hypermasculine machine necessarily entails the breaking of intimate bonds; RoboCop has to push his wife away and keep her at a distance, as stressed by the continuous presence of diegetic screens like fences, windows or his own digital vision when he looks at her.

RoboCop can thus be seen as a figure of sexual impotence, which is suggested in the narration itself through the questions asked by the heartless (one could even say castrating) OCP lawyer before the meeting: "Do you think you could ever be a husband to her? What can you offer her? Companionship? Love? A *man's* love?" As Murphy, the protagonist is, indeed, allowed tantalizing glimpses of the eroticized female body—the flashback includes several POV shots from his perpsective of his wife's bare feet and legs, as he follows her up into their bedroom, paints her nails or tickles her feet, a sexual intimacy further suggested by his wife's short black silk nightdress and their kiss in the bathroom after her shower [14:23]. The emphasis on bare skin in the flashback contrasts with the rest of the film, where the women RoboCop comes into contact with are always fully clothed and generally in uniform, wearing lab coats or police clothing. RoboCop's female partner, Ann Lewis, is an interesting case in this regard, since her first appearances in both *RoboCop* and *RoboCop 2* desexualize her, presenting her first and foremost as a police officer on duty and in full gear, including helmet and bullet-proof vest, as she efficiently subdues violent criminals. Lewis is more of a mother figure than a lover when she brings RoboCop baby food or helps him repair his targeting system by aiming for him, standing close behind him in *RoboCop* [83:09]. As an embodiment of hypermasculinity, RoboCop cannot become truly intimate with a woman: consequently, his calling Lewis by her first name and complimenting her on her hair are seen as signs of his dysfunction in *RoboCop 2*.

The Terminator and *The Fly* go even further by linking hypermasculinity to domination and violence against women, echoing sociological and psychological research on hypermasculinity that associates it with physical and sexual aggression against women (Mosher and Sirkin 1984; Parrott and Zeichner 2003). Both the Terminator and Brundlefly (post-transformation Seth) are presented as dominating males who seek to assert power and control over the women around them. The Terminator's mission is to kill Sarah Connor, and he proceeds by methodically killing all the Sarah Connors listed in the phone book, as well as Sarah's roommate, Ginger, whom he mistakes for her. His attack on the first Sarah Connor [15:14] and on Ginger [30:12] are depicted in a much more detailed, violent and frightening manner than his attacks on men, in the police station for example. In both cases, the Terminator forces entry into these women's homes, remaining calm and composed in front of any obstacle (dog, boyfriend), while the women react with terror, an emotion underlined by the closeups of their frozen faces and the utilization of slow motion to depict the Terminator's movements, as he points his gun at them and shoots repeatedly, even after they have fallen to the floor, standing high above their agonizing bodies. The Terminator's coldness, dominating position and casual use of violence thus echo the categories of Mosher and Sirkin's Hypermasculinity Inventory, which include "calloused attitudes to women" and "violence as manly," and to which J.A. Hall has added "toughness as self-control over emotions."

Likewise, Seth becomes aggressive towards women after his transformation, relentlessly dragging them towards the telepod to subject them to his own intimacy and transform them into perfect partners that will satisfy his increasing sexual needs. He first manhandles Ronnie, yells at her when she refuses to go in and finally abandons her to roam the bars in search of a more willing sexual and teletransportation prey, to the sound of powerful brass music signaling his new-found aggressiveness [45:56–47:24]. His callousness is revealed in the bar scene when he chooses Tawny as a prize, treating her like a prostitute who can be bought in an arm-wrestling match. Yet, as the scene moves on, he becomes creepy and menacing, first when he declares that he "take[s] bodies apart and put[s] them back together again" [49:25], then when he stops and watches the girl intently as they arrive at his deserted warehouse [50:06]. The Gothic setting finally bears out what had only been hinted at in previous scenes, as the characters get out of the taxi in the rain and smoke, and climb the dark stairs up to the isolated apartment, shot in an expressionist style and accompanied by a soundtrack of rapid discordant string music [50:35]. This is the lair of a mad scientist whom all should fear, as Ronnie states at the end of the scene: "Be afraid, be very afraid." Indeed, both *The Fly* and *The Terminator* equate the hypermasculine male to a serial killer, explicitly in the case of the Terminator, whom the police labels a "one-day pattern killer," and implicitly in *The Fly* through location and atmosphere, thus assimilating hypermasculinity to a dangerous psychosis creating aggressive sociopaths.

To conclude, American science fiction films of the 1980s can be seen as products of the hypermasculine ideal of the time, an ideal of muscular masculinity that reflected anxious concern with national military strength as well as individual bodily strength. However, the films discussed above counter the exhibition of hypermasculinity by deconstructing this ideal in scenes of intimacy that expose the vulnerability of a hybrid and unnatural hypermasculinity, further undermining this ideal by highlighting the impossibility of shared intimacy for the hypermasculine protagonists. Ultimately, the films are more ambivalent than what critics like Claudia Springer, Susan Jeffords and Pauline Kael have acknowledged. Indeed, as genre films, they have what Thomas Schatz calls the "capacity to play it both ways" (35), both enacting the fantasies of the audience by upholding and exhibiting the ideal of hypermasculinity through iconic heroes, but also criticizing hypermasculinity as alienating and unfulfilling on an intimate level, perhaps as a soothing response to the anxieties of the male audience in front of an unrealizable masculine ideal of invulnerability and bodily prowess.

WORKS CITED

The Fly. 1986 [2006]. Dir. David Cronenberg. With Jeff Goldblum (Seth Brundle), Geena Davis (Veronica Quaife), John Getz (Stathis Borans) and Joy Boushel (Tawny). Brooksfilms. DVD. Fox Pathé Europa.
Hall, J.A. 1992. *Development and Validation of the Expanded Hypermasculinity Inventory and the Ideology of Machismo Scale*. Unpublished Master's thesis. University of Connecticut, Storrs.
Jeffords, Susan. 1994. *Hard Bodies: Masculinity in the Reagan Era*. New Brunswick: Rutgers University Press.
Kirkham, Pat and Janet Thumim. 1993. *You Tarzan: Masculinity, Movies and Men*. London: Lawrence and Wishart.
Lacan, Jacques. 1949. "Le stade du miroir comme formateur de la fonction du je, telle qu'elle nous est révélée, dans l'expérience psychanalytique." *Revue Française de Psychanalyse* 13.4: 449–55.
Levy, Donald P. 2007. "Hypermasculinity." *International Encyclopedia of Men and Masculinity*. Eds. Michael Flood, Judith Kegan Gardiner, Bob Pease and Keith Pringle. London: Routledge.
Mosher, Donald and Mark Sirkin. 1984. "Measuring a Macho Personality Constellation." *Journal of Research in Personality* 18.2: 150–63.
Mulvey, Laura. 1975. "Visual Pleasure and Narrative Cinema." *Screen* 16.3 (Autumn): 6–12.
Nishime, LeiLani. 2005. "The Mulatto Cyborg: Imagining a Multiracial Future." *Cinema Journal* 44.2 (Winter): 34–49.
Parrott, Dominic, and Amos Zeichner. 2003. "Effects of Hypermasculinity on Physical Aggression Against Women." *Psychology of Men & Masculinity* 4.1: 70–78.
RoboCop. 1987 [2002]. Dir. Paul Verhoeven. With Peter Weller (Officer Alex J. Murphy / RoboCop) and Nancy Allen (Officer Anne Lewis). Orion Pictures. DVD. MGM / United Artists.
RoboCop 2. 1990 [2002]. Dir. Irvin Kershner. With Peter Weller (Officer Alex J. Murphy / RoboCop) and Belinda Bauer (Dr. Juliette Faxx). Orion Pictures. DVD. MGM / United Artists.

Roche, David. 2010. "L'horreur viscérale de David Cronenberg ou l'horreur de l'anti-nature." *CinémAction* 136 "Les cinémas de l'horreur": 141–49.
Schatz, Thomas. 1981. *Hollywood Genres: Formulas, Filmmaking and the Studio System.* New York: McGraw-Hill.
Sharrer, Erica. 2001. "Tough Guys: The Portrayal of Hypermasculinity and Aggression in Televised Police Dramas." *Journal of Broadcasting and Electronic Media* 45.4: 615–34.
Springer, Claudia. 1993. "Muscular Circuitry: The Invicible Armored Cyborg in Cinema." *Genders* 18: 87–101.
The Terminator. 1984 [2004]. Dir David Cameron. With Michael Biehn (Kyle Reese), Linda Hamilton (Sarah Connor) and Arnold Schwarzenegger (Terminator). Hemdale Film, Pacific Western, Euro Film Funding and Cinema 84. DVD. Universal Music.

"I've got you under my skin"
No Exit from Insane Intimacy in Bug

CHRISTOPHE CHAMBOST

Bug is adapted from Tracy Letts's play, which was written and staged in 1996. Though written by Letts, the film enables Friedkin to tackle his favorite theme: the portrayal of the human soul in all its complexity. *Bug* tells the story of two lonely misfits who share a crazy kind of love that leads them to their deaths. We first meet Agnes White, a tough-looking barmaid who lives alone in a seedy motel room; subsequently, we learn that she suffers from a deep psychological trauma, presumably linked to the fact that her son Lloyd was inexplicably abducted in a grocery store several years ago. Then enters Peter Evans. He appears from nowhere, and appears to be very sweet and understanding. One night, he confesses that he is a deserter who had egg sacks of bugs called aphids injected into him during a military experiment that went wrong. He is now on the run, hunted by scientists who want to get their guinea pig back so as to improve their potential weapon of mass destruction. These two characters find in one another the caring person they are unconsciously looking for. They develop an intimate relationship in which they share delusional beliefs about a scientific conspiracy, which gradually lead them to cut themselves off from the rest of the world and cut their bodies open to remove the bugs that supposedly infest their flesh. The film ends with a hysterical scene where they kill themselves by burning their bodies and the motel room so as to stop the spread of the bugs they think they have bred.

The film maintains the play's unity of space. Most of it is set inside the small motel room, creating a claustrophobic atmosphere and stressing the growing and devouring intimacy that unites the two main characters. The intimacy that is here portrayed is extreme, and I will focus on its characteristics in order to observe the deadly consequences that such a desire for oneness entails. I will therefore concentrate, first, on the nature of the intimacy that Friedkin portrays in this *huis-clos*. This peculiar sort of "behind-closed-doors" intimacy will bring to the fore the ideas of isolation, of "being inside," and, on a psychological level, the refusal of the Other and the preference for the realm of the Imaginary rather than the Symbolic. I will then explore the brutal way Friedkin films the bodies of his characters. The fact that these bodies appear as a sort of problematic threshold will ultimately lead me to focus on the grotesque and the Lacanian notion of "extimacy."

Intimate Inmates or How to Dissect Intimacy Behind Closed Doors

Intimacy has something to do with what is secretly inside (Jeudy 7). Even if it should not be confused with privacy and interiority, these notions do overlap. The specificity of intimacy is that it insists on a form of emotional communication that can be defined as the intimate knowledge of the other's Self, in which a relationship of pure love can be founded (Giddens 163). Intimacy is also much closer to the ideas of corporality and immediacy than those of spirituality and mediation. This closeness even enables Henri-Pierre Jeudy to link intimacy with smiling, both being inexplicable (9). Predictably, then, much of the intimate atmosphere in the film comes from the silences and gazes the two characters share. Of course, as *Bug* is adapted from a play, dialogues are of the utmost importance, but attention should also be paid to the skill with which the film manages to make us *feel* the characters' immediate connection, thanks to the smallness of the room, the many medium closeups and closeups, and the soundtrack in which we can hear Agnes and Peter breathe.

Intimacy has much to do with the non verbal. Sociologist Irène Théry shows that an excessively developed private life where intimacy prevails turns out to be nefarious, socially speaking (81). Indeed, intimacy can imply a loss of collective norms: when only private life matters, then that life becomes a place of servitude and ghastly delusions. This is blatantly the case in *Bug*.[1] In *Intimate Revolt*, Julia Kristeva gives a balanced view of intimacy. Though she mentions its emotional nature, the role of drives and of perception, she also links it to sensation and reason. For her, intimacy can also be found within enunciation when one tries to express one's sensations through words, and when one approaches communication, some deep pleasure is obtained.

In *Bug*, we can sense this intense feeling of deep communion when, in the first part of the film, Peter and Agnes confide in each other in successful scenes that could belong to what David Sylvester calls "kitchen sink realism."[2] In such moments, the two characters share everything from the tritest remarks of every day life to the deepest secrets buried within their hearts. As they get to know each other, they take off their social masks, and Peter is the first to let the darker side of his personality surface. On the DVD commentary, Friedkin says that, as the plot unfolds, the characters "take their masks of sanity away" [1:20]. This seems to happen, for instance, when Peter starts explaining why he is a deserter [46:30]. The scene almost resembles a confessional: the characters are separated by a closed door, as he speaks and she listens silently. Agnes is moved; she opens the door to embrace both Peter and his conspiracy theory. This embrace will prove to be deadly, for they are about to enter a shared spiral of delusion and self-mutilation. As they hug, their madness is symbolically shown onscreen: the scene ends frantically in the tumult caused by a nearby helicopter whose vibrations make the room start to disintegrate. The helicopter noise is first heard in the background when Peter starts to "infect" Agnes's mind with his talk of the army's botched experiments, but it is only when she opens the bathroom door that the din hits the viewer full blast. Thus, the commotion could be the symbolic rendering of the chaos spreading in their minds as they share the same space. Agnes and Peter's motel room can, in effect, be seen not simply as the locus of their intimacy, but also as the symbolic representation of their mental space. This seedy place is a kind of sick sanctuary where two bodies and two minds merge into one delusional entity. When opening the bathroom door that previously separated Peter's space from hers, Agnes removes the last structure that held confusion at bay. If, according to T.J. Lustig, "thresholds only exist within reason" and "lie on this side of chaos" (12), then by suppressing them, reason is likely to crumble away under chaotic waves. The couple's motel room appears, then, to be anthropomorphized: in traditional Gothic fashion, it represents the characters' joint psyche; and when it quakes under the effects of the helicopter or of their deepest fears, the House of Usher, whose fall into the tarn swallows up other troubled minds, obviously comes to mind.

Houses are usually linked to the topography of intimacy, just like shells, nests or chrysalis, as Jean Clam has noted when adopting a Bachelardian perspective on intimacy (25). *Bug* is a case in point. The aluminum foil that eventually covers the room from floor to ceiling is the perfect embodiment of the characters' desire to be insulated/isolated from the rest of the world [69:20]. The nest they build enables their intimate relationship to "hatch," but the unusual interior they conceive is also the telltale sign of their mental unbalance. Poe comes to mind yet again, since Peter's ratiocinations regarding the conspiracy organized by the FBI are not that different from the narrator-character's delusional beliefs about the three policemen at the end of "The Tell-Tale Heart." The discreet young man that Peter first seemed to be turns out to be more and more talkative; he drags Agnes into his delusional theories, his arabesques, so much so that, in the end, it is Agnes who gives the last turn of the screw by updating their shared delusion: *she* is the "super mother bug" and Peter is the innocent "drone" (the male bee) sent by the army to fertilize her.

This flow of words has a double function: it provides evidence of the protagonists' delirious states of minds, but also contributes to their growing mental confusion in some kind of self-generating dynamics. Indeed, their convoluted reasoning only makes their psychological conditions more acute: as their delusional plot thickens, their clear-sightedness darkens. Their words lead them to irreversible psychological damage, which brings to mind Roland Barthes's idea that "words are irreversible, it is their destiny. What is said cannot be taken back, *only more words can be added*. Strangely enough, 'to correct' here becomes 'to add'"[3] (1984, 99, my translation). Conspiratorial words having been spoken, madness creeps in in its coherent disguise.

In *Madness and Cinema,* Patrick Fuery insists on the fact that madness is not nonsense, but a site of resistance where some knowledge can be found (5). To prove his point, Fuery calls on Foucault, for whom "the ultimate language of madness is that of reason, but the language of reason enveloped in the prestige of the image" (95). Fuery distinguishes between two types of films dealing with madness: those that describe it from the outside—like *Psycho* (Hitchcock, 1960) with its scientific conclusion—and those that make the audience feel madness from the inside. Like *Clean, Shaven* (Lodge Kerrigan, 1993), *Bug* clearly belongs in the latter category. With the initial aerial shot that closes in on Agnes's motel, the viewer is, from the start, made to enter the characters' minds.[4] Once inside the motel room, the camera relentlessly tracks the characters down, never giving them the chance to escape. In *Bug*, the succession of closeups and medium closeups insists on how cramped space is and conveys an acute awareness of the "aesthetics of proximity," responsible for the "violent and impressionistic intimacy" of the cinema (Madelénat 120).[5]

However, the film does not simply rely on camerawork to make us experience the characters' madness. It gives us a thoroughly detailed and accurate account of what is known as "delusional psychotic disorders." The film is not a case study properly speaking, but Tracy Letts did use some elements of Oklahoma bomber Timothy McVeigh's story to create Peter's character.[6] Much like Peter, McVeigh fought in the Gulf War, had relational problems with women and believed the army had implanted a microchip in his body. In the script,

Letts also alludes to other events that are related to madness and conspiracy; for instance, he mentions Ted Kaczynski, the Unabomber, as well as the Reverend Jim Jones and his People's Temple. Letts and Friedkin also portray Peter as suffering from the Ekbom's syndrome or "delusional parasitosis." In this kind of psychosis, the patient believes he is infested with bugs, which can lead to self-mutilation. This kind of psychotic disorder can be shared, and the condition is then aptly called "*folie à deux*" (madness shared by two), as it is characterized by an "emotional contagion" which could be likened to an extreme form of uncontrollable empathy. Some reviewers criticized Friedkin for making his film swerve too suddenly into madness and hysteria, but they might not have paid enough attention to the cleverness of the dialogues in the first part of the film. Thus, when commenting on a painting, Peter indirectly introduces the idea of persuasion [15:35]. In this scene, the script also links delusion, insects and hazardous technology, thanks to a noise which sounds like the chirping of a cricket, but which comes from a smoke detector supposedly containing Americium 241, a highly radioactive element. Thus, the filmmakers have skillfully sown the seeds (or laid the eggs) of the regressive dynamics that will rapidly gain momentum to reach a destructive climax, as the protagonists' psyches merge in the mythical state characterized by what Lacan calls the Imaginary.

By creating their own hermetic world, Agnes and Peter aim at recreating the lack of distinction caused by the blurring of Self and Other. This regressive desire to reach back to a psychological entity akin to some omnipotent Self obviously shows the characters' extreme state of mental confusion. The return to the Imaginary can be seen as the protagonists' attempt to flee their painful traumas. It is, therefore, not surprising that, in their final and most convoluted version of the army conspiracy, Agnes reintroduces her missing son into their delirious scenario: "[The army] took Lloyd to the lab, and they cut him open, and the stuff matched with whatever ... the DNA ... and the blood and all ... and they started to build the queen, the mother ... and ... they gave it to me, they gave it to me... I am the super mother bug! I am the super mother bug!" With this deadly triad composed of Agnes's son's DNA, Peter in the role of the drone and Agnes in that of the queen bee, the womb-like tinfoiled motel-room can give birth to the hallucinatory entity desired by the delusional couple.

In the last seconds of the film, when Agnes and Peter believe that self-sufficiency is at hand and that the Symbolic is no longer needed, they even lose their command of language [91:40]. Indeed, having rejected Otherness and mediation, they are now unable to make complete sentences as they splash themselves with gasoline. In their final and deadly embrace, the couple whispers a string of disconnected words with no grammatical coherence. In this shared delirium, the words they use belong to both entomology and the early stages of psychic life when a full-fledged personality has not yet developed. The final dialogue makes it clear that they are engaged in a paradoxical rebirth:

> AGNES: ... under the skin ...
> PETER: ... breeding ground ...
> AGNES: ... egg sack ...
> PETER: ... larva pond ...
> AGNES: ... baby bug water ...
> PETER: ... feeding pupa ...
> AGNES: ... feeding baby bug ...
> PETER: ... imago den ...
> AGNES: ... skin and ground breeding eggs ...

Despite the chaos that has spread in the room, Peter and Agnes now seem to understand each other perfectly, having reached a symbiotic relationship that abolishes distinction and makes their deadly embrace a primal one.

The final scene also emphasizes specularity—they face each other, act the same way, and ultimately both say: "I love you" (Fig. 13)—which also brings them back to the Mirror stage[7] and its inherent narcissism, so that when they willingly ignite the match that puts an end to their lives, the viewer understands that they want to reach some kind of twisted wholeness. At the same time, it is difficult not to react to the violence that they have been inflicting on their own bodies in their attempt at sharing this most brutal intimacy.

"Open Up and Bleed" or Friedkin's Cinema of Brutal Intimacy

Using the phrase "brutal intimacy" is by no means fortuitous. Tim Palmer uses it in the title of his book on what Anglo-American critics also call "the French cinema of the body." Attention has been paid to some of the recurring characteristics of these French films, notably the filmmakers' tendency to film the human body from up close and stress the intensity of the protagonists' emotions. In these films, sensation takes precedence over abstract reasoning; in other words, immediacy prevails over mediation. In its own way, *Bug* participates in this kind of cinema by insisting on the brute force of the body and the raw power of skin. This extreme proximity creates some corporal dynamics that can, at times, be very trying, for instance when Peter pulls out his tooth [66:50]. The visceral response that is triggered has a purpose: the film's hysterical crescendo is meant to make us feel the protagonists' hopeless attempts at getting rid of their supposedly contaminated earthly frames.

The immediacy felt in *Bug* creates an instinctive physical reaction that blocks the intellect and triggers fascination. In this respect, the film neatly exemplifies what Denis Mellier says about the mesmerizing power of the horrific image and the "scopic vertigo" it entails (244). Despite the gaping holes induced by self-mutilation, the body, in *Bug*, is conferred concreteness, and its presence matters. The protagonists' bodies take up so much onscreen space that we can almost feel what phenomenologist thinkers have put into words, that is to say the fundamental role of corporal sensations over abstract thinking.[8] Sharing many ideas with French director Claire Denis, philosopher Jean-Luc Nancy argues, in *Corpus*, that the body cannot be said: it simply acts and goes without saying. In *Bug*, we can find one scene that clearly shows the prevalence of the body over reasoning when Peter, who wants her best friend R.C. out of the picture, tries to cut Agnes off from her previous connections [63:10]. After a useless talk in which he vainly tries to convince Agnes not to listen to R.C., his body is seized with convulsions, which deeply frighten Agnes who then slaps her friend in the face, as she holds her responsible for Peter's fit. Peter's "body language" has thus achieved what his conspiracy theory had failed to do: rid the tragic couple of R.C.

In emphasizing the protagonists' corporeal presence, Friedkin had to be

Fig. 13. Agnes (Ashley Judd) and Peter (Michael Shannon) facing the lure of the Mirror stage in William Friedkin's *Bug* (2006).

very careful about the actors he cast. His choice turned out to be flawless, as actors Ashley Judd and Michael Shannon both manage to physically inhabit the screen. The initial slowness of their movements gradually gives way to the frenzy of their growing hysteria, and much can be felt thanks to the texture of their voices. More than the ideas uttered, what is at stake, here, is the physicality of their voices, the fleshiness of the sounds. Barthes beautifully defines this texture of the voice in *The Pleasure of the Text*:

> In fact, it suffices that the cinema capture the sound of speech *close up* [...] and make us hear in their materiality, their sensuality, the breath, the gutturals, the fleshiness of the lips, a whole presence of the human muzzle [...] to succeed in shifting the signified a great distance and in throwing [...] the anonymous body of the actor into my ear: it granulates, it crackles, it caresses, it grates, it cuts, it comes: that is bliss[9] [67].

In *Bug*, one can feel that the voices are "lined with flesh" (Barthes, 1973, 66). This is particularly the case when Peter, in a tremoring voice and with a dry mouth, confesses to Agnes that he would like to go to bed with her [35:50].

Thus, it is impossible to ignore the bodies and their raucous presence in the film, but what is also striking is the gruesome impression that emanates from this corporality. Echoing Nancy's ideas on *Trouble Every Day* (Claire Denis, 2001), we can feel that, in *Bug*, the body is also a source of a paradox, since it is both the positive limit that constitutes the protagonists and the negative limit that prevents them from reaching their ontological core (2001, 60). Tearing one's flesh open is, therefore, an ambivalent act, because it simultaneously enables the protagonists to look for their own Self while destroying it. In *Bug*, this paradox is darkened by the fact that the characters seem to gain very little relief from their bodies. This is particularly blatant when dealing with the way bodily fluids appear onscreen.

Sometimes, these fluids connote a positive feeling, as when Peter and Agnes make love [36:40]. Here, the saliva and sweat they exchange are the (somewhat conventional) symbols of an orgasmic union. Yet, in other instances, the same fluids are tinged with darker hues. Thus, sweat is also shown to be the mere consequence of a sultry atmosphere in an oppressive room [3:40], and the sperm they share when making love is connoted in the most negative way, owing to a very brief cut-in of swarming cells which is inserted in the intercourse scenes and alludes to some kind of threatening contamination [37:22]. As for blood, it has none of the dynamic qualities that can be found in the carefree gory geysers of splatter films like *Braindead* (Peter Jackson, 1992). On the contrary, the thick streaks of blood oozing from the protagonists' gashes have an ominous aspect, which is all the more felt as those self-inflicted wounds do not alleviate the protagonists' anxiety in the least.

Indeed, as is shown by Armando Favazza in his study of self-mutilation, patients with delusions of parasitosis do *not* experience relief from excoriation (149). All they can do is keep on hurting themselves in their self-probing for imaginary bugs.[10]

Grotesque Bodies, Hysterical Flesh and "Extimacy"

These remarks on bodily fluids inevitably lead me to a discussion of the grotesque, with its emphasis on gross physicality and the fusion of human and animal, a fusion that is suggested in *Bug* with the insert on the praying mantis that abruptly ends the love-making scene [37:47]. When considering the way bodies are manhandled in the film, there is, indeed, little surprise at calling on all the paraphernalia of the Bakhtinian carnivalesque.[11]

The excessive nature of *Bug* can mainly be found in its second part, when hysteria reaches its peak and chaos rules supreme. In these moments, Friedkin uses a wide variety of means to take his audience on a rollercoaster ride without leaving the motel room: the editing is sharp, there are many closeups and extreme closeups of moving and bleeding protagonists, e.g., the extreme closeup of Peter's bloody face looking straight at the camera and yelling: "Machine!" repeatedly while stabbing an intruder [79:55]. The soundtrack is also likely to set the audience's nerves on edge: the characters yell at each other or they just scream. And on top of it all, the soundtrack includes the recurring racket of helicopters, the buzzing sound of insects, a pinch of hard rock music and even, coming from nowhere, some metallic clangs that reverberate much in the same way as in the soundtrack of *The Texas Chain Saw Massacre* (Tobe Hooper, 1974).

All these sights and sounds are aggressive and transgressive; they evoke a kind of Dionysian celebration in which cruelty and uneasiness prevail. The brutality of these moments is akin to the "mystical ecstasy" Daniel Madelénat analyzes when dealing with Georges Bataille's thoughts on inner experience. Madelénat speaks of the "explosion of intimacy under the shock of excessiveness" (70), and such an explosion does, indeed, echo what can be felt in *Bug*. The notion of excess and the emphasis on physicality also evoke the notion of the obscene, which implies the prevalence of an ineffable experience over the intellect (Bernas 7). In some extreme circumstances, intimacy and the obscene overlap: both notions have the same raw material: the body. What Estelle Bayon says about skin in relation to the obscene, that it "reveals the exceeding/exasperating secret of the obscene" (34), also applies to the form of intimacy depicted in *Bug*. By forcing us to look at human bodies that are torn open and act in a most animal-like way, *Bug* could be included in Bayon's corpus of obscene films. Cited in Bayon's study, Jean Baudrillard has stated that, "with the obscene, the distance of the gaze disappears" (33). The unnerving quality of the obscene has much in common with the immediacy and horror mentioned earlier as regards intimacy in *Bug*. The film's excessive and pessimistic features, therefore, evoke the darker trend of the "romantic grotesque" that Bakhtin defines at length in the long introduction of his study on François Rabelais.[12]

The absence of spirituality in *Bug* does not come from Friedkin's inability to deal with such themes, but it can be explained by his desire to concentrate on the concrete consequences that a delusional mind provokes on the human body. In *Bug*, Friedkin shows human beings trapped in their bodies and unable to feel complete and serene. This situation is reminiscent of Freud's Uncanny, since their physical home is simultaneously reassuring and disquieting (because of their belief in a foreign body within their body). The association of these two opposing feelings creates a tension that can also be found in the merging of the two antithetical notions of excess and lack: "excess" because of the foreign body that has supposedly been inserted in them, and "lack" as the result of the hollowing out of their bodies. It is precisely this tension that eventually leads them *outside* the sphere of the Self.

The idea of an "outward" dynamics may seem paradoxical at first sight, considering that I have previously insisted on the way the characters are locked up in the prisons of their selves where they cannot escape the snare of the Imaginary. Yet there is no real contradiction here, since the "centrifugal" forces that take the characters' psyches out of their worlds happen to be maddening forces that only accelerate the collapse of meaning and of the Symbolic. In *Bug*, the protagonists resort to self-mutilation to expel foreign bodies from their systems, and they feel more alive thanks to their union in this common experience. In other words, their ontological center is no longer *within* themselves but outside their bodies (*without* their bodies) and within that room, cut off from the rest of the world. They have reached a kind of ecstatic fusion thanks to this de-centering dynamics or violent ex-stasis.

The psychological movement outside oneself in search of an unknown part of oneself evokes the Lacanian concept of "extimacy" ("*extime*" in French). Extimacy can be defined as what is "more intimate than the most knowable, intimate detail" about oneself (Fuery 118). It is something about oneself that one is not aware of and, most importantly, it is something one has to look for in the Other. Extimacy is both fascinating and fearsome, for it is part of our psychological processes, but nonetheless remains foreign to our conscious mind (and it has much to do with the Real and the "*objet petit* a"). By going outside their minds in order to merge, Peter and Agnes fail to inscribe their frantic union in the Symbolic: they do *not* reach accommodation and *cannot* recognize the Other as a distinct, full-fledged entity. Fuery's assertion according to which "the extimacy of our desires resides in a radical evil for they define our subjectivity, and yet resist any Symbolic compromise" seems therefore to theorize the protagonists' inability to reach mediation (118). There is no compromise at the end of the film. What we have, instead, is an indistinct mass of hysterical flesh determined not to take part in the conspiracy of life.

Fuery's notion of "hysterical flesh" is especially relevant here, for hysteria implies the conflation of the mental and corporal, and it emerges out of extimacy (119). For Fuery,

> Hysterical flesh is the representation of the body when it exceeds, transgresses, challenges, and resists its moral, ethical, social status and in doing so comes to problematize meaning systems and interpretations. It is the subject made flesh by a collapse in the systems of signification. [...] Hysterical flesh is a challenge to meaning initially through the body [119–20].

Likewise, in *Bug*, the body and its self-destructive drives are untamable and they alter the intellectual understanding of things. The bodily (the hysterical flesh) "says" something that is turned into some (twisted) meaning the protagonists try to reach by violently extracting it from their body. Such an attempt is doomed to fail, their extimacy being inaccessible and therefore equated to a fundamental lack of being. The "whole" they aim for is grotesquely scaled down to the ghastly holes they inflict on themselves. These holes are, in effect, the physical inscription of a more fundamental lack of being which cannot be filled by their increasingly delirious quest for extimacy. Unable to remain under the regressive spell of the Imaginary, unable to transform the transgressive desire for extimacy into something else than self-harming acts, Agnes and Peter are only left with one more delusion, that of union through cremation. It is tempting, then, to ultimately liken the protagonists of *Bug* to Icarus, as they literally burn their wings in their final attempt to reach an elusive and burning object of desire.

Notes

1. Intimacy may, however, also be beneficial when dealing with the everyday life of those who are not delusional patients. In *La Pornographie et ses images*, sociologist Patrick Baudry shows that the most intimate relationship still triggers intersubjectivity, thereby strengthening social links. Didier Le Gall also says that intimacy simply cannot be outside the social (11).
2. David Sylvester used the phrase "kitchen sink realism" to describe the emphasis on the banality of everyday life shown in British paintings of the 1950s. He also applied the

terms to British playwrights, novelists and filmmakers of the time, in the December 1954 issue of the art journal *Encounters*.

3. Original text: "La parole est irréversible, telle est sa fatalité. Ce qui a été dit ne peut se reprendre, *sauf à s'augmenter* : corriger, c'est, ici, bizarrement, ajouter."

4. Of course, this initial aerial shot easily relates to the surveillance program mentioned by Peter, but it could also be taken as the God-like gaze of the filmmaker, inviting us to witness his scrutiny of the human mind.

5. When evoking cinema, Madelénat refers to what Jean Epstein and Henri Agel wrote on the cinematographic means of conveying intimacy.

6. Timothy McVeigh was responsible for the "Oklahoma City bombing" that killed 168 people in 1995.

7 For Jacques Lacan (2004), the mirror stage represents a permanent structure of subjectivity. It initially takes part in the formation of the Ego through identification with one's image in the mirror. The visual identity that can be grasped from the mirror conveys an imaginary wholeness, but it also implies alienation from oneself.

8. This tendency to stress the major role of the body goes against Western rationalistic thought, but it is also advocated by psychoanalysts like Alain Amseleck (325), and by neurologists like Antonio Damasio who contends that we think with our body and our emotions (173).

9. Original text: "Il suffit en effet que le cinéma prenne de très près le son de la parole [...] et fasse entendre dans leur matérialité, dans leur sensualité, le souffle, la rocaille, la pulpe des lèvres, toute une présence du museau humain [...] pour qu'il réussisse à déporter le signifié très loin et à jeter [...] le corps anonyme de l'acteur dans mon oreille : ça granule, ça grésille, ça caresse, ça râpe, ça coupe, ça jouit" (89).

10. For patients with delusions of parasitosis, self-mutilation is not a reassuring way of perceiving the limits of their bodies, as is the case for cutters who suffer from depersonalization.

11. An even more obvious literary trend with which to connect *Bug* might be the Southern Gothic. Indeed, the film takes place in Oklahoma and its protagonists' lives could embody the "caught condition" Carson McCullers describes in her fiction (Spencer Carr 40). Similarly, Agnes and Peter are not that far from the self-mutilating freaks that can be found in Flannery O'Connor's *Wise Blood* (1952). Yet, as said before, no spirituality is alluded to in *Bug*, whereas religion is a source of torment in O'Connor's novel.

12. This dark hue of the romantic grotesque can be felt in *Bug*, as the viewer might smile uneasily in some of the most excessive scenes, for instance, when Agnes grandiloquently states that she is the "super mother bug." This may explain why Friedkin described the film as a "black comedy love story" when promoting it in 2006.

WORKS CITED

Agel, Henri. 1952. *Le Cinéma a-t-il une âme?* Paris: Editions du cerf.
Amselek, Alain. 2006 [2010]. *Le Livre rouge de la psychanalyse : L'écoute de l'intime et de l'invisible*. Paris: Desclée de Brouwer.
Bakhtine, Mikhaïl. 1965 [1970]. *L'Œuvre de François Rabelais et la culture populaire au Moyen Age et sous la Renaissance*. Paris: Gallimard.
Barthes, Roland. 1984. "Le Bruissement de la langue." *Le Bruissement de la langue. Essais critiques IV*. Paris: Seuil. 99–102.
_____. *The Pleasure of the Text*. 1973 [1975]. New York: Hill and Wang.
Baudrillard, Jean. 2000. *Mots de passe*. Paris: Pauvert.
Baudry, Patrick. 1997. *La Pornographie et ses images*. Paris: Armand Collin.
Bayon, Estelle. 2007. *Le Cinéma obscène*. Paris: L'Harmattan.

Bernas, Steven, and Jamil Dakhlia, eds. *Obscène, obscénités*. Paris: L'Harmattan, 2008.
Bug. 2006. Dir. William Friedkin. Written by Tracy Letts (based on his play). With Ashley Judd (Agnes White), Michael Shannon (Peter Evans), Lynn Collins (R.C.) and Harry Connick, Jr. (Jerry Goss). Lyons Gate Films. DVD. Metropolitan Filmexport.
Clam, Jean. 2007. *L'Intime:Genèses, régimes, nouages: Contributions à une sociologie et une psychologie de l'intimité contemporaine*. Paris: Ganse Arts et Lettres.
Damasio, Antonio. 1994. *Descartes' Error: Emotion, Reason, and the Human Brain*. New York: G.P. Putnam's Sons.
Epstein, Jean. 1974. *Écrits sur le cinéma*. Paris: Seghers.
Favazza, Armando. 1987 [1996]. *Bodies Under Siege: Self-Mutilation and Body Mortification in Culture and Psychiatry*. Baltimore: Johns Hopkins University Press.
Foucault, Michel. 1964 [1987]. *Madness and Civilization: A History of Insanity in the Age of Reason*. New York: Vintage.
Fuery, Patrick. 2004. *Madness and Cinema: Psychoanalysis, Spectatorship and Culture*. New York: Palgrave McMillan.
Giddens, Anthony. 2004. *La Transformation de l'intimité : Sexualité, amour et érotisme dans les sociétés modernes*. Rodez: Les Editions du Rouergue.
Jeudy, Henri-Pierre. 2007. *L'Absence de l'intimité : Sociologie des choses intimes*. Belval: Circé.
Kristeva, Julia. 1997 [2003]. *Intimate Revolt: The Powers and Limits of Psychoanalysis*. New York: Columbia University Press.
Le Gall, Didier, ed. 1997. *Mana:revue de sociologie et d'anthropologie* 3 "Approches sociologiques de l'intime."
Lacan, Jacques. 1949 [2004]. *Écrits: A Selection*. New York: Norton.
Lustig, T.J. 1994. *Henry James and the Ghostly*. Cambridge: Cambridge University Press.
Madelénat, Daniel. 1989. *L'Intimisme*. Paris: PUF.
Mellier, Denis. 1999. *L'Écriture de l'excès : Fiction fantastique et poétique de la terreur*. Paris: Honoré Champion.
Miller, Jacques-Alain. 1985. "Extimité." *Séminaire de l'Orientation lacanienne*, lesson given on November 13, 1985.
Nancy, Jean-Luc. 1992. *Corpus*. Paris: Métailié.
_____. 2001. "Icône de l'acharnement." *Trafic* 39 (Fall): 58–64.
Palmer, Tim. 2011. *Brutal Intimacy: Analyzing Contemporary French Cinema*. Middletown: Wesleyan University Press.
Spencer Carr, Virginia. 2005. *Understanding Carson McCullers*. Columbia, SC: University of South Carolina Press.
Théry, Irène. 1996. "Différence des sexes et différence des générations. L'institution familiale en déshérence." *Esprit* (December): 65–90.

Filming Fantasy, Imitating the Intimate in *Eyes Wide Shut*

Yann Roblou

> Art treats appearance as appearance; its aim is precisely not to deceive. It is therefore true.
> —Friedrich Nietzsche

Cinema's power to represent animate life and produce a strong impression of reality warrants and supports its other fascinating capacity, namely, to fabricate honest yet appealing illusions. In certain instances, audiences may respond to the cinematic realism as if to actual reality, particularly when the characters of a fiction are interpreted by actors whose real-life relationship cannot but affect the way their imaginary alter egos are perceived when depicted in a similar relationship. At the heart of this complex issue lies the notion of intimacy. Indeed, Lauren Berlant reminds us that intimacy is connected to the verb "to intimate," which posits that something is communicated "with the sparest of signs and gestures" (281). She immediately adds that "intimacy also involves an aspiration for a narrative about something shared, a story about oneself and others, [...] set within zones of familiarity and comfort" (281). The features evoked by Berlant (sharing, familiarity, comfort) are among the characteristics usually employed to define the close relationship one can have with another individual, and any material and symbolic extension thereof. To which it is also necessary to add relying on the verbal and physical as the privileged modes of expression, thus allowing for "dialogue, transparency, vulnerability and reciprocity" (Ridley-Duff x).

Intriguingly, although this aspect of the relationship between the protagonists of *Eyes Wide Shut* is of paramount importance, intimacy has merely been evoked, in the wake of Kubrick's death, as a characteristic of the original situation the film describes or as anecdotal,[1] but not as an apt and astute means for his last statement on the power of cinema. As a matter of fact, most critics tended to focus—and, arguably, rather rightly so—on the psychological (Carnicke 2006, Gross 1999, Vachaud 1999), social (Starfield 2006, Williams 1999) and political (Kreider 2000) overtones of the film. And even if sex traverses most critical analyses, it seems to be the only way to subsume Alice and Bill's relationship, thus failing to take into account another significant facet of this work.

Drawing his inspiration from Arthur Schnitzler's 1926 novella *Traumnovelle*, Kubrick's long-standing project and last film explores the uncertain boundaries between dream, fantasy and reality, i.e., the stuff "psychological reality" is, according to Freud, made of. Though originally set in a different time and place, *Eyes Wide Shut* retains the essential components of the story—a woman admits to having erotic desires which remain pure fantasy, and her husband tries to avenge his wounded pride by pursuing a series of real erotic adventures which, in fact, never go beyond the state of desire and dream—but places the argument and the unfolding of the male protagonist's physical and fantasized wanderings in the final year of the 20th century.

This essay aims at examining a very short scene [19:03–19:50], which, I will argue, offers some keys to understanding the rest of the film, in order to uncover the essence of Kubrick's aesthetic treatment of the tension between desire and frustration, his particular use of dramatization, and the displacement of a discourse on intimacy onto the exposition of the shortcomings of visualizing fantasy.

The scene does not exist in Schnitzler's novella. The fact that it was invented for the film prompts a series of remarks both on the scene itself and the film in general, as the scene cannot be read without including it in a broader context. The apparently frontal nudity is essential to the sequence and serves several purposes. First, as a privileged mode of suggesting intimacy, it allows the spectator to determine the space of the action. Where else than a bedroom would a couple, with a young daughter to boot, we have been shown as perfectly aware—and observant—of social norms allow themselves such a degree of intimacy? Within the spheres of privacy, that of the bedroom's inner sanctum stands prominent. It is also noteworthy that further key scenes also take place in the couple's bedroom, though they are presented in a very different manner, both in terms of *mise en scène* and tone.[2] Everything here suggests shared warmth—as the colors of the image, the paintings and the wooden objects suggest—and wealth—as the sheer number of paintings, columns, and the size and quality of the mirror indicate.

Secondly, Nicole Kidman's physical presence is a sign of visual desire. For the second time in the film,[3] her nudity is what is most ostensibly visible in the scene, first to us, but also to her partner. Significantly, Tom Cruise is looking at her body when he enters the shot, and it seems to stimulate his desire, as the rest of the scene suggests (Fig. 14). However, the spectator can only witness the exterior signs of their upcoming intimate relation. We see the pair kiss, but the rest—their real intimacy, as it were—can only be found in the following black fold of the cinematic text and in the imagination of the viewer. Bearing this in mind, it is necessary to evoke what precedes the scene. During the Christmas party given by a rich client of Bill's, both he and Alice are flirted with, respectively by a couple of young models who offer to take Bill "where the rainbow ends" and by an old Hungarian beau who insists he must see Alice again [18:43]. Though Alice is shown observing her husband in such charming company, it is not clear whether he has seen her. Thus, it is tempting to think that Bill's apparent desire for Alice may also have been prompted by his yet unformulated jealousy or by a form of mimetic desire. Similarly, her lukewarm reaction to his advances could also be interpreted as a reaction to the previous events.

Yet nudity serves as a red herring: it hides more than it reveals. While

Fig. 14. In Stanley Kubrick's *Eyes Wide Shut* (1999), Alice Harford (Nicole Kidman) undresses in front of the mirror as her husband William (Tom Cruise) embraces her.

the spectator's gaze cannot but wander over Kidman's body, several other features are likely to be overlooked in the brief scene. First, that there is, in fact, nothing to see. Indeed, though the actress's body may appear to be completely naked, it is shown neither frontally, as the reflection in the mirror would have us believe, nor in its entirety. And its most intimate parts are hidden from view: her arms cover her breasts and a pile of books ingeniously hides her genitals. What is more, caught between the mirror and the camera eye which keeps getting closer, her body becomes fragmented as the zoom focuses on the actress's face and eyes. Kidman's nudity can, then, be understood as a mental image more than the actual exposure of flesh. From this perspective, the nudity we are confronted with may be perceived as a double of the reflective surface of the mirror. It is just as smooth and flawless—and, one might add, uninteresting. Unless one were to look for something that is not there, that is to say, something that is only projected. When taken in the broader context of the whole film, the relationship between surface and superficiality at work in the scene obviously echoes the uncanny presence of all the feminine figures Bill Hartford comes into contact with. Thus, while bent on seducing/being seduced by a series of women, he apparently fails to grasp (or feigns to ignore) that their physical appearance is systematically based on his wife. As all these feminine figures appear to share a perfect—at least according to the canons of the late 20th century—physique, without asperity, they become interchangeable and eventually lose their identity. This also concerns the spectator's own interaction with the images presented in the film. The naked figures inhabiting this fiction are meant to be nothing but images, and as such are devoid of any erotic charge—which might account for the frustration of a number of critics who deemed the film cold and unsexy.

Intimately connected to the pseudo-erotic dimension of the scene is the presence of the mirror and the way it is used. Materially, the mirror seems to be an apt element of decoration with a certain usefulness (Alice uses it to take off her makeup and jewelry). However, this is not what we are shown: at the beginning of the scene, she is watching herself, and the mirror could, therefore, serve as a substitute for someone else's gaze. But as it also reflects her own gaze, it may signify both her frustration and narcissism. In this intimate confrontation with herself, Alice represents both an object being looked at and a subject of the gaze: she looks in the mirror, looks at herself, then looks at herself being looked at by Bill. She only closes her eyes to better abandon herself to his embrace, but cannot resist coming back to her reflection and, at the last moment, she gazes deeply into the camera eye. The multiplication of gazes exposes the mirror for what it is: simultaneously a magical surface, a "snare for the soul" in keeping with the classical tradition, it reveals Kubrick's aesthetic strategy. By connecting the mirror and the gaze, the film seems to foreground Alice's superficiality and, through her, that of all the women who will appear in the rest of the film. The mirror also echoes the Borgesian symmetries at work in the global dramatic structure of the film, as well as in the construction of the scene. When one looks carefully at the setup of the initial shot, the impression of perfect symmetry (a common feature in Kubrick's films) needs to be specified. The exact line forming the center of the frame lies in between Kidman and her reflection. The mirror and the actress are, in a sense, both "pushed aside" to let the space thus created act as a gaping hole in the visual fabric. The viewer's gaze is, then, caught in the interstitial void, unable to choose between elements made equal by their position: that of the body and its reflection.

Besides imprisonment, the mirror also evokes a division of the body. As mentioned above, a physical distance is created between the actual body of the actress and her reflection in the mirror. What is more, the beveled edges of the frame fragment and expand the bodies of the subjects caught in the mirror. Symbolically, the mirror is an apt means to manifest the divisions at work within the Hartford couple, as well as within the individuals themselves. The juncture for Bill and Alice will come soon after the present scene, when Alice evokes an adventure she could have had with a naval officer, which will sting Bill's assumptions on their individual status as desiring subjects and prompt his wounded pride to try to compensate for his frustration [30:20–34:44]. In this scene, however, both Alice and Bill complacently seem to relish their individual and collective reflections, unaware that they are caught in a visual extension of the scene's meaning, which is associated with both duplication and duplicity.

Though they claim to be telling the truth about what they have done or what they feel, there is no way for the spectator to be able to confirm or contradict the validity of both protagonists' earnestness. We can only base our opinion on the general discourse of the fiction they are a part of. In this respect, the scene under consideration is indicative of Kubrick's overall intent, for looking into the mirror determines the self-conscious reference to artifice. Regarding the setting, it is necessary to point out features that can easily go otherwise unnoticed, but make sense when considered as indicative of a very carefully constructed *mise en scène*: the makeup and skin-care products on the pedestal table, but also the indirect presence of pillars and red curtains—all signs of a certain theatricality. It is also in this light that Alice's seduction dance should be analyzed in connection with the usage made of Chris Isaac's 1995 song. Synchronized with the images, the drum and guitar chords of the intro pave the way to the meaningful first verse of "Baby Did a Bad Bad Thing."

It should be observed, first, that there is no clear indication as to the source of the music. We cannot determine whether the song is being played on a device in the room or if it is a projection of Alice's unconscious mind. This uncertainty reinforces its second characteristic: its presence on the soundtrack imposes itself as a means to compensate for the absence of dialogue in the scene. As a matter of fact, since verbal exchanges between protagonists are recurrently most unreliable (a constant in Kubrick's films, which were envisaged by the director as non-verbal experiences), "Baby Did a Bad Bad Thing," with its theme of jealousy, becomes a sort of dialogue: the singer uses the first and second person pronouns, asks questions and provides answers. The spectator is, thus, invited to make sense of the lyrics in connection with the situation, what happened before and, possibly, his/her own experience of similar situations, but also to acknowledge potential associations to come, as if the song contained something prophetic connected to the interpellations the pronoun "you" implies. This is undeniably the case when one considers the whole film.

It is also intriguing to try to connect the title and chorus to something one of the protagonists might have done. One could easily suggest that both Bill and Alice have transgressed by flirting with other people, though it remains to be justified to what extent flirting is inherently "bad." But the sentence could also proleptically announce troubles to come: Alice may have done wrong by fantasizing about a naval officer; Bill will (try to) flirt with disaster. The lyrics might even refer to the fact that Bill and Alice are about to engage in sexual intercourse. More challenging is the use of the chorus when Nicole Kidman looks at the mirror as the image fades to black: this mode of address to the spectator could, in effect, be deemed perverse because of the voyeuristic posture it entails. Kubrick's ironical comment on the ease with which the spectator-voyeur has fallen into the trap laid for him is perceptible in the duration of the connection between the end of this sequence with the opening of the following one, and the echoing of the song's chorus while the screen remains black.

The half-hidden strategy of the *mise en abyme* of the medium itself is also determined by Alice's final gaze. It constitutes the most appropriate conclusion of the process induced by the utilization of the zoom which provides the only movement of the recording apparatus in the scene. Like the film director, Alice may be directing her own mental representation of a seduction scene. Bill's embrace could, then, be conceived as an enactment of what she fantasized both with the naval officer in a former moment of her intimate life and with the Hungarian fop; the proximity of both experiences may be suggested by the abrupt cut between the end of the party and the present scene. As if contaminated, Bill will create and indulge in his own "blue movie," revealed by the grainy amateur-like black and white images of what he imagines could have happened between his wife and the naval officer, after Alice's (undeterminedly true or false) revelation. It may also be possible to envisage the decidedly mechanically arranged series of events in Bill's wanderings as fantasies of his own frustrated psyche, the theatricality of the masked orgy being a case in point. As was suggested above, the viewer has also been caught in a voyeuristic trap without an object, as s/he was led to believe s/he was going to watch what the promotion campaign termed "The Sexiest Movie Ever" (Krieder 41). Overdetermining the process of staging and directing may also be considered as a last reflexive, self-conscious acknowledgement of Kubrick's debt to the nostalgic voyages of Ulysses in Homer's *Odyssey*, a text he had always been fascinated by, as well as to filmmakers he admired, such as Max Ophüls with *La Ronde* (1950), Luis Buñuel with *Belle de Jour* (1967) and Michelangelo Antonioni with *Zabriskie Point* (1970), to name but a few. This tribute cannot be disconnected from the intertextual references to his own cinema, from *Fear and Desire* (1953) to *Full Metal Jacket* (1987), either.

To this effect, and to point out just a few themes connected to intimacy and encountered in *Eyes Wide Shut*, one could evoke the prominent double tension in the binary fascination/seduction present in all of Kubrick's films, or the equally important sex/death binary. Interestingly, both themes allow for the presence of motifs that also denote intimacy and are emblematic of all other social rituals of privacy, notably dancing scenes—the predatory evolutions in the night-club world of *Killer's Kiss* (1955) or the high-school dance in *Lolita* (1960) are preludes to Sandor Szavost's barely disguised advances to Alice during the Zieglers' Christmas ball—and bathroom scenes—which offer, from *Dr. Strangelove* (1964) to *The Shining* (1980) or even *Full Metal Jacket*, hints of the potential nightmares that, as Larry Gross (1999) has noted, exist beneath the apparently calm surface of normality.

In spite of Alain Masson's contention that Kubrick has relinquished the use of certain recognizable stylistic traits in this film (131), *Eyes Wide Shut* remains a Kubrick film, be it only because of two notable features: the symmetrical composition that has already been evoked and the utilization of sinuous tracking shots. A permanent feature of his films since *Paths of Glory* (1957), the latter device puts the viewer in a paradoxical position. It allows us to grasp the energy of the movement of the protagonists as they move towards the camera, while simultaneously destabilizing us as we progressively discover the setting. This device is traditionally combined with a reverse shot, with the camera moving forward this time, presenting the setting as it is perceived by the protagonist. This composition appears three times in the film—thus reinforcing the effect of global symmetry—and, significantly, at key moments when the private and public meet. The first occurs during the Christmas party at the Zieglers' [2:38–3:17], the second during the orgy scene [76:21–77:55], and the last one during the final Christmas shopping sequence [142:57–144:10]. All three concern Bill and suggest a tension between his intimate feelings of (some form of) desire (respectively for the two models, the naked women and Alice) and the socially contingent situations in which he is present (a party, an orgy and shopping). The dialectics of his (and the spectator's) emotions is the result of a possible transgression of boundaries (between intimate emotions and public display of affect) that is negotiated here in cinematographic terms by simultaneously involving (tracking towards) and keeping out (tracking backwards) the protagonist (and, consequently, the viewer), a technique which stands as an equivalent to the use of the almost unnoticeable zooming in in the second shot of the scene under study.

Thus concatenated into two shots which last less than one minute, the fundamental elements that are used through the film are present in this scene: the juxtaposition, coexistence and eventual porosity between the public and private spheres, and the social and the intimate. This problematic connection between the two poles can be particularly felt in the cuts connecting this scene to the rest of the filmic fabric. The initial cut clearly separates Bill and Alice from the party they participated in, yet the way she looks at him during their embrace blurs this caesura. In complementary dynamics, the final fade to black veils the rest of the logical continuation of the scene, but leaves open the possibility of a dramatic development: how will the situation evolve between the two partners?

What also makes this scene singular is its dream-like quality, the camera almost floating into and through the couple's intimacy. It is therefore a paradoxical experience we are invited (even forced) to share: the spectator must imagine the mental state, the feelings of the characters, while being simultaneously kept at a distance. We are given a position and a role that can only be apprehended in an ever-shifting fashion.

If the meaning of all the elements (visual and aural) composing the scene, not unlike the gaze itself, is in constant circulation, it finally sets Alice and Bill apart—though they are thus paradoxically joined—just as it holds a mirror up to the spectator who cannot but identify with either of them and must be content with looking at his/her own expectations and frustrations. For ultimately, the film is not so much about sex as it questions sexual fantasies. It seems that Kubrick's ambition was to locate pornography not on the surface of images, but in the social designs one can find exposed in the depiction of a rich omnipotent oligarchy present in turn of the century Manhattan. From this perspective, perhaps, the general unease expressed by critics was not so much generated by the purely mechanical movements of the participants at the orgy, caught silent both in long shots and in a dramatic development—all characteristics foreign to ordinary pornographic fare, as Nadia Meflah (2006) has noted, thus making the scene devoid of any titillating effect—as by the capacity of a class of (masked) "untouchables" to possess the right of life and death over the general population and to remain unseen and unnamed, preserved by the elaborate narrative of Ziegler, acting as intermediary and mouthpiece, and by the fear distilled in the Hartfords.

Like any other Kubrick film, *Eyes Wide Shut* should not be interpreted in psychological terms, but rather in sociological ones, as it deals with human history and evolution, not individuals. The focus, then, is not on the subtle illumination of psychological nuances and reflections of the protagonists, but rather on a no less subtle metafilmic reflection on the act of seeing. This tension leaves us with no other alternative than to be aware of the director's determination to call on the spectators' conscious minds and make them stay wide awake, with their eyes wide open.

Notes

1. Nicole Kidman and Tom Cruise separated not long after the film's release.
2. Bedroom scenes abound in *Eyes Wide Shut*: from Marion's father's death bed to Domino's small apartment, Bill Hartford seems to forever wander from one to another. Three other scenes take place in the Hartfords' bedroom. The first follows closely on the scene under study and is devoted to the argument between Bill and Alice after the party at Ziegler's. The second takes place after Bill's narrow escape from the orgy: Alice tells him the dream she was having when he walked into their bedroom. The last one is set immediately after Bill's visit to Ziegler and his demand for an explanation concerning the death of a woman he believes helped him escape the orgy. Seeing the mask he was wearing that night but had misplaced on the pillow next to Alice sleeping, Bill breaks down in tears and confesses everything he has (not) done. The three scenes share two similar components: the prominent presence of the bed itself and the disturbing atmosphere conveyed by the omnipresent color blue.
3. The film actually opens on the actress putting on her dress, the camera revealing her from behind in full shot, entirely naked.

Works Cited

Berlant, Lauren. 1998. "Intimacy: A Special Issue." *Critical Inquiry* 24.2 (Winter): 281–88.
Carnicke, Sharon Marie. 2006. "The Material Poetry of Acting: 'Objects of Attention': Performance Style, and Gender in *The Shining* and *Eyes Wide Shut*." *Journal of Film and Video* 58.1–2 (Spring/Summer): 21–30.
Gross, Larry. 1999. "Too Late the Hero." *Sight and Sound* 9.9 (September): 20–23.
Kreider, Tim. 2000. "*Eyes Wide Shut* by Stanley Kubrick." *Film Quarterly* 53.3 (Spring): 41–48.

Masson, Alain. 1999. "Fin d'un empire imaginaire." *Positif* 464 (October): 131–34.
Meflah, Nadia. 2006. "Le cinéma × et le corps conducteur de sensations." *CinémAction* 121: 40–44.
Nelson, Thomas Allen. 2000. *Kubrick: Inside a Fim Artist's Maze*. Bloomington: Indiana University Press.
Raphael, Frederic. 1999. *Eyes Wide Open*. London: Orion Books Ltd.
Ridley-Duff, Rory. 2010. *Emotion, Seduction and Intimacy: Alternative Perspectives on Human Behaviour*. Seattle: Libertary Editions.
Starfield, Penny. 2006. "Masques du pouvoir, pouvoirs du masque dans *Eyes Wide Shut*." *CinémAction* 118: 85–95.
Vachaud, Laurent. 1999. "Identification d'une femme." *Positif* 464 (October): 134–36.
Williams, Linda Ruth. 1999. "Mister Strangelove." *Sight and Sound* 19.3 (March): 18–22.

J. Edgar
Staging Secrecy

Anne-Marie Paquet-Deyris

A few minutes after the opening scene which roots the title character in the first decades of the 20th century, J. Edgar Hoover's biographer asks him whether he was present when Attorney General Mitchell Palmer's house was bombed in 1919. The Federal Bureau of Investigation Director answers:

> Let's leave that to the reader's imagination. You see, it's important we give our protagonist a bit of mystery. [...] I don't need to tell you that what determines a man's legacy is often what isn't seen. What's critical at this moment is that we clarify the difference between villain and hero [5:20–5:53]

These programmatic words illustrate the very nature of the central figure and serve as guidelines for Eastwood's film. Both the art of manipulation and mastering secrecy, both Hoover's own and the intimacy of others, are at the core of the film's narrative logic. The very notion of intimacy comes to operate, then, in two ironically opposed ways. In its most broadly accepted sense, a close intimacy or friendship with someone, intimacy is mostly associated with the hero's hidden private life, also euphemistically referring at times to sexual intercourse. In its second meaning, it partly defines Hoover's professional life, also ironically tainted by the same secretive, illicit dimension as his life-long personal relationship with Deputy Director Clyde Tolson. Intimacy becomes synonymous with another kind of closeness, the closeness of observation or knowledge illegally acquired of other people's compromising secrets. This twofold articulation of the sense of intimacy is also reflected in the dual narrative structure.

Starting in 1972, a short while before Hoover died after thirty-seven years at the head of the Federal Bureau of Investigation, the narrative hinges around a twofold temporality: the highlights of his career at the Justice Department from 1919 onward, and later at the Bureau he joined in 1924 before becoming its Director, and the current moment in the narrative which ends with his death at age seventy-seven. The process of narration alternately features the older man dictating his memoirs to a series of FBI agents and the younger agent in flashbacks that are sometimes commented on by Hoover in voiceover. Toying with various narrative fragments, the flashback structure captures in detail the manner in which Hoover patiently and expertly wove a parallel system of control and perfected the intelligence business thanks to the progress of forensics and police investigation methods. But the twofold narrative mechanism only documents part of the character's complexity. Showing the Bureau's backstage, the film constantly addresses the issue of how to stage a public figure's intimacy and inscribe the twists and turns of his private life—without ever fully addressing it: how could this figure who *manufactured* his own legend so consistently and obsessively conceal the various facets of his private life? Operating as a *trompe-l'œil*, the apparent polar opposites of the private and public dimensions in the movie manufacture competing fictional levels, which create narratives that are above all dissonant. The as-yet untold story of Hoover's intimacy unfolds against the generic framework of the biopic. It collides frontally with a mode of display including various markers of public recognition, such as press conferences, newsreels or trial scenes. As Steve Neale has underlined,

> [B]iopics deal with notoriety as well as with fame, with tyrants, villains and outlaws as well as with exemplary figures, with those who are willing to ignore or destroy the rules and the boundaries of communities as well as those who wish to reformulate them [64].

The Arrangement

The film's heavy reliance on flashbacks, and therefore its constantly moving back and forth between time periods, enables it to focus both directly and indirectly on the intimate dimension of the character. Within a few shots, a heavily made up DiCaprio goes from embodying an old man restaging his entire life to an ambitious young novice eager to prove himself among Washington government officials. As a visual echo of the official strata of memory, the key scene at the Library of Congress already establishes secrecy as the heart of Hoover's life [10:13–14:17]. Having just realized Miss Gandy won't marry him, he immediately asks her to become his personal secretary and never to breathe a word about their brief romantic interlude. The entire scene is actually emblematic of J. Edgar's consummate skills for orchestrating and performing.

Even during the brief exchange between two young people who could have been lovers, everything is already skewed, deflected from the more conventional course, as when Edgar decides to be called by his second name instead of "John" [6:30]. The private and emotional side is immediately circumvented, somehow covered up by the professional and functional dimension Hoover favors in his relationships with others. In a strange effect of symmetry, Hoover is duplicated and amplified by Helen Gandy, his perfect female double. The music score bridges the gap with the previous scene and further blurs the distinction between the various spheres. Edgar has just told his mother of his recent promotion at the State Department and he is about to meet with a new "very organized" typist. When Mrs. Hoover asks him whether it is a date, he answers: "I think so. I'm going to show her my old card catalogue system at the Library of Congress" [9:51–9:56]. The straight cut and the Goldberg Variations crescendo abruptly foreground Helen and Edgar first in a low-angle shot in the vast space of the Library Hall, before being shot from various angles in the next scene. Their bodies only partly register onscreen, thus creating an optical illusion: the giant architectural body of the library dwarfs the individuals, rendering them insignificant in such a disproportionate space, and hence metaphorically erasing the private dimension.

At this early stage, Edgar already resembles the organic monster acting "with precise and mechanical violence"[1] Philippe Ortoli mentions when describing Eastwood's portrayal of the hero in *Pale Rider* (Eastwood, 1985). Every single camera angle highlights the artificial dimension of the scene specifically choreographed to feature prominently in Hoover's memoirs. Functioning like a sequence, as the Library's different spaces open up one after the other like some giant labyrinth, this extraordinary scene lays the foundations for the legendary America Hoover so ardently wishes to hand down to posterity. Most shots inside the temple of knowledge are actually highly emphatic crane shots capturing the two heroes as if they were part of the majestic scenery. After the changes of perspectives in the stately hall and once the golden cupola has been magnified in a low-angle shot, the camera moves back down to the protagonists' level to, paradoxically, better emphasize the erasure of any form of intimacy. The hero has been reduced to his function, and from now on, his intimate dimension will only resurface in a few brief scenes of both literal and symbolic exposure: the stuttering scene when his mother is forced to calm Edgar down and eventually teaches him how to dance [78:34–81:05], the erotically-charged fight with Clyde which ends on a bloody kiss in a hotel in La Jolla, California [90:30–94:12], the

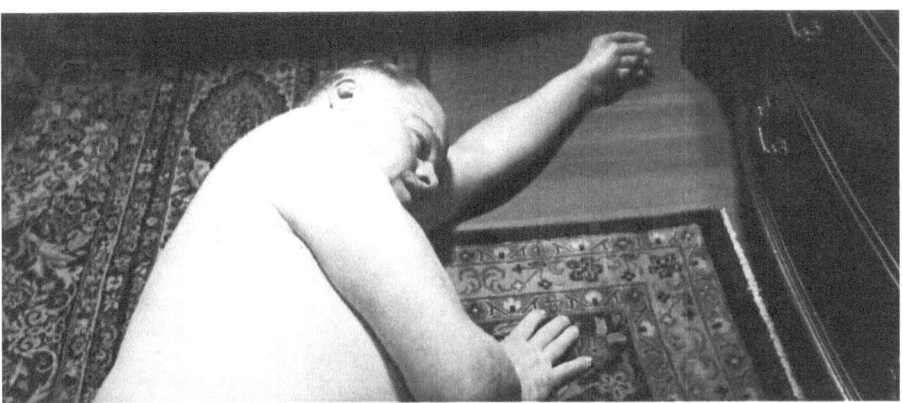

Fig. 15. A figure of ultimate secrecy: Edgar's half-naked body carrying his secrets to the grave in Eastwood's *J. Edgar*.

cross-dressing scene after his mother's death [117:49–119:40], and the final exposure of Edgar's half-naked body struck dead by a heart attack [125:02–125:50] (Fig. 15).

The spectacular volume and architecture of the Library are emblematic of the secret and intricate layers of Hoover's system. Under the stately dome of the Library, his unique and ground-breaking work is showcased and beautifully highlighted by the camera angles and chiaroscuro lighting, as well as by the technical words he uses when speaking to Miss Gandy: "See, every item is assigned its own index card with its own completely unique code" [10:37–10:42] (Fig. 16). Besides being an awkward courtship, the seminal scene truly epitomizes the implacable precision mechanism of Hoover's information classification system. It is also the moment when Edgar and Helen seal their lifelong pact of mutual assistance and discreet work cooperation. When Helen Gandy picks the topic "indiscretion" so that her new boss can make a catalogue search, he immediately interprets the term in its strictly private meaning. His prophetic guess announces the vast file collection on people's dirty secrets he will spend his life perfecting. From the onset, the two partners' relationship is clearly built on trading and archiving secrets. The scene serves as a synecdoche of their symbiotic work relationship, as the first secrets they share are actually their own: Edgar's unsuccessful proposal and Helen's unusual lack of interest in marriage. The uncanny symmetry between the ways the Library and the Bureau are organized is also clearly underscored by the older Hoover's voiceover. The camera frames from high above and a quasi-divine and prophetic viewpoint the brand-new colleagues' tiny forms leaving the Library, thus further emphasizing the odd couple's extraordinary destiny.

Fig. 16. J. Edgar Hoover (Leonardo DiCaprio) showing Helen (Naomi Watts) his card catalogue system in Eastwood's *J. Edgar* (2011).

Fault Lines

The entire sequence materializes the great divide between the characters' intimate and public facets. From the Library of Congress scene onward, Edgar's professional life will take on an increasingly political dimension author Marc Dugain calls "the power to deter"[2] in his literary docufiction *La Malédiction d'Edgar* (311, my translation). The final shot in chiaroscuro of the reading room and its concentric tiers is a striking visual inscription of the importance of mastering the type of "indiscretion" Miss Gandy has just alluded to [14:31]. The camera movements, the types of shots as well as the lighting serve as metafilmic comments on the tight, ritualized organization of the strange threesome composed of Hoover, Gandy and soon Tolson.[3] They also provide a metaphor for the film's structure that is equally cyclical and closes in on itself, eventually staging Hoover's dead body with crosscuts on Miss Gandy erasing all traces of his precious "system of indiscretions."

Hoover constantly reshapes the different versions of his personal myth, as the film's diverse and sometimes competing strata show. The play on the different stories, and the interaction between fifty years of American history and Edgar's tight mechanism of information control, map out a more intimate tale. From the outset, the film focuses on staging the Bureau chief and his collaborators' paranoia and mythomania. The inscription of human flaws on screen shapes the narrative, as if these cracks were the sign of systemic flaws. Some of the most fascinating moments in the movie have to do with the way the director charts affects and intimacy which are by definition unacceptable because uncontrollable. The shots of the fight and kisses between Clyde Tolson and his boss tell an alternative, literally *behind-the-scenes* story. Briefly registering within the frame, the very fact that they temporarily exist disrupts Edgar's official grand design "to put everyone's secrets on file"[4] (Lalanne 2012, my translation). The narrative of his intimate relationship with Tolson can only be related in some indirect, roundabout way, stealthily resurfacing in scenes where the unconstrained body takes center stage.

Even though he was able to survive most of the great economic, political and cultural upheavals of 20th-century America, Hoover is constructed as an unstable character living in denial, who goes from the heights of omnipotence to the lows of powerlessness, especially when facing his mother. At no other moment in the film are pathos and helplessness better transcribed than in the cross-dressing scene following Mrs. Hoover's death [117:55–119:40]. The partly blurred and redoubled image of Edgar's miserable face in the mirror materializes onscreen the most secretive and *uncertain* side of the other Hoover.

The real issue however seems to be: Who has made him this way? To what extent did he will himself to become this persona? How did screenwriter Dustin Lance Black, director Clint Eastwood and the spectators contribute to creating a character so deeply and paradoxically linked to the notion of intimacy? Eastwood discusses Hoover's selective memory in an interview he gave Franck Garbarz in 2011: "What's certain is that he considered himself as a heroic figure meant to play a crucial part in the nation's destiny. [...] At times, the image he desperately tries to create cracks and something else emerges from beneath the mask"[5] (10, my translation). Positing that what lies beneath and suddenly resurfaces is also part of Hoover's "true" personality, Eastwood not only shows alternately the hero and the villain, but simultaneously the conflicted heroic villain. His own orchestration of such a dubious figure somehow redoubles the character's own maneuvering.

The series of vignettes, which places the character at the center of the frame while he's posing for posterity before his staff and journalists, is part of the great manipulation scheme at the core of the Hoover enigma. In the scene depicting the arrest in May 1936 of Alvin Karpis, one of Depression America's most wanted gangsters, the camera tracks the FBI chief through a car window [71:36]. The double-framing effect foregrounds the artificial dimension of his heroic gesture. Once on location with his men, Hoover pushes aside the agent who already has his gun trained on Karpis so as to reap the benefit of appearing as the most effective G-Man. Even in the line of fire, J. Edgar Hoover still finds the time to stage himself in the roles he's carefully picked, concealing his dark side the way he has manipulated his victims' for five decades and under eight presidents, from Calvin Coolidge to Richard Nixon.

The Body Exposed

One of the rare instances in the movie when Hoover loses control is when he gets in a fight with Deputy Tolson. While the two men are sharing a room, Edgar tells Clyde he plans to marry American actress Dorothy Lamour, causing a memorable fit of jealousy and despair. Even in the most private of moments, menace and violence still permeate the two lovers' intimate relationship. Tolson's frantic kiss turns into savage biting explicitly materialized onscreen by blood trickling from Edgar's mouth. It harks back to the dual tradition of the gangster and vampire film. Love can only be of a vampiric nature, even if this time, Hoover is the one being preyed on. The two men confront each other with the same violence as the gangsters they fight in their professional lives. The shots of Edgar's bloodstained mouth and their dual generic heritage inscribe within the frame the impossible combination of the private and public facets. One can only develop at the expense of the other.

The sudden eruptions of intimacy in the narrative and Hoover's official biography mainly function as glitches in the seamless and broad pattern, providing glimpses of an alternate story highlighting bodies which are by no means under control. In this covert story, the shot of Edgar's dead body struck down by a heart attack next to his bed may be the crudest disclosure of intimacy. As it exposes to the viewer's gaze a flesh that is usually forbidden (Fig. 15), the scene seems to be the only one Hoover could not direct himself. It actually provides a clear and intensely physical image of a troubled, constrained and eventually sacrificed interiority. Vulnerable like an old man's stranded corpse, it is also a hermetically closed container, letting no secret escape. The body's state of abandonment paradoxically translates restraint and constraint.

In the final series of shots, Eastwood toys with visual echoes and brilliantly suggests the impenetrable spiral of secrecy. The low-, then high-angle shots of Miss Gandy by the paper-shredder [126:41–126:58], the insert shots of Edgar's fantasized and untitled autobiography and of his secret file on Eleanor Roosevelt [126:59–127:04], and eventually the high-angle shots of Tolson reading his dead lover's memoirs [127:07–127:23]—all interact as paradoxical figures of secrecy. The insert shot of the title page of the file on the First Lady serves a dual purpose: it proves the existence of the "personal and confidential" file and reasserts the effectiveness of Edgar's system of secrecy. Ironically, while its very existence has repeatedly been denied by Bureau officials, its actual contents forever seem to elude the spectator's gaze. In his book on Hoover, Curt Gentry relies on Agent Sullivan's claim that, contrary to her secretary Edith Helm, she had never been put under FBI surveillance despite her liberal political and social opinions.[6] Hoover was mostly interested in uncovering what could potentially become the most damaging elements of her sex life if exposed. This obsessive propensity to excavate the most intimate parts of other people's lives defines Hoover's persona most. Eastwood also tracks down these upsurges of affects and intimacy the better to delineate the characters of Hoover, Tolson and, though to a lesser extent, Gandy, most of all when he shows the Director and his deputy delighting in discussing a wire-tap of Mrs. Roosevelt, apparently engaged in an affair with another woman [58:33–59:07].

However, the mute eloquence of these bodies and objects exposed to the inescapable eye of the camera still does not fully inscribe the secrets of both characters and compromising files. Even if the latter end up in Miss Gandy's paper shredder, Eastwood's camera endows them with the impregnable and diffuse dimension of the ambiguous constructs that keep on haunting politicians and the collective unconscious. The final high-angle shot of Clyde reading Edgar's memoirs materializes onscreen the fictional distance created around the main character and his tactics. Once dead, Hoover still leaves behind impenetrable strata of secrets in the meanders of his own false (auto-)biography and behind the cover sheets of the various volumes framed in insert shots. The final zoom-out on Tolson holding the book as the ultimate relic and the fade-to-black chart Hoover's incessant self-reorganizations, which eventually remain as opaque as any of his other creations [127:20–127:23].

With its brief incursions into J. Edgar Hoover's intimacy, Eastwood's biopic departs from more traditional approaches of the genre. Rather than generating an aura of respectability, his treatment of the subject ushers in doubt, questioning and controversy on all interpretative levels. Like Charlie Parker in *Bird* (Eastwood, 1988), Hoover is one of those hybrid protagonists possessing talent and ambition counterpointed with failure in another field or in parts of the same field. This opens up onto "another set of traits—a further dimension of character" (Neale 209), that vitalizes the stereotypical traits of the historical hero. But it also deliberately undermines the genre's stable patterns and motifs by borrowing from other genres—the gangster or adventure movie, or even the romantic comedy at times—thereby reformulating their combined boundaries and bringing about varying and unpredictable resolutions. The term biopic may, in the end, not be absolutely adequate in the case of *J. Edgar*, as showing Hoover's pathetic death interrupts his grand opus, as well as a trajectory marked by deviance "where the drive for success is coded as a form of megalomania" (Neale 64).

Notes

1. My translation of Ortoli's words in the centerfold of his book.
2. Original text: "le pouvoir d'empêcher."
3. Armie Hammer played both twins in *The Social Network* (David Fincher, 2010).
4. Original text: "archiver tous les secrets des autres."
5. Original text: "Ce qui est sûr, c'est qu'il se considérait comme une figure héroïque appelée à jouer un rôle crucial dans la vie du pays. [...] Parfois, l'image qu'il s'évertue à créer craque et l'on aperçoit autre chose derrière ce masque."
6. Gentry chronicles Eleanor Roosevelt's unwavering support for Martin Luther King or the communist activist, Earl Browder, which used to infuriate Hoover: "More than most women, Eleanor Roosevelt lived a highly public life. Astonishingly busy, she even chronicled her activities in a newspaper column entitled 'My Day.' It was her private life, however, that most interested Hoover" (301).

Works Cited

Dugain, Marc. 2005. *La Malédiction d'Edgar*. Paris: Gallimard.
Garbaz, Franck. 2012. "Clint Eastwood, *J. Edgar* : Citizen Hoover." *Positif* 611 (January): 6–13.
Gentry, Curt. 1991. *J. Edgar Hoover: The Man and his Secrets*. New York: Norton.
J. Edgar. 2011 [2012]. Dir. Clint Eastwood. With Leonardo DiCaprio (J. Edgar Hoover), Judi Dench (Annie Hoover), Armie Hammer (Clyde Tolson) and Naomi Watts (Helen Gandy). Written by Dustin Lance Black. Warner Bros. Pictures. DVD. Warner Bros.
Lalanne, Jean-Marc. 2012. "*J. Edgar*, portrait d'un homme complexe et frustré." *Les Inrocks* 866 (July 4). http://www.lesinrocks.com/cinema/films-a-l-affiche/j-edgar-portrait-dun-homme-complexe-et-frustre, retrieved on 15/1/2013.
Neale, Steve. 2000. *Genre and Hollywood*. London and New York: Routledge.
Ortoli, Philippe. 1994. *Clint Eastwood : La figure du guerrier*. Paris: L'Harmattan.

Intrusions of the Other
Intimacy in the Films of Atom Egoyan

JEAN-FRANÇOIS BAILLON

> Brooding at the end of the world on my island of Sal in the company of my prancing dogs, I remember that month of January in Tokyo, or rather I remember the images I filmed of the month of January in Tokyo. They have substituted themselves for my memory, they are my memory. I wonder how people remember things who don't film, don't photograph, don't tape.
> —Chris Marker (1983)

When it comes to discussing intimacy in film, the name of Atom Egoyan quickly comes to mind. Taking as a starting point the fact that several commentators have clearly identified intimacy as a central theme in his films, this essay will try to establish how problematic the relationship of most of Egoyan's characters is to their own intimacy, as well as to that of other characters, and how this, in turn, says much about Egoyan's specific use of the cinematic medium. The omnipresence of the theme of intimacy and privacy in Egoyan's films has often been remarked upon. Here is what we can read in *The Canadian Encyclopedia Online*:

> Stylistically and narratively, Atom Egoyan's work has been influenced by Cronenberg's clinical detachment, expositional minimalism and resolute intellectualism. But Cronenberg's remoteness from the emotional undercurrents of his characters is counterpointed by Egoyan's genuine interest in the causes, effects and permutations of diminished human interaction in the electronic era. Egoyan's films all end on nearly operatic emotional epiphanies and are rooted in the romantic search for self-fulfillment through intimacy.[1]

On other websites, we can read that "Atom Egoyan is known for his dramas about intimacy and the nature of truth, whether familial or sexual,"[2] or that "Egoyan's nine feature films to date reflect his unique aesthetic and explore his own very personal thematic obsessions, delving into issues of intimacy, displacement and the impact of technology and media in modern life."[3] Leaving aside some questionable assumptions—Egoyan a romantic, *really*?—we can but notice how vague and general such descriptions are. This essay will attempt to be much more specific about the way intimacy and privacy are handled in Egoyan's cinema by focusing on strategies developed by several of his protagonists to retrieve lost intimacies through technology.

It is safe to say that intimacy in Egoyan's films is rarely a given. Tom McSorley, in his brilliant full-length study of *The Adjuster* (1991), has written about the theme of "impeded intimacy" pervading all of Egoyan's early works (41). One can undoubtedly add that the premise of most of his films is the loss of intimacy between lovers or parents, as is the case of Mitchell Stevens's broken relationship with his daughter, beautifully rendered in the opening credits of *The Sweet Hereafter* (1998). Egoyan's fictions are about characters attempting to reconstruct some form of privileged contact through displacement and substitution, often relying on the assistance of recording machines. Intruding upon the private circle and territories of some "significant others" is often part of the fantasmatic scenario implied by such a quest. Many characters in Egoyan's films are actually in the position of intruders, and one often gets the sense that privacy and intimacy are defined in terms of what someone intrudes or pries on; this is the case of Peter in *Next of Kin* (1984), Van in

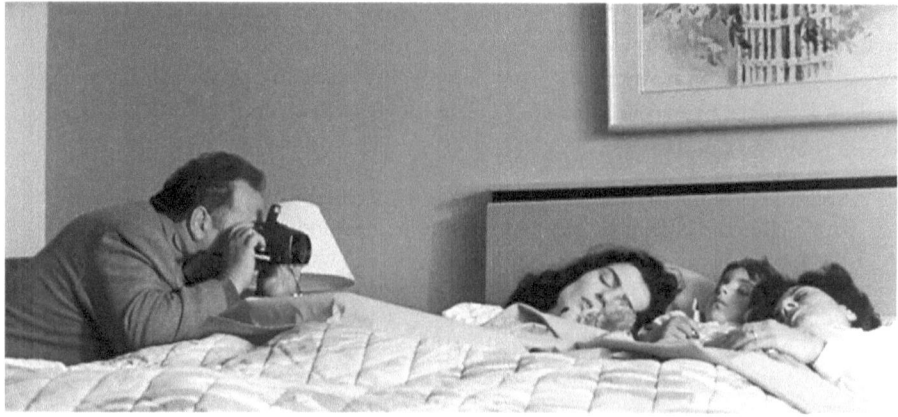

Fig. 17. Bubba (Maury Chaykin) violating the intimacy of Hera (Arsinée Khanjian) and her children in Atom Egoyan's *The Adjuster* (1991).

Family Viewing (1988), Lance in *Speaking Parts* (1989), virtually everyone in *The Adjuster* (Fig. 17) and Mitchell Stevens in *The Sweet Hereafter*.

Many characters in Egoyan's films have jobs that allow them to probe into other people's lives and even to search their personal belongings or explore forbidden, intimate images, to gain access to those parts of people's lives that usually belong to the private sphere: Mitchell Stevens is a litigation lawyer in *The Sweet Hereafter*, Noah Render an insurance adjuster in *The Adjuster* and David a customs officer in *Ararat* (2002). To psychologists, customs officers, gynecologists, lawyers, private investigators—the list is both various and strikingly consistent—can be added hotel or motel workers like Lisa and Lance, and home movie directors like Eddy in *Speaking Parts*. And yet what is even more striking is that they all go out of their way to do more than what their jobs strictly require in order to get to know as much as they can, in what often seems to be a process of substituting one life (or lives) for another (or others). In *Ararat*, customs officer David projects his relationship with his son onto the tale told by Rafi; in *The Sweet Hereafter*, lawyer Mitchell Stevens's personal difficulties with his own daughter interfere with the case of the lost children of a whole community; and, as the final flashback of *The Adjuster* reveals, Noah's own family was the result of the same kind of reconstruction that we see at work throughout the film.[4]

The intrusion-of-the-other motif obviously brings to mind Pier Paolo Pasolini's *Teorema* (1968) as a prototype, an influence acknowledged by Egoyan himself (Tschofen 348; McSorley 70). The fact that many of Egoyan's characters engage in relationships with the past or with others that are mediated by recording machines suggests another strong influence, that of Michael Powell's *Peeping Tom* (1960). Indeed, as we shall see, one of the basic questions in Egoyan's cinema is that of who or what occupies the site behind the camera, a problem that was also raised by Powell in the opening of his 1960 film: Mark Lewis's disease can, in a sense, be described as intimacy with the screen or with the gaze of the camera—in other words, as Christian Metz's primary cinematographic identification brought to a crisis. The theme of substitution as an excuse for intruding on the other's territory, therefore, entails a view of responsibility as defined by Emmanuel Levinas—according to him, my responsibility for the Other stems from my absolute passivity (Butler 85–86)—which, in turn, implies cinematic choices.

From this situation, which Levinas describes as a form of "persecution" (Butler 85–101), Peter in *Next of Kin* wishes to "take control" through a literalization of substitution. At this point, it should be recalled that, for Levinas, the presence of the Other in me both calls for responsibility and makes ethics take precedence over ontology in the structuring of subjectivity; in simpler terms, I am a "me" before being an "I." Through this process of literalization, Peter turns himself over to another family, thereby becoming "hostage" to their hospitality. In cinematic terms, this implies a shift from a definition of the cinema as an ontology of the image (the Bazinian scheme) towards an ethics of the image. This also involves a questioning of the relationship between the filming subject and the filmed subject, the two "I"s/eyes of the camera, as it were, to quote William Rothman's classic 1989 study.

By drawing our attention to the "man (or woman) behind the movie camera," Egoyan's films precisely engage with such a questioning and, in so doing, echo Levinas's thesis of the primacy of ethics over ontology. Actually, neither the camera, nor the profilmic material in front of it can be said to be passive in any meaningful sense of the term, and very often we find that the filmed subject refuses to become a mere object and resists the passiveness which the filming process presupposes. This is exemplified in a film like *Calendar* (1993), which is really about what Marc Vernet, elaborating upon Noel Burch's sixth portion of the offscreen in *Praxis of the cinema*, calls "the underside or the gaze of the camera"[5] (29, my translation). This is deeply related to Egoyan's preoccupation with "the man behind the movie camera":

> To my eyes, he wrote to Paul Virilio, the act of filming cannot be separated from the idea that *someone* is filming the image [...] In all my films there are always key characters, or a central character who is missing, absent from the drama. I often entrust the camera with the task of impersonating that missing character, of giving it body and mind [Virilio 114].

One of the recurrent figures of this "intrusion of the other" is that of the character reaching out with her/his hand. The sense of touch, with all its ambiguities, is the sense of intimacy—often forbidden or transgressive—in Egoyan's cinema. Fingering the other's archives is one of its key structuring motifs. It is also one of the entries into the metafilmic dimensions of the way Egoyan handles his theme, as the other's archives very often become some sort of script or character definition that lead to identification; this is very much the case in *Next of Kin*, when Peter discovers the files and videotapes of the Armenian family, whose son Bedros will later define a role he will perform, and in *Speaking Parts*, the whole plot of which revolves around the writing of an actual screenplay for a television show. As Peter puts it in *Next of Kin*, part of him is spectator, part of him is an actor performing different roles. This is what film critic Peter Harcourt described as Peter's "chiasmatic sense of self" (4); it is only part of a more general chiasmatic structure of visibility at work in Egoyan's cinema. I have in mind Maurice Merleau-Ponty's description of that structure in *Le Visible et l'invisible*: "As soon as I see [...] sight must be doubled by a complementary sight or by another sight: myself seen from outside, such as another would see me, settled in the midst of the visible and contemplating it from a certain place" (175, my translation). In the same passage, Merleau-Ponty, who establishes the equation of sight and touch, talks about the "identity of seeing and the visible." The credit sequence of *Adoration* (2008) provides a perfect illustration of this, as the camera slowly tracks right to reveal that the female violinist is actually under the gaze of a young man, who is both her son and the protagonist of the film [1:30]. Much later in the film, an extended version of the same shot will reveal that the young man was himself the object of his father's gaze [69:25–69:50]. This chiasmatic structure of the visible is what makes it possible for protagonists to reverse the relationship of viewer and viewed, to take upon themselves the responsibility for the images and narratives of which they initially formed a part.

Exploring another person's archives can also be seen as another instance of the transformation of a passive situation into something more active, taking responsibility for what are mere chance circumstances, as more often than not characters in Egoyan's film "happen upon" private spaces or archives and rise to the occasion by making the most of it. Happening upon the other's intimacy is a situation described in *The Adjuster* by Bubba in answer to Noah's need of some further explanation as to why he wants to use his house as a location for his film:

> for no reason you can see a house and you're wondering "what's going on inside of those walls?" and sometimes the opportunity comes to find out. And it could be an open door that you're passing at night, it could be a good peek at someone else's family ... or it could be ... an invitation to dinner, though that's rare. You have to have friends. And other times you would find alternatives [53:10–54:17].

In *Next of Kin*, Peter happens upon the file of the Deryan family very much like Lance happens upon the script left in Clara's room in *Speaking Parts*—or, albeit a bit differently, Karen O'Connor in *Where the Truth Lies* (2006). The invention of the other will, then, become an invention of the self and the video screen will, in effect, turn into a "psyché," which is both a mirror (a "cheval glass mirror" in English) and refers to the mind or the inner self or interiority (Derrida 1988). The "cheval glass mirror" actually has a very special structure which can be used, here, as a metaphor for the reversal of gazes implied in the process I am attempting to describe: it usually swings on a frame so that the direction of the mirror can be inverted. The "mirror-role," to borrow D.W. Winnicott's notion, of the video image of the (m)other is obvious in *Felicia's Journey* (2001): Hilditch looks for an image of himself through the gaze of his mother, just as the protagonists of the earlier films look for traces of themselves in the gazes of meaningful others.[6] According to Winnicott's analysis of the mirror stage, which differs from Jacques Lacan's, what matters is not so much the look the infant *gives* as the look the infant *receives*: "What does the baby see when he or she looks at the mother's face? I am suggesting that, ordinarily, what the baby sees is himself or herself. In other words the mother is looking at the baby and *what she looks like is related to what she sees there*" (Burgin 48). Hence, the profusion of looks-to-the-camera in Egoyan's films: the viewer's gaze looks for signs that her/his presence is being noticed in a way that reflects on the features of whoever appears on an image that somehow functions as a mirror. Hence, also, for much the same reason, the profusion of two-way mirrors in Egoyan's films.

Indeed, the function of looks-to-the-camera in Egoyan's films is complex and would deserve a full-length study in its own right. Within the scope of this essay, it is perhaps relevant to note that many of them are rooted in the practice of home video and amateur photography—hence, in the capturing of ordinary private situations supposedly not meant to be watched by outsiders or by the general public. However, in several instances, Egoyan resorts to the look-to-the-camera as a device whose function is clearly to expose the cinematic illusion and point to the cinematic frame as a construct, sometimes through reference to previous films such as Alfred Hitchcock's *Suspicion* (1940) or *Psycho* (1960). In *Felicia's Journey*, for instance, Hilditch carries a glass of milk to Felicia, echoing a similar scene in *Suspicion* where Johnnie (Cary Grant) brings a glass of milk to his wife Lina (Joan Fontaine). Having reached the top of the stairs, Hilditch looks at the camera, the scene thus drawing the viewer's attention to the reference [87:09]. The allusion to *Psycho* is more subtle in *Next of Kin*: the face of the psychiatrist playing the part of Bedros in a psychodrama significantly fades out to reveal that of Peter looking at the camera (he will later impersonate Bedros in real life) [14:33], just as the grin of Mrs. Bates' skull appeared in superimposition over the final shot on Norman Bates' face in *Psycho*.

As the references to Hitchcock suggest, one can never be sure that the memories apparently triggered by the spectacle of video archives are anything but hallucinatory projections. In *Felicia's Journey*, Hilditch remembers being present during the shooting of the television program featuring his mother and being smothered by her as she forced some of the liver he had spilled into his mouth [59:40–1:00:00] ... but does he really? Perhaps it never happened, or not quite the way he remembers it. Perhaps, more to the point, Hilditch is now choking on his food not because of what he remembers, but because of who he has become. This could, then, be interpreted as an instance of what Jacques Derrida calls "half-mourning," i.e., what happens when you can neither vomit nor assimilate the dead, neither take them inside you nor leave them outside of you (Derrida 1980, 543–44; Derrida 1992, 161).

As the case of Hilditch makes clear, the use of recording machines and archives triggers a process of mourning that verges on illusion and fantasy. Another clear instance is the ending of *Speaking Parts*, when suddenly the editing process takes the viewer from the stage of the television show to the hospital room and allows different levels of narrative to interfere [84:40–85:53]. The characters of Egoyan's films engage with machines in processes of "half-mourning," in which characters prove unable to retrieve the past or come to terms altogether with a traumatic experience. As Egoyan himself puts it, they "have a sensory contact to something that they don't have the means to possess anymore. [...] They become drunk with the possibility of contact and therefore remove themselves from the possibility of genuine restitution" (Wilson 2008, 260). In the words of Peter Harcourt, "[i]t is as if Egoyan's characters, in their imaginings, have irretrievably abandoned their 'originary' homes" (13). This melancholy view of the relationship between memory and machines might well be described in deconstructionist terms, as Tollof Nelson has done when talking about the photographer of *Calendar*:

> the photographer can never simply return or rewind the singular alterations of his experience. His entire life and memory is organized by the impossible attempt to align experience with memory, identity with history: he is stuck irrevocably in the temporality of the re-play, a replay that is never identical to the original experience, but must be re-lived and acted as the blurred life of the fast-forward or the rewind functions of his video machine [139].

In an interview with Monique Tschofen, Egoyan actually revealed his interest in "faulty mourning," in which "rituals we set up to deal with grief and mourning [...] may only serve to exaggerate these feelings" (Tschofen 352; Romney 119). Egoyan said this in answer to a question about the presence of ghosts in his work. This recalls Derrida's definition of a crypt as the place within us where the other is present and acts as a ventriloquist for us (Derrida, 1976, 9–25). Egoyan's protagonists are often confronted with video images of their dear departed, which can be rewound and watched again in a way that not only suggests a process of faulty mourning, but also invites endless repetition, as if they were caught in a loop.

The beginning of *Speaking Parts*—yet another chiasmatic opening in Egoyan's oeuvre—intertwines the parallel situations of Clara and Lisa, each watching images of a distant loved one on a screen: Clara endlessly watching the video image of her dead brother in a mausoleum, Lisa compulsively watching the image of her workmate Lance who works as an extra in exploitation films (she rents copies at the local video store) [0:53–5:05]. The ritual devised by Lisa in her apartment unmistakably echoes the Japanese tradition of the *toko no ma* or alcove, described by Junichiro Tanizaki in *In Praise of Shadows* (1933), thus emphasizing its intimate dimension.[7] Each situation is framed as an intimate act of watching: each woman is performing a ritual, alone in some private room or mausoleum built for some specific purpose. The variations in framing (as the video image expands to full screen) and zooming in insist on the link of intimacy established with an *image* rather than with a real flesh-and-blood person—thereby emphasizing absence rather than presence—whereas the utilization of reverse shots of the diegetic viewer can be interpreted as suggestions of voyeurism or eavesdropping. As Hamid Naficy has aptly put it,

> Self-consciousness is an aesthetic principle in his films [...] a self-consciousness derived from the idea that one is always being watched and must therefore put on a public face, even in moments of privacy, because of the possibility of being subjected to voyeurism or eavesdropping [Morris 33].

Such a possibility is suggested by the presence of a curtainless window behind Lisa as she is watching videos of Lance and touching her hair or breast, and by the establishing shot that closes the sequence as the video of Clara's brother is replaced by a blank screen [5:22]. In both cases, the viewer becomes visible, and we are also made aware that we are being offered some twisted version of the situation of spectatorship. Something like a deconstruction of the essence of spectatorship is, here, proposed: in terms of loneliness, ritual, of being forever at a distance from the object of the gaze, and of the materiality of the screen and the ultimate reduction of the illusion to artefacts.

In short, what we are offered in the first five minutes of *Speaking Parts* is the spectacle of spectatorship as performance. Lisa and Clara perform the intimate in terms of longing, but also in terms of relating with the image of both the loved one and the dead one. Separation and absence produce intimacy through machines of vision—this could be Egoyan's definition of the cinema, especially since his experience has much to do with exile and diasporic identities. The closer we get to the grain of the video image, the less we get the sense either of an image or of the illusion of a body. Hans Belting's remark about the relationship between ghosts and images, which is at the heart of Egoyan's film, immediately comes to mind: "It is precisely in the closest intimacy with the body that the photographic image turns into a ghost which is neither body nor image" (269). During the second discussion with the television producer over the production of the film based on her story, Clara looks at the camera, and this look is followed by one of the appearances of her brother on video, giving the sense of a spectral presence that haunts the film as it haunts her conscience [28:41–28:43].

The rituals performed by Lisa and Clara, like those performed by many other characters in Egoyan's films (Singer 2012), are strongly reminiscent of the audience's own immediate experience of watching a film. Could it be, then, that the darkness surrounding some of Egoyan's characters is offered as an analogon for the condition of the audience watching films? In *Family Viewing*, we hear the voice of a colleague of Aline's addressing an invisible client (it might as well be one of us), saying: "I think it's better—in the dark ... turn off the lights ... that's better" [3:12–3:23]. This is the first, but not the last time that the film thus alludes to the conditions of the cinematic experience. It echoes what Egoyan had to say—in different circumstances—in 2002 about *Whispering Room* (1991), an installation by contemporary Canadian artist Janet Cardiff:

> I had the sensation of being in the middle of a film that was still being formulated; that was still in someone else's mind. I was completely overwhelmed by the collision of technological artifacts—speakers, projectors, lights, wires—and narrative abstraction. I found myself drifting through the emotional residue of a personal trauma that was both immediate and distant, visceral yet disembodied.

Thus, the theme of intimacy has to a lot do with the essential darkness in which cinema-going is experienced, as described by Egoyan again: "I love to drift. There's no better place for me to just let go than in a dark room that's projecting images at twenty-four frames a second" (Morris 113). Elsewhere, Egoyan has linked this sense of intimacy to the experience of children being read to, an experience that, in a 2003 documentary, he compared to that of entering a movie theater:

> That's a formula ultimately. The moment we see something projected as a film. It's almost as though it's like a child to have a parent come into a bedroom at night and open a book. As a child, you expect to then hear a story. And it's the same gesture when you walk into a cinema and the lights go down and the image begins, you expect to hear a story.[8]

Egoyan's own installation *Hors d'Usage* (Montréal, 2002) was set in darkness and dealt with intimacy and memory. It staged recording devices (mostly tape recorders) with images of people using them projected onto them, that were visible only as the visitor got closer to each exhibit, some of which were lit by a single, naked lightbulb. This invitation to explore various people's intimacies was described by Egoyan himself as a "mausoleum dedicated to the memory of tape recorders."[9] In a 1993 interview with Marc Glassman, Egoyan explained his choice of film as a medium by the fact that he "felt that in some ways it allowed [him] to become more private. Film by nature doesn't require the same type of interaction as the theater. It's a much more solitary experience, watching a film, than going to a theatrical presentation" (Egoyan 1993, 51). To explain his choice of embracing his craft in terms of the experience of watching films in a theater is a somewhat curious explanation on the part of a filmmaker. However, the analysis of what it really means to watch an image lies at the heart of Egoyan's relationship to his own art:

> We refuse to recognize that our experience of certain feelings is a direct result of our inability to fully confront what it means to watch a mechanical image. How much of the nostalgia we feel when we watch an artefact of personal memorabilia has its source in the sad realization that we have come to need such devices to retain these experiences? [Egoyan 1993, 26].

This statement implies an awareness of the difference between memory and archive, or perhaps of the interrelatedness of memory and archive, the dependence of memory on archives, at least in Egoyan's films, where so many characters, instead of relying on their own personal capacity to conjure up mental memories, actually rely on recorded images and sounds, film archives that often take the form of home videos.

The visual impact of Egoyan's installation is strikingly reminiscent of the setting of the censoring board's headquarters in *Exotica* (1994), and both works invite some concluding remarks on the strange link between privacy, intimacy and pornography. In his video correspondence with Paul Virilio, Egoyan defines pornography as "watching something you are not supposed to watch," having "access to an image that was not meant for you" (111). The stolen intimacy of home videos is one example, although any kind of infringement of privacy is liable to apply to Egoyan's definition; examples in his films abound. Seen in that—admittedly shady—light, pornography and privacy are, therefore, not a function of the objective or legal contents of the image, but of its uses. The intention behind the construction of an image, the *postal* structure of the video image, are what makes it possible to talk about voyeurism and pornography, even in the case of superficially trivial situations. In *The Adjuster*, the incident with the flasher who masturbates at Hera's sister's window suggests that we are dealing with some sort of pornography of the trivial [47:55–48:35]. Although Hera purportedly smuggles censored material for her sister's private enjoyment (she has become "addicted" to the stuff), the angle from which the man was looking into the room makes it unlikely that he was getting his kicks from the same stuff. It is much more likely that voyeurism as such turns everyday reality into its own simulacrum, as if the footage from diegetic home movies in Egoyan's films were actually to be viewed as real "snuff movies." Hence, the obscenity of the situation and the abjection of the peeping tom: not unlike Noah's own abjection when, at the end of the film, he walks backwards in horror from the spectacle of Bubba surrounded by "some of his favorite things" [93:22–93:32]—Bubba being of course his own grotesque *doppelgänger*, a substitute who, like Noah, intrudes on other people's privacy.

Conversely, one can also consider how the human beings whose lives are being captured on video or film attempt to devise strategies to elude the voyeuristic gaze of the camera in ways that suggest that actual intimacy—provided there is such a thing—is always achieved beyond the scope of what the camera is able to record. One such example occurs in *Calendar* when the photographer's wife and their guide disappear inside a cave, and is strongly reminiscent of what Homi K. Bhabha wrote in *The Location of Culture* about the Marabar Caves in E.M. Forster's *A Passage to India*: "*there* the implausibility of conversation and commensurability" (180). The whole ritual that gives *Calendar* its structure, with the combination of foreign languages and the departure of each woman invited by the photographer towards the background of the frame, is like an echo of the unbearable emptiness that disrupted the continuity of representation when the guide took Arsinée inside the black hole. Bhabha also writes of the "momentous, if momentary, extinction of the recognizable object of culture in the disturbed artifice of its signification, at the edge of experience" (180).

Something needs to be said about the language of the other, too. Egoyan's films are profoundly multilingual films, and yet there is a sense in which some characters are isolated within their own language. They are made to measure the distance from the other's inner life through language, and as a result they measure their own distance from others through their own idiosyncrasies. In *Speaking Parts*, Aline may claim that "there is nothing special about words" [14:53–14:55], yet there is a sense in which *speaking parts* us. The sound that we hear once the screen turns black is undecidable, like Christina's fate at the end of *Exotica*, as musical echoes of Armenia accompany her disappearance into another black rectangle within the vanishing point of the image, before the whole screen, once again, turns black [95:52–96:23]. We have returned to the initial darkness that made the experience of cinema-going possible at all. It is also one of the sites of the ungraspable otherness of the other, the crypt where the other turns out to be radically unlike me—perhaps the last refuge of intimacy or secrecy, as Isabelle Singer (2011) has convincingly demonstrated (172–78). What is left once communication has been attempted and failed? The untranslated remains of a conversation, the ashes of a few family photographs, white powder in film cans, the blurred hand of the painter's mother on a canvas, the charred remains of a mobile phone? Perhaps the last words should be left to Eric in *Exotica*:

What is it that gives a schoolgirl her special innocence, Her sweet fragrance? Fresh flowers ... light as a spring rain? ... Or is it her firm, young flesh inviting your every caress ... enticing you to explore ... her deepest and most private secrets? Well, gentlemen, I'm gonna let you decide that one for yourselves [7:15–7:37].

Notes

1. *The Canadian Encyclopedia Online*, author Geoff Pevere, revised Tom McSorley, http://www.thecanadianencyclopedia.com/articles/atom-egoyan. Retrieved on 11/30/2012.

2. Tribeca.com, "Director Atom Egoyan on *Chloe*," by Jenni Miller, http://www.tribecafilm.com/news-features/features/Director_Atom_Egoyan_on_Chloe.html#.T-GpIWjkyWc. Retrieved on 11/30/2012.

3. National Film and Television School, http://www.nftsfilm-tv.ac.uk/index.php?module=People&people_id=525&courseName=Masterclasses&searchtype=listVisitTutor&type_id=4&ma_dip_course_id=204. Retrieved on 11/30/2012.

4. Egoyan's own reflexive views on this theme draw a parallel between this list of characters and his own plight as a filmmaker: "If you are an insurance adjuster, if you are a tax auditor, if you are a litigation lawyer, if you are a film censor, if you are a customs agent, all of these professions give you access to other people's experience in a way that otherwise would be an invasion of privacy. But suddenly you have this reason or this excuse to investigate other people. As a film director I get to make other people behave in a way that they wouldn't be acting otherwise. And that is either a perversion or it's a natural aspect of your job. It depends on your perspective" (*La Revue*, 2003). Egoyan further relates this to his belief in the heightening effect of recording devices: "When you are being recorded you perform or behave differently. This whole interview, the access you've had into my private life, or I've had glimpses into yours, has certainly been heightened by the fact that the interview is being recorded. We both have the sense that there is something here that is artificially heightening this discourse" (Morris 60).

5. Original text: "[L]'en-deçà ou le regard de la caméra."

6. According to Winnicott, the baby, then the child, see their selves in the mother's face: this is what he calls the "mirror-role" of the mother. In *Felicia's Journey*, Hilditch replaces the closeness to his mother he did not have as a child with present intimacy with archive images of her: "now, because of the lack of attention that Hilditch felt, he has a ritual where he can command Gala's full attention. He can play her films and redirect her gaze electronically, to be watching him" (Morris 117). Egoyan claims in another interview: "Through this ritual of the tapes, she's able to look at him all the time. And it is a very intimate, very adoring relationship that they have, which never existed in his childhood" (Morris 121). "With his mother never giving him attention as a kid, and suddenly through this ritual of the tape, he is able to maintain an intimacy in a relationship. He's able to construct an electronic gaze where there wasn't any attention directed to him as a kid. He's able to make that happen" (Morris 124). Egoyan adds: "It's similar to the situation in *Family Viewing*, with the father trying to erase over the tapes of the home video. I'm very interested in those points where the technology, as I said, can serve as a metaphor but also as a way of having these characters think they are dealing with issues of experience" (Morris 124).

7. Typically, a *toko no ma* would include the display of a calligraphic or pictorial scroll and an arrangement of flowers (*ikebana*). Actually, the link with Japan and the Far East is not so far-fetched: in an interview with Peter Harcourt, Egoyan confesses to having heard about film mausoleums being developed in Japan from a friend who went there (Morris 86).

8. This immediately brings to mind the ending of *The Sweet Hereafter*, with Nicole Burnell reading *The Pied Piper of Hamelin* to Billy Ansell's children, and the narrator's anticipation of his mother's reading of George Sand's *François le Champi* in Proust's *Swann's Way*—the latter experience being deeply connected with intimacy and memory, darkness and the projection of images (the magic lantern), as Raoul Ruiz's adaptation of *Time Regained* (1999) wonderfully captured.

9. The exhibition itself was the result of an appeal by Egoyan (2002) to the people of Montréal to send him their old tape recorders and, most importantly, to tell him their own personal memories related to their own tape recorders.

Works Cited

The Adjuster. 1991 [2007]. Written and directed by Atom Egoyan. With Elias Koteas (Noah), Arsinée Khanjian (Hera), Maury Chaykin (Bubba) and Gabrielle Rose (Mimi). Ego Film Arts. DVD. TF1 Video.
Adoration. 2008 [2009]. Written and directed by Atom Egoyan. With Devon Bostick (Simon), Rachel Blanchard (Rachel) and Arsinée Khanjian (Sabine). Ego Film Arts. DVD. TF1 Video.
Ararat. 2002 [2007]. Written and directed by Atom Egoyan. With David Alpay (Raffi), Charles Aznavour (Edward Saroyan), Christopher Plummer (David), Bruce Greenwood (Clarence Ussher / Martin), Elias Koteas (Ali / Jevdet Bay) and Arsinée Khanjian (Ani). Ego Film Arts. DVD. TF1 Video.
Bhabha, Homi K. 1994 [2007]. *The Location of Culture*. London and New York: Routledge.
Belting, Hans. 2004. *Pour une anthropologie des images*. Paris: Gallimard.
Burgin, Victor. 2004. *The Remembered Film*. London: Reaktion Books.
Butler, Judith. 2005. *Giving an Account of Oneself*. New York: Fordham University Press.
Calendar. 1993 [2007]. With Atom Egoyan (Photographer), Arsinée Khanjian (Translator) and Ashot Adamian (Driver). Ego Film Arts. DVD. TF1 Video.
Derrida, Jacques. 1976 [1999]. "Fors." *Le Verbier de l'Homme aux Loups*. Eds. Nicolas Abraham and Maria Torok. Paris: Flammarion. 7–73.
———. 1980. *La Carte postale : De Socrate à Freud et au-delà*. Paris: Flammarion.
———. 1988. *Psyché : Inventions de l'autre*. Paris: Galilée.
———. 1992. *Points de suspension : Entretiens*. Paris: Galilée.
Desbarats, Carole, Daniele Rivière, Jacinto Lageira and Paul Virilio. 1993. *Atom Egoyan*. Paris: Éditions Dis Voir.
Egoyan, Atom. 1993. "Surface Tension." *Speaking Parts*. Toronto: Coach House Press. 25–38.
———. 2002. "Janet Cardiff by Atom Egoyan," *Bomb* 79. http://bombsite.com/issues/79/articles/2463. Retrieved on 12/14/2012.
Exotica. 1994 [2007]. Written and directed by Atom Egoyan. With Elias Koteas (Eric), Arsinée Khanjian (Zoe), Bruce Greenwood (Francis), Don McKellar (Thomas), Mia Kirshner (Christina), David Hemblen (Inspector) and Sarah Polley (Tracey). Ego Film Arts. DVD. TF1 Video.
Family Viewing. 1988 [2001]. Written and directed by Atom Egoyan. With David Hemblen (Stan), Aidan Tierney (Van), Gabrielle Rose (Sandra) and Arsinée Khanjian (Aline). Ego Film Arts. DVD. Zeitgeist Video / Ego Film Arts.
Felicia's Journey. 1999 [2001]. Written and directed by Atom Egoyan. Based on the novel by William Trevor. With Bob Hoskins (Joe Hilditch), Elaine Cassidy (Felicia) and Arsinée Khanjian (Gala). Alliance Atlantis Communications, Icon Entertainment International. DVD. Studiocanal.
Harcourt, Peter. 1995. "Imaginary Images: An Examination of Atom Egoyan's Films." *Film Quarterly* 48.3: 2–14. Retrieved on 11/30/2012.

McSorley, Tom. 2012. *Atom Egoyan's* The Adjuster. Toronto: Toronto University Press.
Merleau-Ponty, Maurice. 2011. *Le Visible et l'invisible.* Paris: Gallimard.
Morris, T.J., ed. 2010. *Atom Egoyan: Interviews.* Jackson: Mississippi University Press.
Nelson, Tollof. 2005. "Passing Time in Intercultural Cinema: The Exilic Experience of the Time-Passer in Atom Egoyan's *Calendar* (1993)." *SubStance* 34.1: 129–44. Retrieved on 11/30/2012.
Next of Kin. 1984 [2001]. Written and directed by Atom Egoyan. With Patrick Tierney (Peter Foster / Bedros Deryan) and Arsinée Khanjian (Azah Deryan). Ego Film Arts. DVD. Zeitgeist Video / Ego Film Arts.
La Revue—ARTE. 2003. Dir. Alain Fleischer. La Sept-ARTE.
Romney, Jonathan. 2003. *Atom Egoyan.* London: BFI.
Rothman, William. 1989. *The "I" of the Camera: Essays in Film Criticism, History and Aesthetics.* Cambridge: Cambridge University Press.
Singer, Isabelle. 2011. "'Il y va d'un certain pas': l'expérience de la réserve chez Atom Egoyan." *Paradoxes de la réserve.* Eds. Jean-François Baillon, Véronique Béghain, Lionel Larré and Paul Veyret. Pessac: CLIMAS. 167–78.
_____. 2012. "Le Cinéma d'Atom Egoyan: vers une description de l'image-obsession." *L'Obsession à l'œuvre : Littérature, cinéma et société en Grande-Bretagne.* Eds. Jean-François Baillon and Paul Veyret. Pessac: CLIMAS. 227–39.
Speaking Parts. 1989 [2001]. Written and directed by Atom Egoyan. With Michael McManus (Lance), Arsinée Khanjian (Lisa), Gabrielle Rose (Clara) and David Hemblen (Producer). Ego Film Arts. DVD. Zeitgeist Video / Ego Film Arts.
The Sweet Hereafter. 1997 [1998]. Written and directed by Atom Egoyan. Based on the novel by Russell Banks. With Ian Holm (Mitchell Stevens), Sarah Polley (Nicole Burnell), Gabrielle Rose (Dolores Driscoll), Arsinée Khanjian (Wanda) and Bruce Greenwood (Billy). Ego Film Arts. DVD. New Line Home Video.
Tschofen, Monique and Jennifer Burwell, eds. 2007. *Image and Territory. Essays on Atom Egoyan.* Waterloo, Ontario: Wilfrid Laurier University Press.
Vernet, Marc. 1988. *Figures de l'absence : De l'invisible au cinéma.* Paris: Éditions de l'Étoile.
Where the Truth Lies. 2005 [2006]. Written and directed by Atom Egoyan. Based on the novel by Rupert Holmes. With Kevin Bacon (Lanny), Colin Firth (Vince) and Alison Lohman (Karen). Serendipity Point Films. DVD. TF1 Video.
Wilson, Emma. 2008. "The Senses and Substitution: A Conversation with Atom Egoyan." *Paragraph* 31. 2: 252–62. Retrieved on 11/30/2012.

Hidden Worlds and Unspoken Desires
Terence Davies and Autobiographical Discourse

WENDY EVERETT

At the basis of this essay is an exploration of the complex relationship between intimacy and desire, with specific reference to the cinema of the British director Terence Davies. Intimacy and desire are, of course, closely interwoven, and it is possible that the relationship between them is fundamental, even inevitable. Perhaps it is *only* intimacy that permits the compelling and private discourses of desire, or the secure context in which taboo can be transgressed (Harvey and Shalom 1987). Such ideas are particularly pertinent to autobiographical discourse since, like the diary—or *journal intime*—autobiography constitutes a privileged space of intimacy in which to explore one's identity, and articulate and (re)consider one's innermost thoughts and desires. Leaving to one side the spurious discussion of the differences between diary and autobiography—often simplistically characterized as an awareness of whether or not the work will be viewed by others—it is the case that desires, hidden, perhaps forbidden, sometimes merely implied, permeate the pages or images of such works: from Rousseau to Virginia Woolf, from Bergman to Godard, from Anne Frank's passionate jottings to those of any school child scribbling beneath the blankets. In cinema, of course, a multitude of directors have engaged with the mobile and intimate discourse of autobiography in an open-ended dialogue between their present and earlier selves.[1]

Not surprisingly, therefore, this essay on representations of intimacy and desire in the films of Terence Davies will begin with the privileged inner-outer topography of his early films, all of which are autobiographical and explore memories of growing up in Liverpool in the 1950s, in a working-class, Irish Catholic family, with an abusive father who died when Davies was about ten, and an adored mother and older siblings. What I find particularly compelling, however, and this will constitute the main focus of this essay, is the way in which Davies's later literary adaptations are no less deeply imprinted by his personal and subjective experiences and desires. Whereas in the autobiographical films, these desires lie on or just below the surface, in the later works, they must be read through the films' visual and sonorous textures: unworded subtexts, lacunae or voids which we, the spectators, must discover or create for ourselves.

The Autobiographical Project

Davies's early works are, as he freely acknowledges, intimate, personal autobiographies, however fluid, experimental and innovative they appear. His "Trilogy"—*Children* (1976), *Madonna and Child* (1980), and *Death and Transfiguration* (1983)—which dates from his student days, looks both backwards to early childhood and forwards towards an imagined, lonely old age and death, all within the non-linear, non-chronological, fluid temporality that is the hallmark of all his work. *Distant Voices, Still Lives* (1988), quickly achieving international cult status, and still regularly appearing in lists of the greatest films ever made, articulates the memories and stories told to him by his mother and older siblings. Davies himself does not appear, but his presence haunts the narrative at all times, just as the film's images haunt all his subsequent works. In *The Long Day Closes* (1992), the most directly personal of his autobiographical works, Davies, through his young alter ego, Bud, traces approximately one year in his childhood, marking the transition from infant to adolescent and, with it, his growing self- and sexual awareness.

It is not unusual for directors of autobiographical films to return repeatedly to their childhood memories—witness the number of autobiographical trilogies that abound.[2] Presumably, we are all, to varying degrees, obsessed with our childhood, and there is a widespread belief that it is in those early days that can be found the key to our adult selves. For Jacques Lacan, the compulsion to revisit our memories and narrate our desires stems from the impossibility of their fulfillment: narration thus becomes a substitute for the blissful *jouissance* of our earlier union with the mother, that state which we, as adults, perpetually strive for but can never attain (166–67). Desire is, thus, seen as a defining feature of humanity, stemming from this doomed quest and feeding off its own articulations. It is not difficult to apply such theories to Davies's autobiographical films, with their shifting, intimate topographies in which certain key landmarks can be identified, not least the inextricably interwoven themes of Davies's problematic sexuality and his enduring position as outsider. Of course, if adult desires are sourced in early childhood, then the privileged discourse of autobiography, the intimate relationship between remembering adult and remembered child, is ideal terrain for their articulation.

The relationship between sexual desire and identity is seen by Michel Foucault to be fundamental to the development of self-knowledge. In *Technologies of the Self*, an exploration of the various processes whereby an individual develops an awareness of self, he highlights the fact that self-knowledge, or individual truth, is, inevitably, dominated by personal sexual desires and, in particular, by one's experiences of sexual interdiction (16–18). In other words, the search for self-knowledge and truth which underlies the autobiographical impulse is inextricably bound up with forbidden sexual desires. Such ideas offer further understanding of Davies's autobiographical films in that all of them are fundamentally marked by his forbidden, thus unresolved, sexual desires. Indeed, he has never fully come to terms with being gay, has never been able to see this identity as other than a curse—an insurmountable barrier to the "normality" of the worlds which, as a child, he glimpsed through his family life and in the romantic Hollywood musicals and songs that so influenced him.

Given how important sexuality and sexual interdiction are in the development of self-knowledge, it is helpful to situate Davies's childhood experiences within their wider social context.

- Even between consenting adults, homosexual activity was a criminal offence in Britain until the implementation of the Woolfenden legislation in 1967.
- In 1950s Britain, there was increased pressure by the U.S. government to link homosexuality with communism and moral corruption. As a result, in 1952, there was a threefold increase in prosecutions of gay men. Nighttime raids were common, and letters or even the privileged intimacies of diaries were used to provide evidence leading to prosecution and imprisonment (Jivani 98–116).
- Seen as a moral plague, homosexuality was also presented as a physical and/or mental illness, and medical "cures" were attempted well into the 1960s. It has recently emerged (Chesal 2012) that, in the 1950s, the Catholic Church in Holland used the castration of gay men as one of its "cures."

- Being brought up in a practicing Catholic family, within a wider Irish Catholic community, Davies was painfully aware of the Church's condemnation of the "vice" of homosexuality as a mortal sin, i.e., a form of eternal damnation.

Surely, it would have been hard for any child in Davies's position to accept his sexuality in a positive way. Without any role models to guide him, his desires had to be tightly hidden, never admitted or discussed—a heavy burden for a child to shoulder.

One of the direct ways in which Davies's sexuality impacts on his identity is that he perceives himself as an outsider. This understanding enables the spectator to approach more perceptively the deeper layers of meaning in repeated shots which tightly frame and contain his younger self or position him as looking out at the world through barriers: windows or net curtains, for example. To illustrate this contention, this article will begin by considering a few brief sequences from *The Long Day Closes*, since, in this very personal account, forbidden and hidden desires, more deeply encoded in Davies's later films, can be found on, or just below, the surface.

In one early sequence, Bud is asked by his mother to go upstairs to his brothers' room and bring down the net curtain for her to wash [7:06]. Instead of carrying it down to her, he drops it out of the window as she stands in the yard below. The curtain floats down, landing softly on the mother's head, briefly transforming her into a bride. As the child looks up and away from his smiling mother, he notices the figure of a workman, stripped to the waist, on the building site opposite. They look at each other briefly and the man smiles and winks, before joking and laughing with his mates. Overcome by embarrassment, Bud slowly ducks out of sight and sits huddled in the corner. Gradually, his gaze fixes on the camera, suggesting that autobiography evokes a space of intimacy between remembering adult and remembered child [8:05].

This brief scene lasts just a few seconds. Although, at first viewing, its significance may seem minimal, in terms of direct articulation of intimate desires usually far more deeply embedded, it is significant, as the following brief deconstruction reveals:

1. The image of the mother veiled in white is linked to images of the Virgin Mary, seen throughout the film, but also to the Oedipal desires of childhood. This desire for union with the mother is directly juxtaposed with an expression of homosexual, homoerotic desire through the exchanged gazes of the child and the man.
2. The child's embarrassment reveals his vulnerability to the hostile out-

side world; his acute awareness that his desires are forbidden and of the danger of admitting, even to himself, what he is feeling.
3. The scene reveals his isolation first by containing him within the framing of the window, and then by positioning him in the tiny space below the window, alone and hidden from view.
4. Finally, the look at the camera, expressing, as we have seen, the close intimacy between child and adult subjects, also engages with the spectator, making us complicit in the uncomfortable questions it raises.

Later in the film, another short sequence depicts Bud in church, praying to be delivered from mortal sin [49:52]. Suddenly, horrifyingly, we share his vision of nails being hammered into live hands; slowly, with much creaking, the cross is raised up, and the Christ figure nailed onto it lifts his head and screams. In this fleeting image, lasting scarcely a second, it is just possible to identify his features as those of the workman from the earlier scene [57:45].

Of course, the child's unresolved sexuality is woven deeply into the fabric of the film in multiple and complex ways, just as it is woven into the director's self-knowledge: his truth. As has already been intimated, one of the ways that it impacts on the film is through recurring presentations of the child as a watchful, solitary and reflective outsider. Even within the haven that is home, Bud is repeatedly positioned on the stairs, "caged" behind the banister rails, or tightly framed in windows or doorways, in visual acknowledgement of his "difference." Some of the most poignant of these scenes occur as his older brothers and sisters develop their own "normal" romantic attachments. Excluded from their activities, Bud is left alone, gazing longingly after them as they set off for parties or picnics, or quietly observing a romantic kiss through the frosted glass of the closed front door [56:09].

If unresolved sexual desire, coupled with a strong sense of isolation and exclusion, constitute key landmarks in the intimate topographies of his autobiography, what happens when Davies moves into fiction, or rather, into his adaptations of other people's fiction? The rest of this chapter shall consider this question briefly in relation to his three literary adaptations, *The Neon Bible* (1995), *The House of Mirth* (2000) and *The Deep Blue Sea* (2011), before exploring in greater detail a number of the ways in which intimate desire is encoded in the most recent of these.

However personal, Davies's adaptations are, in my opinion, honest and sensitive, insomuch as they respect and respond directly to the original works they "translate." Is it therefore possible, or even legitimate, to seek to identify in them expressions of Davies's personal desires? Normally, I would be critical of any such attempt. However, in Davies's unashamedly palimpsestuous, multi-layered and intertextual adaptations, the possibility of a more personal subtext should be considered, not for what it reveals about Davies, but in order to recognize and deconstruct some of his more complex filmic strategies, and in so doing, to gain fresh insight into the nature of filmic adaptation.

The first thing to consider is the significance of Davies's choice of texts. The three works span diverse times and spaces, differing widely in their structure, form and language, and while two are novels which had long been important to Davies, part of his internal cultural landscape, the third is a play with which he was not previously familiar and which, in terms of adaptation, confronted him with very different challenges. Nevertheless, common features can be identified. In all three, the protagonist is an outsider, struggling against a hostile, patriarchal society, vulnerable, yet refusing to conform to society's hypocritical rules, thus incurring social exclusion with all the painful consequences. *The Neon Bible*, a semi-autobiographical, first novel by the young John Kennedy Toole, set in the American Bible Belt in the Deep South in the 1930s and 1940s, and telling the story of an introvert, solitary young boy growing up in a homophobic, narrow-minded society, closely echoes Davies's own experiences, and, unsurprisingly, the film replicates many of the techniques used in his earlier autobiographies. The child's isolation is, for example, articulated through tight framings [3:58–4:18]; his intimate desires are merely implied via elliptical, fragmentary references to poetry and music, and past and present interweave in a fluid, non-chronological structure. *The House of Mirth*, an adaptation of Edith Wharton's classic 1905 novel, set in the upper echelons of New York society at the turn of the 20th century, recounts the story of the beautiful, but penniless Lily Bart who is doomed both by her rejection of social convention and her essential vulnerability as a woman within a patriarchal and materialistic society. Female, single, poor, Lily's desires are no less forbidden than are those of Davies's alter ego in the autobiographies; they are expressed indirectly through intimate gesture, complex patterns, textures and music, which draw us ever deeper into her claustrophobic world.

The Deep Blue Sea (2011)

Sir Terence Rattigan (1911–1977) was a successful and prolific author who published some twenty-nine plays between 1934 and 1975, although his popularity waned somewhat in the 1960s. Like Davies, Rattigan was gay and, in fact, *The Deep Blue Sea*, reputedly inspired by the recent suicide of a former lover, was highly controversial at the time of its first performance in 1952, both because of its explicit expression of heterosexual desire and for its implicit homosexual themes.

Davies was invited to make this film for Rattigan's centenary celebrations. Thus, for the first time, he adapted a work that had no particular historical or emotional significance for him, although, given its deeply personal nature (Rattigan described it as the "hardest" of all his plays to write for that very reason), its appeal was perhaps inevitable. It follows the story of Hester, luminously played by Rachel Weisz, who leaves her safe, comfortable marriage to a high court judge to live "in sin" with a dashing, but damaged ex-RAF fighter pilot, with whom she has fallen passionately in love. Beginning with her unsuccessful suicide attempt, the action covers a period of twenty-four hours and takes place in a dingy bedsit in war-damaged London in the early 1950s.

Aspects of the play which appealed to Davies are predictable: Davies is unparalleled in his depictions of the 1950s, and the world Rattigan references is, therefore, very much his own. Furthermore, Hester's character and situation are, as we have seen, ones with which he empathizes. Hester has given up everything for the sake of sexual passion at a time when women were not supposed to even discuss sex, let alone enjoy it. Indeed, in post-war Britain, female sexuality was only slightly less of a taboo than gay sexuality, and for a woman to live with a man to whom she was not married was a scandal that inevitably resulted in social ruin. In Hester's case, she has abandoned a particularly "successful" marriage, which conferred social prestige and financial security. To make matters worse, the feckless Freddie, for all his charms, is shallow and unreliable, and as she soon realizes, incapable of loving her in the way that she loves him. So the play is about despair and exclusion, but it is also about integrity, honesty and, above all, desire.

It may well be argued that the desire we are dealing with here is the blatantly heterosexual desire Hester feels for Freddie. She sees no need to conceal her feelings, freely acknowledging her passion, both verbally and physically. And yet in subtle and powerful ways, by showing us the world entirely from her perspective and establishing our close intimacy with her, Davies's film communicates other powerful desires—hidden, secret, encoded—using complex strategies of intimation and suggestion. It is this process of filmmaking that I want to explore briefly here.

One of the many significant changes Davies makes to the original play is his rejection of Rattigan's chronological structure, which he found boring and predictable. Instead, his film adopts the temporal and spatial fluidity of his autobiographies, since, for him, this fluidity is characteristic of the very processes of remembering, and memories are what give Hester her sense of identity. The film thus interweaves unmarked flashbacks from her past; there are no fewer than thirteen different moments in time prior to the narrative's present. While a few of these moments can be sourced in the play, the majority are of Davies's own devising and, significantly, draw repeatedly on the personal memories and experiences articulated in his autobiographical films. In this way, from the start, the identities and desires of Davies and Hester are brought together through the process of remembering to create an intimate, hidden space in which the usual boundary between creator and protagonist is irrevocably transgressed. It is within this unworded, invisible space of intimacy that forbidden desires can be situated.

Music

Amongst the most powerful means of conveying desire is, of course, music, that "symbolic key to the unconscious mind whose symbolism we shall never be able to fathom" (Ehrenzweig 164–65). Music is one of Davies's passions; indeed, he contends that film itself should be structured *as* music.[3] In *The Deep Blue Sea*, the emotional impact of the music results from its contrast with the densely textured silences that reproduce Hester's claustrophobic world as much as from its dynamic relationship with the film's visual rhythms and textures. Interestingly, music in this film is, at the same time, both sparse and overwhelming, with only six pieces throughout its ninety-eight minutes running time. As in Davies's autobiographical films, various popular songs from the period are foregrounded because of their unique potential to recall distant and intimate memories and situations (Everett, 2000, 99–117). These songs provide a form of counterpoint with a single classical piece: the second movement of Samuel Barber's *Concerto for Violin and Orchestra*, Op. 14. If the popular songs pinpoint individual memories of intimacy for Hester—dancing in Freddie's arms, sitting close to him during a pub sing-song or gazing into his eyes, variously evoking her passion and their stormy romance [56:19–57:48]—the Barber offers unique access to the deeper, intimate spaces of desire discussed earlier. This work is one of Davies's favorites, and is emotionally and intellectually important to him. Indeed, he claims that it was the original inspiration for the film, and it was played on set throughout the filming to establish pace, mood and rhythm. The music starts as we hear Hester's voice reading her suicide note and, in a particularly daring move, plays without interruption throughout the first nine minutes of the narrative, replacing language, as we watch Hester's unsuccessful attempt to gas herself and then drift with her through the fluid times and spaces of her memories [1:28–10:22]. Thereafter, that music *is* Hester: we access the deeply hidden interstices of her memory and desire through its repetitions, but importantly, those intimate spaces are also those of the director, and in them, his and her identities fuse.

Camerawork

The camera must also be recognized as an active agent in the creation of intimacy and desire. Like music, Davies's fluid camera transports us beyond or between the images that are shown. Just as music can reorder time and space, slowing the narrative and causing us to reflect more deeply on what we are seeing, so, too, do devices such as closeups of Hester's face and intimate gestures, or the textures and patterns of her world, images which draw the spectator deep below their surfaces, creating a strong sense of intimacy and involvement (Epstein 1921; Branigan 1984). The utilization of dissolves and ellipses links different times and spaces in a logic that is entirely internal, so that we are drawn into this inner world without rational understanding; we accept it on Hester's terms, in an emotional process of identification, not a logical process of understanding.

Gesture

Far more than her words, Hester's tiniest gestures indicate her deepest, most intimate feelings. In flashbacks of earlier moments with Freddie, we glimpse an intensely private language through the coded moves of the lovers [7:20]. Dance sequences provide examples of the most intimate of such gestures: dancers moving together in harmony create, in Sawyer and Thomas's words, "a kind of microcosmic world of their own" (5), an intimate space in which nothing matters beyond their closeness. For Laura Mulvey, discussing the films of Max Ophüls (which are directly referenced by Davies in this film), dance sequences are "ultra-cinematic moments" in which the rhythms of repetition, as two bodies move in harmony, slow down the narrative in a self-conscious reference to film's illusion of movement, and transport us to the realm of the Symbolic, through their creation of an erotic space of desire outside time (78, 87). The powerful intensity of such instances is revealed in *The Deep Blue Sea* in a lengthy sequence in which Hester and Freddie dance slowly and sensuously to the song "You Belong To Me"[4] [57:48–59:47]. Just as the song's melody and lyrics transport us—and them—from the public space of a pub singsong to the private space of home, so too, the rhythmic movements of the couple draw us into an intimate space of desire, outside both time and

Fig. 18. Hester Collyer's (Rachel Weisz) and Freddie Page's (Tom Hiddleston) bodies creating an intimate space of desire through a choreography of abstract patterns in Terence Davies' *The Deep Blue Sea* (2011).

language. In another sequence, the abstract patterns and rhythms of Hester and Freddie making love function in a similar manner [8:30–10:12] (Fig. 18). Filmed entirely in high angle, with a constantly mobile camera, their bodies execute a choreography of shifting, abstract patterns which, this time in conjunction with Barber's concerto, draw us deeply into the complex layers of reference and reflection.

Adaptation and Citation

Finally, I want to turn to the question of adaptation, for I suspect my comments might suggest that the original text has all but disappeared from Davies's interpretation. Like all creative acts, adaptations are, in effect, inherently palimpsestuous, since the very act of writing/filming across the surface of the *hypotext* automatically involves the heterogeneous polyphony of the influences and experiences that have shaped the adapter's interpretation. Among the competing voices that we have already identified in Davies's film are countless others: references to art (for instance, through the textured shadows in interior shots that speak of Davies's passion for Vermeer), to literature (quotations, asides, shots of books, including Shakespeare's sonnets) and, of course, to film. Filmic references abound, and include, notably *Now, Voyager*

(Irving Rapping, 1942), *Brief Encounter* (David Lean, 1945), *It Always Rains on Sunday* (Robert Hamer, 1947), *Letter From an Unknown Woman* (Max Ophüls, 1948) and *All That Heaven Allows* (Douglas Sirk, 1955).

Such multiple references do not reflect a conscious attempt by Davies to impress, far from it. Just as in the autobiographical films, similarly filled with personal references, what we are seeing are the cultural landmarks that have shaped his identity and become an intimate part of the way he sees and makes sense of the world. They can, therefore, act as signposts indicating the deeper meanings encoded in the narrative we are watching. Even more interestingly, depending on the spectators' familiarity with these films, their inclusion opens up new potential pathways and connections, leading to new layers of meaning that they themselves create.

The previously mentioned films are predominantly so-called "women's films" of the 1940s and 1950s. The genre, which has attracted a good deal of critical attention in recent years, is primarily distinguished by its female protagonists and perspectives, placing a woman "at the centre of the story universe" (Basinger 13), and by narratives that revolve around the traditional realities of female experience: family, home and romance (La Place 139). Breaking away from the norms of classical, male-driven narrative, such films are deemed subversive by critics like Mary Ann Doane (1987). It is this aspect, the fact that they explore difference and are fundamentally critical and oppositional, that has led a number of critics, including Vito Rosso, to argue that such films play a vital role in expressing gay sensibility. Rosso points out that, because gay sensibility is largely a product of oppression and the need for concealment (particularly in an era of rigid conformity), its presence can be identified in certain films even when they contain no open signifiers of homosexuality (92, 99).

Such ideas are worth considering, albeit cautiously, when we approach the cinema of Terence Davies, and by way of conclusion I should like to consider briefly, in this context, the relationship between *The Deep Blue Sea* and *Brief Encounter*, the film it references most frequently and most directly. The plots of both center on an unhappily married woman's memories of transient romantic fulfillment, and both are largely narrated through flashbacks. Both works originate from the writing of gay playwrights (Noël Coward and Terence Rattigan), and it is possible that Davies is particularly responsive to the displaced gay sensibility in their work. Images of Hester in *The Deep Blue Sea* directly reflect images of Laura (played by Celia Johnson) in *Brief Encounter*, so that the identities of the two women repeatedly merge. Given that both Rattigan and Coward used straight female characters as a dramatic vehicle through which to narrate stories of unhappy (because impossible) love, one might argue that the traumatic awareness that true desire between two people is routinely forbidden by social convention might, just as easily, be read as the product of male homosexual identity and experience.

It is clear that such ideas would merit further analysis and development, but I hope to have succeeded, at the very least, in opening up some of the strategies used by Terence Davies to create the multiple, shifting subtexts of desire which both haunt and ultimately escape the film's apparent narrative content. The essential intimacy at the heart of a film like *The Deep Blue Sea* is formed by and within these palimpsestuous layers, transforming the public discourse of cinema into the intimate discourse of desire.

Notes

1. Ingmar Bergman, John Boorman, Bill Douglas, Federico Fellini, Jean-Luc Godard, Louis Malle, and Andrei Tarkovskii, among others, come to mind.
2. Examples of such Trilogies include Bill Douglas's *My Childhood* (1972), *My Ain Folk* (1973) and *My Way Home* (1978), and Márta Mészáros's *Diary for my Children* (1984), *Diary for my Lovers* (1987) and *Diary for my Father and Mother* (1990).
3. For a more developed exploration of the role of music in Davies's films, see Everett (2004) 167–200.
4. The song, in which the singer reminds her/his lover that whatever exotic journeys s/he experiences, ultimately "you belong to me," dates from the early 1950s. Davies uses its most successful recording, by Jo Stafford, which, in 1952–1953, topped the charts in both the U.S. and the U.K., where she was the first female vocalist ever to reach this position.

Works Cited

Basinger, Jeanine. 1994. *A Woman's View: How Hollywood Spoke to Women, 1930–1960.* London: Chatto and Windus.
Branigan, Edward. 1984. *Points of View in the Cinema: A Theory of Narration and Subjectivity in Classical Film.* New York and Amsterdam: Mouton Publishers.
Chesal, Robert. 2012. "Time for the Truth about Catholic Sex Abuse in the Netherlands." *Radio Netherlands Worldwide*, 19 March. www.rnw.nl/English/article/time-truth-about-catholic-church-sex-abuse-netherlands. Retrieved on 1/16/2013.
The Deep Blue Sea. 2011 [2012]. Written and directed by Terence Davies. Based on the play by Terence Rattigan. With Rachel Weisz (Hester Collyer), Tom Hiddleston (Freddie Page) and Ann Mitchell (Mrs. Elton). Camberwell / Fly Films, Film4, UK Film Council. DVD. Artificial Eye.
Doane, Mary Ann. 1987. *The Desire to Desire: The Woman's Film of the 1940s.* Bloomington: Indiana University Press.
Ehrenzweig, Anton. 1975. *The Psychoanalysis of Artistic Vision and Hearing.* London: Sheldon Press.
Epstein, Jean. 1921 [1974]. "Grossissement." *Écrits sur le cinema* I. Paris: Seghers. 93–99.
Everett, Wendy. 2000. "Songlines: Alternative Journeys in European Cinema." *Music and Cinema.* Eds. James Buhler, Caryl Flinn and David Neumeyer. Hanover: Wesleyan University Press. 99–117.
_____. 2004. *Terence Davies.* Liverpool: Liverpool University Press.
Foucault, Michel. 1988. *Technologies of the Self.* Amherst: University of Massachusetts Press.

Harvey, Keith and Celia Shalom, eds. 1987. *Language and Desire: Encoding Sex, Romance, and Intimacy*. London: Routledge.
Jivani, Alkarim. 1997. *It's Not Unusual: A History of Lesbian and Gay Britain in the Twentieth Century*. London: Michael O'Mara Books Limited, by arrangement with the BBC.
Lacan, Jaques. 1966 [1977]. *Écrits: A Selection*. Trans. Alan Sheridan. London: Tavistock Publications.
La Place, Maria. 1987. "Producing and Consuming the Woman's Film: Discursive Struggle in *Now, Voyager*." *Home Is Where the Heart Is: Studies in Melodrama and Women's Film*. Ed. Christine Gledhill. London: BFI. 138–66.
The Long Day Closes. 1992 [2008]. Written and directed by Terrence Davies. With Marjorie Yates (Mother), Leigh McCormack (Bud) and Anthony Watson (Kevin). BFI. DVD. BFI
Mulvey, Laura. 2011. "Max Ophuls's Auteurist Adaptations." *True to the Spirit: Film Adaptation and the Question of Fidelity*. Eds. Colin MacCabe, Kathleen Murray and Rick Warner. Oxford: Oxford University Press. 75–89.
Rosso, Vito. 1981. *The Celluloid Closet: Homosexuality and the Movies*. New York: Harper and Row.
Sawyer, Larry M. and Irene D. Thomas. 2005. *The Temptation to Tango: Journeys of Intimacy and Desire*. Victoria, Canada: Trafford.

"Extimacy" and Embodiment
in Hunger *and* Shame

ISABELLE LE CORFF

Explorations of the physical limits of the human body, the conscious and the unconscious are clearly at stake in Steve McQueen's two feature films *Hunger* (2008) and *Shame* (2011). McQueen's previous work in different media is already very much preoccupied with the representation of the human body in situations that symbolize the contradictions within the subject. These include several short films, which were projected in art galleries, notably "Bear" (1993), a sexually charged encounter between two naked men, one of them McQueen himself, and a clip entitled "Deadpan" (1997), a riff on Buster Keaton's *Steamboat Bill, Jr.* (1928) in which McQueen stands in front of a collapsing house frame. McQueen won the Turner Prize with "Drumroll" in 1998 and "Deadpan" in 1999. A war artist in Iraq in 2006, he exhibited "Queen and Country" at the Imperial War Museum the following year, a piece which comprises a series of postage stamps bearing the faces of British soldiers killed during the war.

Hunger and *Shame* have little in common: one is a non-classical biopic, the other complete fiction. However, our acquaintance with the now notorious star Michael Fassbender, who embodies Bobby Sands on his deathbed in *Hunger*, instantly circumscribes the narrative terms of *Shame*, in which the actor plays the role of the main protagonist, Brandon. Embodiment is investigated through extreme starvation in *Hunger* and through sexual addiction in *Shame*. In each film, however, the human experience assumes a phenomenological structure where spatial and temporal forms are meaningful. The aim of this essay is to examine the aesthetic treatment of the intimate mysteries of human suffering as they are epitomized in both films, and to question the importance of language as well as the significance of repetitions and rituals in the relationship between intimacy and the body. It also exposes how personal experience is made into an allegory of the public sphere, the "outside" becoming the metaphor of the subjects's most intimate core, as figurations of imaginary geographies emerge to symbolize the deepest inside. McQueen's understanding of human desire is, I will argue, very Lacanian, insomuch as desire constitutes the subject rather than the form of that desire.

Naming the Intimate Mysteries of Human Suffering

Based on actual events and set during the 1981 hunger strike at Long Kesh prison in Belfast, *Hunger* recounts the final weeks of the imprisoned IRA hunger striker Bobby Sands, who decided to use his body as the ultimate weapon in a conflict with the British government, Prime Minister Margaret Thatcher having refused to grant political status to Irish Republican prisoners. The film, however, does not engage in the political debate; its preoccupations are more existential. McQueen examines how Sands made his decision to starve to death and the physical decline that ensued during his sixty-six-day fast. McQueen's aim was to give the audience an insight into the enigma of ultimate commitment. As he pondered in an interview in *The New York Times*, "It takes a long time to die that way. Is there a worse way to die than starving yourself? I don't know."

Indeed, exploring the intimate mysteries of human suffering through films with one-word titles (*Hunger*, *Shame*) that evoke the seven deadly sins seems to be part of the project: hunger is the exact opposite of gluttony in the Christian religions, and lust is the very reason for Brandon's shame. The 2011 film relates the story of a successful thirty-year-old man working in New York and living in a classy, minimally furnished apartment. The viewer is soon made aware of the fact that Brandon suffers from sex addiction, an affliction that dominates his whole life. His sister Sissy, a nightclub singer, imposes herself on him by coming to stay in his apartment. In so doing, she destroys the superficial balance he had struggled to maintain up to that point. Although very little is said of their past, except that they were born in Ireland, it is obvious that they both have painful childhood memories and come from a dysfunctional family. *Shame* opens on a high-angle shot of Brandon lying in bed, naked, half-covered in blue bedsheets, staring at the ceiling [0:37]. The establishing shot immediately suggests suffering as well as entrapment and powerlessness, not only because of the actor's expression, but also because it is reminiscent of Bobby Sands's agony in *Hunger*. Yet Bobby and Brandon have nothing in common. One is incarcerated in a maximum-security prison, but nonetheless finds his own freedom by abstaining from eating. The other lives in an up-to-the-minute city and imprisons himself in excessive sexual activity. However, both situations raise the question of what we, as humans, are capable of, morally, physically and psychologically: How much can we inflict on ourselves? What can we endure? What context does each event relate to? Through the representation of these experiences, the spectator is drawn into the core of the relationship between outside and inside, body and self, and between intimacy and what Jacques Lacan called "extimacy."[1] Indeed, the distinction between exteriority and interiority fades away, as the presence of exteriority in the character's intimacy becomes more obvious. The outside interpenetrates the subject's inner world and progressively comes to constitute it.

The "Extimacy" of Language and Culture

The memory of Bobby Sands has spread all over the world; there are streets named after him in France and Tehran, as well as a large monument dedicated to him in Sydney, Australia. On the contrary, Brandon is anonymous, almost nameless, just like his sister. Indeed, "Sissy," deriving from "sister," is hardly ever a first name, while "Brandon," translating into "firebrand," designates the flaming bodies rising from a fire. This brings to mind Dante's *Purgatorio* where the penitents walk through flames to purge themselves of lustful thoughts and feelings, and his *Inferno* where unforgiven souls are blown about in a restless hurricane to be reminded of their lack of self-control in earthly life. In each film, we are given a hint at what our most intimate core can be and what it may intimately feel like to be in the extreme position of losing oneself through one's body.

Words are scarce in both films, confirming the parasitical presence of language. This is especially true of the first and last parts of *Hunger*. However, while the first part is devoted to the conditions of incarceration, the twenty-two minute mid-section is a long, philosophical and intellectual conversation between the prisoner and a priest [43:46–66.42]. As McQueen has argued in the DVD extra "Steve McQueen réalisateur," the prisoner and the priest push language to an absolute limit in order to get to a point where they can actually understand who they are and what they want. Filmed in a single medium shot, the scene creates no cause-effect pattern and the spectator is free to focus on either Bobby or the priest, and ponder on the deeper meaning of their conversation, a meaning that exceeds by far the limits of their bodies. At the end of this verbal joust, it becomes obvious that everything has been said, that all the words have been exhausted, and there is nothing but emptiness left in the protagonists. Bobby achieves what he deeply felt inside. To put it differently, an otherness lodged at the core of his self calls him to something higher, something transcendent. The third part of the film is free to focus exclusively on his agonizing body.

Likewise, very few words are spoken in *Shame*. There no longer seems to be any form of normal conversation between human beings. The first vocalized words in the narrative come from Brandon's answering machine [2:32]. A woman repeatedly asks him to pick up the phone, but he ignores the message. The second instance of spoken words occurs partly offscreen, when a male voice says: "I find you disgusting, I find you inconsolable. I find you invasive" [8:44]. But the speaker is not visible in the frame, and as Brandon appears on the left-hand side of the setting in the following shot, the positioning functions as a reaction shot emphasizing the statement's effect on the spectator who has previously witnessed Brandon's obsessive behavior. It turns out Brandon's boss is the protagonist uttering these words, and we are surprised to realize that he is actually describing the company they work for: "This is what the cynics used to say. Companies would refuse to look to the future. They'd say, 'Can we stop this virus?' As if it was a negative progression. But it's growing. More and more, with a momentum that is unstopped" [9:08]. The so-called "virus" is not only Brandon's, but the whole company's, and it expands from the personal to the group. Sex has been outlined as a "verbal virus," and whenever words are spoken, they are laden with sexual connotations. "[F]ucking weirdo" [55:41], "he fucks it up" [13:50], "I find you disgusting," "some people fuck up all the time" [69:32], "Look at that ass. I'd follow that forever" [26:50] are the "normal" everyday exchanges depicted in the film. Sissy resorts to the same semantic field, but unlike most characters in the film, she talks a lot. She leaves desperate love messages to men who obviously do not care for her, or worse, on answering machines [21:35]. Her "inside" seems so fragile and insecure that she cannot control herself. Brandon witnesses her lack of confidence, overhears her desperate declarations of love on the phone, and refuses to talk to her: "I don't want to talk. Try not talking. Try just listening, or thinking. For a change" [71:46].

The family conversations of Brandon's boss, David, are similarly exposed to everybody at work. His lack of privacy is implied by the fact that he communicates with his children on video and reveals his differences with his wife to his office staff. Once again, there is no clear limit between inside and outside. He may have sex freely when he goes out at night, but women like Sissy are supposed to notice his ring and respect the fact that he is a married man with a family. It is as if people did not know how to relate to one another, as if language had become useless. Marianne is the only character in the narrative that Brandon will have a sincere exchange with, yet as a result of such closeness, he will be incapable of making love to her. According to Michel Foucault, one's mother tongue, the language one has learned from an early age is the only real homeland, the only safe place where one can find shelter and comfort (31). It is obvious, in *Shame*, that most of the protagonists have lost this deeper part of themselves, and Brandon's intimacy is like a foreign body to himself.

Repetitions and Rituals

According to Vivian Sobchack's theory of embodiment, every experience is necessarily embodied, involving technical and technological mediation of some kind. Personal practice therefore provides "the phenomenological—and embodied—premises for a more processual, expansive, and resonant materialist logic through which we, as subjects, can understand what passes as our objective historical and cultural existence" (Sobchack 6).

McQueen's representations of personal experiences in *Hunger* and *Shame* are grounded in rituals, thus providing the beginning of an inquiry, if not its end. The opening sequence of *Hunger* depicts Bobby's guard Raymond's rituals: the way he washes, gets dressed, has breakfast, checks his car and looks for a hypothetical bomb before he starts the engine, all disclose his physical pains, solitude, preoccupations and fears [1:45–4:35]. In *Shame*, the narrative similarly focuses on the protagonist's everyday gestures: getting up, going to the toilet, having breakfast, taking a shower and taking the subway to go to work [4:26–5:52]. Offscreen sounds expand the image far beyond the confines of the frame and taint it with sexual connotations. Brandon's most vital needs revolve around sex and contaminate all the fundamental rituals. Far from the intimacies of heterosexual romance, the opening six minutes of the film show him having sex with a woman, masturbating, hiring a prostitute at his apartment and flirting with another young woman on a subway train [0:00–6:00]. The editing breaks down the unity of space and time, and imposes an awareness of rhythm and repetition. Brandon's addiction is shaped by a wide variety of devices: graffiti on the train windows [1:43], split screens when he masturbates [5:44], symbolic sound effects such as sounds of orgasm juxtaposed to contrasting images and musical motifs [2:03]. The protagonist enjoys no privacy, no rest. He may shut the bathroom door to the tactless camera, but the next shot depicts him masturbating inside, as if the editing symbolized this lack of privacy and "inner life" [5:42].

The Naked and the Nude

Fassbender appears without clothes on in numerous scenes of both *Hunger* and *Shame*, and as noted above, the presence of Fassbender's naked body links the two narratives. The fact that Bobby Sands was not wearing clothes in jail was highly political. In 1975, when the IRA prisoners were informed that they were being deprived of their political status, they refused to conform to the regime that would classify them as ordinary criminals and refused to wear prison uniforms. They thus went on a blanket and hygiene protest.

In *Shame*, Brandon's walking without any clothes on in his stylish apartment may at first be interpreted as a choice and an act of freedom. Everything is clean and tidy in his apartment, and the design gives an impression of open space. He walks freely as he behaves unreservedly. In French, I would use the word *nu* to describe both situations, but English, as Kenneth Clark has pointed out, distinguishes between naked and nude.

> To be naked is to be deprived of our clothes, and the word implies some of the embarrassment most of us feel in that condition. The word "nude," on the other hand, carries, in educated usage, no uncomfortable overtone. The vague image it projects into the mind is not of a huddled and defenceless body, but of a balanced, prosperous, and confident body: the body re-formed. In fact, the word was forced into our vocabulary by critics of the early eighteenth century to persuade the artless islanders [of the U.K.] that, in countries where painting and sculpture were practised and valued as they should be, the naked human body was the central subject of art [3].

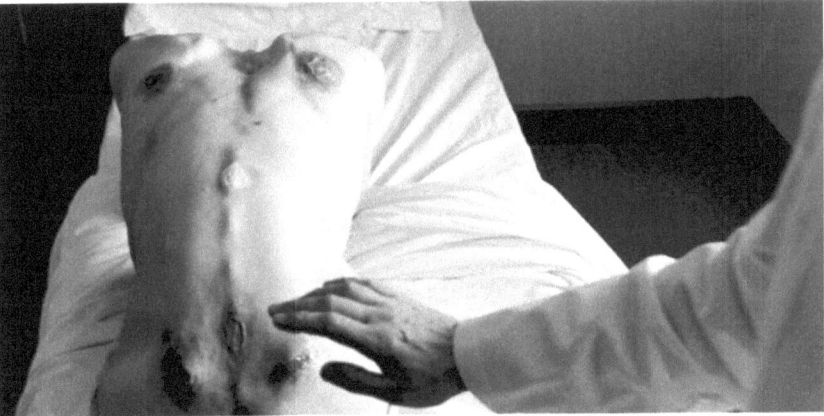

Fig. 19. Bobby Sands's (Michael Fassbender) wounds being healed in Steve McQueen's *Hunger* (2008).

If we go down that path and distinguish between the "naked" and the "nude," the establishing shot in *Shame* might be seen as a nude, except that it is followed by an opening sequence that focuses on a series of creepy visual details and sounds that give the spectator a vivid sense of alienation and "nakedness." In an early scene of *Hunger*, we are shocked by the sight of a prisoner who is dispossessed of his clothes, and then bullied and harassed by guards in uniforms [9:11]. The young man is denied his physical intimacy. Bobby Sands is similarly divested of his personal clothes, like his fellow prisoners. Paul Ardenne has alleged that a body freed of such bonds as clothes and other signs of social or psychological alienation regains an appearance that nothing can obstruct (23).[2] Following Ardenne's appreciation, one can argue that the camera similarly shapes a nude out of Sands's enforced nakedness.

Sands's body is also under constant transformation in the third part of the film. It gets skinnier and weaker scene after scene, as it becomes covered in putrescent wounds (Fig. 19).[3] Corporeal details are inserted in an attempt to represent the "un-representable," to make suffering visible, according to a regime of under-determination. Sands's agony is conveyed through minor physical perceptions added to one another (healing his wounds, changing his bedsheets [74:41]), appeals to minimal auditory experience—we see a person talking to him but cannot hear what is being said [77:29]—and symbolic details like stains on his bed sheets [74:41] evocative of the Shroud of Turin. Sights and sounds concentrate the senses and symbolize the boundary between life and art. As emaciated bodies conjure up the history of religious paintings from early Christian art to the rebirth of Christian fine art, Sands's suffering becomes evocative of the harmony of classical art, the energy and ecstasy of romanticism, and the pathos of the sufferings of Christ and his martyrs, and when we see the beautiful results of such embodiments, it might even seem as if the nude were a means of expression of universal and eternal value (Ardenne 23).

Hyper-Visibility versus Intimacy

Issues of genre are essential to our understanding and assessment of McQueen's movies. In *Shame*, the constant display of naked bodies raises the question of pornography. Is the treatment of sex in his films obscene? Could the young, good-looking women portrayed onscreen "be regarded as objects of fetishist display for male viewer's pleasure," as in Laura Mulvey's thesis (4)? In fact, women are not seen as mere sexual fantasies. Men *are forced to* play a sexual game in order not to offend them. "She'd be so offended if I didn't try,"

David says to Brandon, after trying to seduce a bar hostess and right before he has sexual intercourse with Brandon's sister Sissy [27:24]. A form of contagion operates through language, videos and computer games (at home and at work), through sounds and even visuals, for instance, when, walking in the streets, Brandon witnesses a couple making love against a large windowpane [44:52]. He will repeat the same position while having sexual intercourse with a prostitute at a hotel in a later scene [65:14], thus attesting that visuals function as a type of infection.

Though naked male and female bodies, genitals and sexual intercourse are depicted throughout the film, the images do not have the overtly erotic or pornographic intent of many sex scenes in mainstream cinema. First of all, the camerawork makes it obvious that the protagonists are being watched, so that the spectator can only watch someone watch, a situation that does not allow for direct intimacy with the characters. The persistent repetition of watching and being watched is precisely what the hero undergoes in *Shame*. Every character lacks privacy. Brandon finds Sissy naked in his own apartment [19:08], and on another occasion Sissy arrives at Brandon's apartment and accidentally walks in on him while he is masturbating in the bathroom. As spectators, we witness the scene through the reflection in the mirror so that once more we watch someone watch. Sissy and Brandon belong to the same part of the image, as they did in the previously mentioned scene. This lack of intimacy in the room that should be the most private evokes either an incestuous relationship between brother and sister or a symbolic merging of the two, the feminine and the masculine being one and the same entity, as if "otherness" no longer existed.

In the fragmented time-space continuum of the film, images and sounds of sexual intercourse are constantly intertwined. In such circumstances of hyper-visibility and "hyper-auditory," it becomes impossible for the spectator to adopt a purely voyeuristic gaze. The numerous screens (windows, computer screens, television screens), as well as split screens and closeups on details, tend to distance the viewer from the depictions of sex. At one point, however, McQueen utilizes an intrusive camera in a scene where Brandon has sexual intercourse with two women [80:12]. In the previously mentioned DVD extra, McQueen says that he makes a fourth person take part, namely the spectator, through this specific utilization of the camera. The long series of closeups of naked bodies, lips kissing and penetration produce an intimate exposure of the protagonists, as David MacDougall has argued:

> In films the close-up creates a proximity to the faces and bodies of others that we experience much less commonly in daily life. The conventions of social distance normally restrict proximity except in moments of intimacy. The cinema thus

combines the private view with the public spectacle, creating a sharp sense of intimate exposure of the film subject and a secondary sense in the film viewer of being personally exposed by witnessing the other's exposure [21].

However, the closeups of Brandon's face and eyes are disturbing because they express suffering instead of pleasure [81:28]. The spectator by no means feels manipulated by a lack of proper aesthetic distance, a sense of over-involvement in sensation and emotion, as Linda Williams (1989) has suggested in her investigation of body genres, precisely because the multifaceted editing conveys a sense of entrapment instead of allowing the spectator a sensual experience with powerful physical effects.

"Extimacy," the Opposition Between "Inside" and "Outside"

The slow-paced, melodramatic music Harry Escott composed for *Shame* is in sharp contrast with the rhythm of the images. The spectator cannot watch from a distance, and yet he cannot take part. Neither identification nor empathy can function. The frame works as a kind of symbolic prison, reminiscent of Long Kesh in *Hunger*. The end of the scene produces all the more unease and sadness, as Brandon is at a complete loss. His emotional isolation eventually gives in when he leaves the place with an unexpected feeling of worry for his sister (his feminine alter ego) that suddenly grows into panic. He then has to go through the experience of complete loss to recover and be able to "feel" again, as if he were experiencing a sort of spiritual release.

The absence of natural elements, except for the river, might be a clue to McQueen's message. The viewer who has seen *Hunger* no doubt remembers the drops of snow on Ray's knuckles, the flights of birds and the visions of himself as a child that Sands experiences during his final agony [73:16]. We visualize Brandon's sensory experience of rain at the end of *Shame*, when the track called "Unravelling" is heard. It is the unconscious lodged at the center of the self as an ultimate otherness. In *Hunger*, the desire for a Republican political status emerged in the context of Bobby Sands's life story in Belfast at a young age, just as the appeal for violence arose in the context of Raymond's Protestant environment. In *Shame*, Brandon's desire for more sexual sensations becomes his most intimate need in a 24/7 city where everything is constantly available, where cityscapes (glass, night, subway) are cold (the film's blue, gray and white tones) and soundscapes disquieting (the sounds of traffic, the subway, doors and sirens). As such, both films explore the inter-subjective human structure caught between the inside and outside, and allow the spectators to perceive in detail and without judgment the deep and personal mysteries of human beings.

NOTES

1. In *Le Séminaire XVI*, Lacan applies the prefix "ex" from "extérieur" (meaning "exterior") to the Freudian concept of "intimacy" (225).
2. Original quote: "Certes, en dépouillant le corps, en le dévêtant, on le désocialise. Mais, ce faisant, aussi on le réalise, on le livre au regard comme cette forme évidente que rien n'encombre, à commencer par le vêtement, ce signe de dépendance à la toilette, et par extension, d'appartenance sociale ou d'aliénation psychologique."
3. Fassbender went on a severe diet and lost thirty pounds to play the part.

WORKS CITED

Ardenne, Paul. 2001. *L'Image corps : Figures de l'humain dans l'art du XXe siècle*. Paris: Les éditions du Regard.
Clark, Kenneth. 1956. *The Nude: A Study in Ideal Form*. New York: Pantheon Books.
Foucault, Michel. 2011. *Le Beau danger : Entretien avec Claude Bonnefoy*. Paris: Éditions de l'École des Hautes Etudes en Sciences Sociales.
Hunger. 2008 [2009]. Dir. Steve McQueen. Written by Enda Walsh and Steve McQueen. With Michael Fassbender (Bobby Sands), Stuart Graham (Raymond Lohan), Laine Megaw (Raymond's Wife) and Brian Milligan (Davey Gillen). Film4, Channel Four Film, Northern Ireland Screen. DVD. Mk2.
Lacan, Jacques. 2006. *Le Séminaire XVI : D'un Autre à l'autre (1968–1969)*. Ed. Jacques-Alain Miller. Paris: Seuil.
Lim, Dennis. "History Through an Unblinking Lens." *The New York Times* (March 8, 2009). http://www.nytimes.com/2009/03/08/movies/08lim.html?pagewanted=all&_r=0. Retrieved on 1/5/2014.
McDougall, David. 2005. *The Corporeal Image: Film, Ethnography, and the Senses*. Princeton: Princeton University Press.
Mulvey, Laura. 1975 [1999]. "Visual Pleasure and Narrative Cinema." *Film Theory and Criticism: Introductory Readings*. Eds. Leo Braudy and Marshall Cohen. New York: Oxford University Press.
Shame. 2011. Dir. Steve McQueen. Written by Steve McQueen and Abi Morgan. With Michael Fassbender (Brandon), Carey Mulligan (Sissy), James Badge Dale (David) and Mari-Ange Ramirez (Alexa). See-Saw Films, Film4, UK Film Council. DVD. mk2.
Sobchack, Vivian. 2004. *Carnal Thoughts: Embodiment and Moving Image Culture*. Berkeley, Los Angeles and London: University of California Press, 2004.
Williams, Linda. 1989. *Hard Core: Power, Pleasure, and the "Frenzy of the Visible."* Berkeley: University of California Press.

Keira's Kiss
The Affordance of "Kissability" in the Film Experience

Adriano D'Aloia

Like real life kissing in contemporary Western culture, the cinematic representation of kissing on the lips is a very *intimate* moment, creating both a space of physical proximity and involvement between the characters, and a sense of closeness and sensuality in the spectator. In this essay, I adopt film theory based on cognitive psychology, especially ecological psychology and neurocognitive psychology, to explain how the cinematic kiss turns the film experience into a sensuous and intimate experience. By analyzing a series of cinematic kissing scenes selected from dramas with British actress Keira Knightley as the main female character, I argue that the spectator's desire and sense of intimacy are influenced by prereflexive perceptual dynamics and their neural correlates, in particular on the perception of *affordance*, as psychologist James J. Gibson (1977) posited it at the core of his ecological approach to visual perception. In my proposal, therefore, *osculation*—from the Latin *ōsculātiō*, i.e., the "act of kissing," and, more generally, "a close contact," an *intimate* relationship—meets *philematology*—from *philema*, the Greek for "kiss," thus "the science of kissing" and, more generally, an empirical approach to social and intersubjective dynamics.

On the one hand, kissing can be seen as a metaphor for the encounter between desires emanating from the cinematic screen and the drives projected onto the screen by the spectator. On the other hand, because of the powerful involvement, passion and sensuality that the display of kissing generates in the spectator, the cinematic kiss should be considered as a *concrete experience* that transmits desire and a sense of intimacy directly from the filmic bodies to the spectator's. In this sense, kissing is perhaps the most obvious and effective manifestation of the sensual nature of cinema and its ability to communicate a sense of intimacy. According to Vivian Sobchack's phenomenology of the film experience, cinema offers a relationship between the film-body and the spectator's body. A sentence on the back cover of *The Address of the Eye* perfectly encapsulates this view: "Cinema is a sensuous object, but in our presence it becomes also a sensing, sensual, sense-making subject." The "carnal sensuality of the film experience" (2004 56) has been explored over the 1990s and 2000s by film phenomenologists and has recently begun to gain ground also in cognitive film theory, which traditionally endorsed a more "disembodied" approach to film reception. Carl Plantinga, for example, claims that "[f]ilms are sensual to their very core, in ways that are not widely acknowledged" (114). In light of this "sensual account" of the film experience, I argue that a way to acknowledge *filmic intimacy* is through the study of both the cinematic *representation* of passionate kissing between the main characters in narrative films and, more generally, the way in which certain styles of *presentation* of the lips engage the spectator in the act of kissing, in a manner consistent with her/his tendency to experience emotions, from the most physiological to the most psychological.

Theories of the (Cinematic) Kiss

Traditionally, kissing has been studied in zoology, biology, physiology and anthropology. It is interesting to note that the first extensive studies on kissing date back to the end of the 19th century (Bombaugh 1876; Nyrop 1897). Since the 1960s, it has been thought either to have evolved from the habit of primate mothers of chewing food for their young and then feeding them mouth-to-mouth (Morris 1991), or, psychoanalytically, to be related to sucking on the mother's breast as the individual's earliest form of sexual gratification (Freud 1905). In modern Western culture, kissing is most commonly an expression of affection and intimacy between people. Kissing is almost ubiquitous throughout human cultures (Eibl-Eibesfeldt 1970) and is studied in history, literature (Harvey 2005) and ancient culture (Hawley 2007; Lateiner 2009), not only as the supreme manifestation of romantic love (Blue 1996), but also as a religious symbol (Perella 1969; Frijhoff 1991).

In recent years, the psychological and sociological significance of the act of kissing has re-entered cultural and scientific debates. In natural sciences, recent neuroscientific experiments have revealed hidden complexities behind this simple yet almost impenetrable act of human interaction (Kirshenbaum

2011). Human lips have the thinnest layer of skin of any part of the body and are among the most densely packed with sensory neurons. Kissing triggers sensations in the lips, as well as the tongue and mouth, which are transmitted to the brain and other parts of the body, provoking emotional and physical reactions. "Philematology" was established in 2009 by neuroscientist Wendy Hill of Lafayette College, biological anthropologist Helen Fisher of Rutgers University and psychologist Gordon Gallup, Jr. of the University at Albany–SUNY. According to experimental results published in their books, a kiss mediates hormonal changes and may trigger a cascade of neural messages and chemicals that transmit tactile sensations, sexual excitement and feelings of closeness, motivation and even euphoria. This neurophysiological activation is functional to the selection of a partner. In this sense, kissing is crucial to the evolutionary process of mate selection (Fisher, 2004; Fisher, 2009; Hughes, Harrison and Gallup 2007).

Film theory, a discipline amenable to a variety of methods informed both by the humanities and the natural sciences, offers many options to explain the significance of kissing in the spectator's experience, each with its own specific approach. In order to explore the various meanings of kissing in the film experience, I would like to start with an example from *Atonement* (Joe Wright, 2007), in which privileged Cecilia Tallis (Keira Knightley) and her secret boyfriend, servant son Robbie Turner, first physically express their unbridled erotic love for each other with a confession and passionate kissing, culminating in sexual intercourse in the library [33:43–38:03] (Fig. 20). Their progressive psychological and physical approach is rendered through a series of increasingly *intimate* shots (from medium long shot to extreme closeup) and slow forward tracking shots (toward Cecilia). The low-key lighting and the absence of music create a sort of erotic suspense. The actors' facial expressions, postures and movements in space suggest a melodramatic atmosphere; their whispering voices, long pauses in conversation and the sound of breathing generate a strong sense of proximity. Suddenly, Cecilia realizes that someone is watching them: Cecilia's thirteen-year-old sister Briony accidentally witnesses the scene through the partially open door and misunderstands Robbie's behavior. Later, indeed, this event leads Briony to accuse the innocent Robbie of raping her cousin Lola. The man is arrested and sent to prison. Robbie and Cecilia's love story thus dramatically ends, and they both die during World War II, leaving Briony with the need to atone for what she has done.

Among the explanations that film theory can offer to describe the spectator's experience, a classic narratological account would suggest that the kiss is symbolic of transformation or resolution, e.g., the hero's rebirth, the princess's reawakening, the conquest and completion of love or the lovers'

Fig. 20. From top lefthand to bottom righthand corner: *Atonement* (Joe Wright, 2007), Cecilia Tallis (Knightley) and Robbie Turner (James McAvoy) kiss. *Pirates of the Caribbean: Dead Man's Chest* (Gore Verbinski, 2006): Elizabeth Swann (Knightley) tempts Jack Sparrow (Johnny Depp) with a quasi-kiss. *The Edge of Love* (John Maybury, 2008): Vera Phillips (Knightley) sings "Maybe It's Because I Love You Too Much." *A Dangerous Method* (David Cronenberg, 2011): Sabina Spielrein (Knightley) grimaces during therapy.

farewell. Indeed, in *Atonement*, this kissing scene represents a turning point in the story, as Briony ends up convincing herself that Robbie is a sex maniac who attacked Cecilia. Cognitive theory would support the idea that kissing scenes act as a narrative strategy of emotional involvement. The spectator is aroused by a particular event in the context of a series of past and future events, and s/he cognitively works to infer the meaning of the whole series. One of the inferential factors that contributes to arousing the spectator is the *feeling* that a kissing scene is going to happen. The spectator experiences both the character's intention to kiss the other character and, even before that, the film's intention to set up a kissing scene. One indication of an imminent kiss is the direction of the gaze, when the character looks at the lips, not the eyes, of the other character. Other indications stem from the dialogue or what we know about the character's sentimental situation, which depends on narrative contextualization.

A psychoanalytical theory would have much to say about how Briony watches the scene through the partially open door, as the spectator does in the darkness of the cinema (Metz 1977). With regards to voyeurism and scopophilia, a feminist, psychoanalytically based account of the filmic gaze

(Mulvey 1975) would stress the fact that, in this scene, the representation of the voyeuristic gaze is embodied in a young girl whose immature gaze leads her to misinterpret events and accuse the male character. Indeed, spatial orientation and the characters' movements (Robbie's passion progressively pushes Cecilia against the bookcase behind her) confirms the role of Cecilia/Knightley as the object of male desire.

A phenomenological analysis *à la* Sobchack would view eroticism and desire as being "directly" elicited by a bodily sensation embodied in the film's sensual aspects. The film incorporates desire in its own body and expresses itself as something *vital* experienced by the spectator synaesthetically. In this scene, the formal elements of representation combine to heighten the kiss's bodily and sensuous charge: the trajectory of the characters' gazes directs our gaze to Cecilia's fleshy, quivering, half-open lips at the center of the shot. When Cecilia retreats, the camera advances. The handheld camera is utilized, with out-of-focus closeups and extreme closeups. The intimate contact between the two lovers is embodied through semi-lit lighting that both reveals and hides their faces, with a series of shots of various body parts taking their clothes off. In short, bodily and perceivable elements, such as nudity, skin contact, visible or hidden touching, the intensification of their breathing, the lowering of their voices, the tears on her face, and the senses of taste and smell—all express the tangible and carnal aura of the film.

All these theoretical perspectives (semiotics, cognitivism, psychoanalysis and phenomenology) combine to describe the provocative, sensual and "desirable" experience of intimacy that kissing creates. Yet if all of them are necessary, they do not suffice to provide a full understanding of the cinematic kiss. Desire and arousal depend on, but are not fully explicable in terms of, narrative logic, neurophysiological reactions, aesthetic embodiment, libido, repressed wishes, and so on and so forth. My hypothesis is that, in some cases, when watching a kissing scene, we experience something much more radical.

Lip (Inter)action

If we observe the key protagonists of kissing scenes in film—that is, the lips—we can note that they condense all the characters' actions and gestures, the whole expressive charge of the body in the act of loving or desiring. More precisely, the lips embody the characters' intentionality and (inter)act as if they were the actual characters. The spectator reads this interaction as influenced by causality. A spatiotemporal description of this "reciprocal behavior" in the scene from *Atonement* could go as follows. Initially, the lips are at a distance; they are motionless for a while. The woman's lips back away, seemingly indecisive, doubtful, timorous. Then, suddenly, the man's lips impetuously approach and come into contact with hers. After a few moments, they separate again, but remain very close. They seem to "study" each other briefly. Her lips make three or four movements that seem to simulate an approach, a sort of *invitation* to the man's lips, an assent to a new, longer and more passionate kiss. They seek each other, wait, pull back or escape, invite, hesitate, become closer and connect. The anthropomorphization of the behavior of non-human figures and the attribution of emotions to abstract shapes (in this case, parts of the human body abstracted from their context) obey the principles of *causality* (Michotte 1946; Michotte 1950) and can be compared to experiments on *social cognition* (Heider and Simmel 1944). According to these approaches, if we concentrate on the "reciprocal interaction" of the lips in this scene, we notice that they behave as if they were, in effect, the lovers: they perform a kind of courtship dance and are protagonists of a sort of "love story," independently from the rest of the bodies to which they belong (D'Aloia 2011).

Many kissing scenes are characterized by this "invitation/hesitation" dynamic: the desire to kiss is charged and recharged before the lips touch. Only when peak arousal is reached is this "energy" released, as the characters' lips meet. This oscillation between seeking contact and pulling back, this sustained undecidability, this vacillation, this "sensual shilly-shallying," has a strong sexual effect on the observer. The spectator feels desire in experiencing the intentionality that emanates from this causal relationship. The charge of engagement is obtained by the reciprocal behavior of entities that embody the characters' intentionality.

This is much more obvious in kissing scenes in which the release phase is postponed or even absent. For example, in the *Pirates of the Caribbean* saga, the kiss between Elizabeth Swann (Knightley) and Will is repeatedly postponed. We witness a series of "quasi-kisses," in which the lips are about to touch ... but in the end do not. In a scene from *Dead Man's Chest* (Gore Verbinski, 2006), for instance, Elizabeth *almost* kisses Jack Sparrow [96:30–97:36] (Fig. 20). The effectiveness of this strategy of communicating desire to the spectator depends mostly on Knightley's acting style, especially the way she uses her lips, reflecting the type of interaction described above. Indeed, her acting technique in kissing scenes is very seductive, even provocative: her lips are always half-open, ready to receive a French kiss, but almost as if she were about to bite; drawing much closer towards the other person's most intimate space, she literally speaks into the other's mouth, making them feel her breathing and smell her scent. In other words, she teases and arouses the desire to be kissed by her, the desire to "taste what it is like," as Elizabeth says to Jack.

The Affordance of Kissability

In order to fully understand how the action and rules of engagement of Knightley's lips increase the spectator's desire to kiss, we need to focus on a very basic and unconscious perceptual aspect. My feeling is that Knightley's lips are more "kissable" than those of the average mainstream film actor/actress and that this "kissability" can be related to the notion of *affordance*. Coined by psychologist James J. Gibson (1977, 1979), this term indicates that an object directly offers its behavioral meaning to the observer. Affordances can be defined as all "action possibilities" latent in the environment, that are objectively measurable and independent of the individual's ability to recognize them. The notion of affordance was inspired by Gestalt psychologist Kurt Koffka's concept of *demand character*. As Koffka stated in 1935, "[i]n the pre-scientific stage man behaves in a situation as the situation tells him to behave. To primitive man each thing says what it is and what he ought to do with it: a fruit says 'Eat me'; water says 'Drink me'; thunder says 'Fear me'; and woman says 'Love me'" (7). Drawing on Koffka's idea that "each thing says what it is" (7), Gibson described affordances such as a rigid surface being "step-on-able" or a chair being "sit-on-able" for humans (1979, 127–28). The same is true of the "handling" of objects, depending on their shapes and sizes compared with human hands: a button affords pushing, a knife affords cutting, a ball affords kicking, and so on. Affordances thus link *action* and *perception*.

Now with regards to cinematic kissing as an act perceived by the spectator, it can be argued that lips are "kiss-on-able," i.e., "kissable," that is: lips afford kissing. The reason for choosing Keira Knightley's kissing scenes is that, in my opinion, the characteristics of her face and mouth make her lips particularly "kissable." This probably depends also on the individual physiognomic formation of her face and her way of talking. Protruding lower jaw, slender cheeks, naturally full lips and large teeth are physical elements that directly express a tendency both to "explore" the surrounding environment and engage in intersubjective relationships principally via her lips. In other words, the anatomy of Knightley's lips contributes to magnify the affordance of "kissability."

It is not, of course, a mere matter of physiognomy. Rather, a series of factors contributes to enhance "kissability." First, aesthetic and stylistic factors such as *mise en scène* (especially the makeup and acting style) and shot size (especially the use of closeups of her face and extreme closeups of her lips). Second, cognitive factors, including the narrative construction of the film: the kissing scene is often a climax in melodramas or dramatic scenes in other genres, and its emotional potential is narratively prepared. Kissing scenes in other romantic films starring Knightley as leading female character—for example in *Pride & Prejudice* (Wright, 2005), *The Duchess* (Saul Dibb, 2008), *London Boulevard* (William Monahan, 2010) and *Anna Karenina* (Wright, 2012)—would confirm this hypothesis. Third, extra-filmic factors, such as Knightley's appearance as testimonial in TV commercials or printed magazine ads and interviews, can be considered as paratexts of her "cinematic kissability" and have a considerable impact on Knightley's desirability as a person with regards to current canons of female beauty and fashion. In this sense, her subjectivity and personal attractiveness are not necessarily fetishized in her cinematic appearance, and more or less explicitly influence the spectators' perception of her lips' affordance of "kissability."

The excerpts from *Atonement* and *Dead Man's Chest* clearly demonstrate a crucial point: the "behavior" of Knightley's lips frustrates their own prominent "kissability" because they delay and only hint at the moment of contact with the other characters' lips. In this sense, the spectator's desire is provoked by the *incompleteness* of the observed action, i.e., the delay in the realization of a clear and strong affordance. This frustration or delay generates the desire in the spectator to *complete* the action.

Singing and Biting Kisses

I see as clear evidence of Knightley's "kissability" affordance that her lips afford kissing even when they are not actually kissing. In a scene from *The Edge of Love* (John Maybury, 2008), Knightley's character, Vera Phillips, is singing the 1933 Irving Berlin song "Maybe it's Because I Love You Too Much" in a bar, starting from the lines: "Maybe it's because I've kissed you too much / Maybe that is why my kiss means so little" [12:15–13:35] (Fig. 20). The male character, William Killick, is in the audience, watching and listening to Vera from the back of the room. As a technical and aesthetic vehicle, the film strategically uses the prominence of the "kissability" affordance in order to elicit the desire to kiss in the spectator. Vera looks into the camera, with the effect of directly addressing the spectator. The latter has the impression of occupying male character William's position and of being looked at by Vera, who sensuously moves her shiny red lips as if kissing. Desire is further provoked by the creative use of lighting and a forward tracking shot (the camera moves toward Vera) that progressively reduces the physical and psychological distance, and creates an intimate space in which the spectator gets closer to the character/actress. In short, the style of representation and the choice of shots align the spectator with a contemplating and desiring gaze (William's) that is *directed at* and literally *approaches* Vera's "singing/kissing" lips, although

William is not moving in space physically. Even in this case, however, something is missing in the act of kissing, since there is no physical contact between the two characters, and it is this "lack" that increases the sensual appeal of the spectator's enticement, which depends on perception of affordance.

As an aside, there is a contrasting outcome when the kiss's development results in violent contact, such as a bite. In a scene from *Pirates of the Caribbean: At World's End* (Gore Verbinski, 2007), Elizabeth rejects Sao Feng's attempt to kiss her by biting him [75:03–77:00]. In the dialogue before the "kiss," the bite follows the provocative and sensual style described above. The spectator experiences both Elizabeth's lips' "behavior" and, when the bite actually occurs, a more physiological and instinctive reaction of repulsion. As in *The Edge of Love*, when Vera kisses without kissing, Elizabeth's lips bite even when she is not actually biting. In several scenes in *A Dangerous Method* (David Cronenberg, 2011) depicting therapy sessions between Sabina Spielrein (Knightley) and Carl Jung, the woman gives vent to her taboos and reveals her condition, triggered by the humiliation and sexual arousal she felt as a child because of her short-tempered father's habit of spanking her naked [3:00–4:34] (Fig. 20). Both Sabina and Jung are seated on chairs, the woman with her back to the man. The closeup shows her face full of rage and anguish, as she tells Jung her story: the nervous, contorting twitches of her jaw horribly deform her face. It is as if she were literally biting the air while violently reliving her cruel past.

Neurology of the Kiss[1]

Let us return to the desire to complete incomplete gestures, such as the "inviting/hesitating" kiss (*Atonement*), the "quasi-kiss" (*Pirates of the Caribbean*) and the "allusive" kiss (*The Edge of Love*). We now need to go a bit further. Fairly recent discoveries in neurocognitive research reveal that this perceptual and cognitive dynamics, based on "kissability," i.e., the affordance of the character/actress's lips and its frustration, has a neurophysiological correlate. Neuroscientists exploring the activity of a specific brain area in primates (in particular, the ventral premotor cortex—area F5) have discovered the presence and function of cells called canonical neurons. The peculiarity of these neurons is that they respond during both the execution of actions and object presentation, regardless of whether the subject is anticipating or imagining the action (Rizzolatti and Sinigaglia 2008). A necessary condition, however, is that the observed or imagined action should be *goal-directed*. In other words, canonical neurons respond both when a subject grasps an object and when s/he merely sees an object that can be grasped by a prehensile hand movement—as if the subject's brain were foreseeing a possible interaction with this object and preparing itself accordingly. Thus, these neurons codify not a physical (motor-activity) movement, but the intrinsic properties that allow the subject to interact with the object (sensorimotor activity). This suggests that objects have tactile features that are immediately *grasped*, both literally and figuratively, by the subject, whether s/he is executing the action or simply imagining or observing it.

The immediate comprehension allowed by neural activation relies principally on an intimate connection between *action* and *perception*. It must be conceived as the core of the paradigm of *embodied cognition*, i.e., the idea that "cognition depends upon the kinds of experience that come from having a body with various sensorimotor capacities, and [...] these individual sensorimotor capacities are themselves embedded in a more encompassing biological, psychological, and cultural context" (Varela, Thompson and Rosch 172–73; see also Lakoff and Johnson 1999). Canonical neurons have been linked to the human tendency to instinctively grasp the functional quality of an observed object, i.e., the object's *affordance* (Garbarini and Adenzato 2004).

Before considering the neural substratum of the perception of affordance allowed by canonical neurons, it is important to clarify that they work in association with another class of neurons called mirror neurons. These brain cells respond to observations of actions executed by *other* individuals. While a person observes the action of another subject, his/her neural system evokes a mirrored response, as if s/he were carrying out that action her/himself. Thus, a movement observed visually seems to be *reflected* in the motor representation of the same movement in the observer (Rizzolatti and Sinigaglia 2008). Further experiments have shown that mirror neurons also discharge when a monkey observes another individual moving its mouth. The majority of these "mouth mirror neurons" become active during the execution and observation of mouth actions related to ingestive functions, such as grasping, sucking or breaking food (Ferrari et al. 2003).

The activation of canonical and mirror neurons allows an "internal representation" or an "embodied simulation" (Gallese 2005 and 2009) of the intentional act that would be necessary to reach the observed object or perform the action *afforded* by the object (canonical neurons), or the act executed by another subject (mirror neurons). Neuroscientists argue that, thanks to these mechanisms, the architecture of the human brain is functional to an immediate and prereflexive comprehension of the meaning of goal-directed actions and intentional emotions (Iacoboni 2009).

In terms of film theory, these findings allow new interpretations of the film spectator's psychophysical participation. Indeed, the film experience can be seen as an intensified *sensory* stimulus that does not correspond to any explicit *motor* activation. The engaging nature of the audiovisual experience is specifically functional in the creation of an *intimate* relationship between the spectator and the world of the film, based on the perception of observed intentional actions performed by the film characters. This is especially the case in character-driven narrative films and, all the more so, in sensuous and sensual scenes like kissing scenes. The embodied-simulation hypothesis provides empirical evidence not only that the spectator is a witness to the actions represented onscreen, but also that s/he internally *acts out* and simulates the intentional actions executed by a character in a film (Gallese and Guerra 2012).

According to the neurological account of action simulation, although the spectator's lips do not *actually* kiss, s/he experiences the kiss on a neural level. In this sense, the pertinence of the notions of *affordance* and *mirroring* in neurocognitive science supports the hypothesis that the delay in, or allusion of, the kiss generates an *interference* in the spectator's perception of affordances. Even if the characters delay or do not actually execute the kiss, the spectator's canonical neurons activate to *complete* the experience of that kiss. Once a goal-directed action begins or is suggested by the narrative situation and by the characters' reciprocal orientation in space, in fact, the canonical and mirror neurons activate, allowing the spectator to comprehend the intentions implied in the observed action and experience that action, even if it has no immediate or visible outcome. In other words, if the character's action is *intentional*, i.e., goal-directed, and suggested as such by the representation, then this action and the intentions behind it are *simulated*, and thus experienced by, the spectator.

In conclusion, if the object that affords grasping is the character's mouth in the act of kissing, and if both the "action" of the lips and the formal style of representation are *intended* to suggest a kiss, then the spectator tends to experience a kiss or the desirable charge of a kiss on both mental and neural levels. The delay, the concealing or the slowing-down of the kiss, as in a sort of "courtship dance" performed by the characters' lips, conceived as the protagonists of causal and intentional actions, are strategies that create an *intimate* space of relationships, and heighten spectators' sensual and erotic appetites. This happens because the interference between the perception of the "kiss-ability" affordance and the fictional character's sensual, yet ambiguous behavior generates an energy that accumulates in the spectator and must be released. The spectator "balances" this surplus energy through an instinctive activation of a circuit of perceptual and neurophysiological response that makes the cinematic kiss a bodily experience.

Notes

1. Some of what follows is from my article "The Intangible Ground."

Works Cited

Atonement. 2007. Dir. Joe Wright. With Keira Knightley (Cecilia Tallis), James McAvoy (Robbie Turner) and Saoirse Ronan (Briony Tallis, aged 13). Universal Pictures/StudioCanal/Focus Features. DVD. Universal Pictures.
Blue, Adrianne. 1996. *On Kissing: From the Metaphysical to the Erotic*. London: Victor Gollancz.
Bombaugh, Charles C. 1876. *The Literature of Kissing: Gleaned from History, Poetry, Fiction, and Anecdote*. London: J. B. Lippincott.
D'Aloia, Adriano. 2011. "The (Video) Art of Kissing: Notes for a Philematology of Moving Image." *Cinema, Architecture, Dispositif*. Eds. Elena Biserna and Precious Brown. Udine: Campanotto. 350–57.
———. 2012. "The Intangible Ground: A Neurophenomenology of the Film Experience." *NECSUS* 1.2 (Autumn). http://www.necsus-ejms.org/the-intangible-ground-a-neurophenomenology-of-the-film-experience. Retrieved on 1/26/2013.
A Dangerous Method. 2011 [2012]. Dir. David Cronenberg. With Michael Fassbender (Carl Jung), Keira Knightley (Sabina Spielrein) and Viggo Mortensen (Sigmund Freud). Sony Pictures Classics. DVD. Rai Cinema/01 Distribution.
The Edge of Love. 2008 [2009]. Dir. John Maybury. With Keira Knightley (Vera Phillips), Sienna Miller (Caitlin Thomas), Cillian Murphy (William Killick) and Matthew Rhys (Dylan Thomas). Capitol Films/Lionsgate. DVD. Capitol Films.
Eibl-Eibesfeldt, Irenäus. 1970 [1971]. *Love and Hate: The Natural History of Behavior Patterns*. Trans. Geoffrey Strachan. New York: Holt, Rinehart and Winston.
Ferrari, Pier Francesco, Vittorio Gallese, Giacomo Rizzolatti and Leonardo Fogassi. 2003. "Mirror Neurons Responding to the Observation of Ingestive and Communicative Mouth Actions in the Monkey Ventral Premotor Cortex." *European Journal of Neuroscience* 17: 212–26.
Fisher, Helen. 2004. *Why We Love: The Nature and Chemistry of Romantic Love*. New York: Henry Holt.
———. 2009. *Why Him? Why Her?: Finding Real Love by Understanding Your Personality Type*. New York: Henry Holt; London: Oneworld.
Freud, Sigmund. 1905 [1962]. *Three Essays on the Theory of Sexuality*. Trans. James Strachey. New York: Basic Books.
Frijhoff, Willeim. 1991. "The Kiss Sacred and Profane: Reflections on a Cross-Cultural Confrontation." *A Cultural History of Gesture: From Antiquity to the Present Day*. Eds. Jan Bremmer and Herman Roodenburg. Oxford: Polity Press. 201–36.
Gallese, Vittorio. 2005. "Embodied Simulation: From Neurons to Phenomenal Experience." *Phenomenology and the Cognitive Sciences* 4: 23–48.
———. 2009. "Mirror Neurons, Embodied Simulation, and the Neural Basis of Social Identification." *Psychoanalytic Dialogues* 19: 519–36.
Gallese, Vittorio and Michele Guerra. 2012. "Embodying Movies: Embodied Simulation and Film Studies." *Cinema: Journal of Philosophy and the Moving Image* 3: 183–210.
Garbarini, Francesca and Mauro Adenzato. 2004. "At the Root of Embodied Cognition: Cognitive Science Meets Neurophysiology." *Brain and Cognition* 56: 100–6.
Gibson, James J. 1977. "The Theory of Affordances." *Perceiving, Acting, and Knowing. Toward an Ecological Psychology*. Eds. Robert Shaw and John Bransford. Hillsdale, NJ: Lawrence Elbaum. 127–43.

_____. 1979. *The Ecological Approach to Visual Perception*. Boston: Houghton Mifflin.
Harvey, Karen, ed. 2005. *The Kiss in History*. Manchester and New York: Manchester University Press.
Hawley, Richard. 2007. "'Give Me a Thousand Kisses': The Kiss, Identity, and Power in Greek and Roman Antiquity." *Leeds International Classical Studies* 6.5: 1–15.
Heider, Fritz, and Marianne Simmel. 1944. "An Experimental Study of Apparent Behavior." *American Journal of Psychology* 57: 243–59.
Hughes, Susan M., Marissa A. Harrison and Gordon G. Gallup, Jr. 2007. "Sex Differences in Romantic Kissing Among College Students: An Evolutionary Perspective." *Evolutionary Psychology* 5.3: 612–31.
Iacoboni, Marco. 2009. *Mirroring People: The Science of Empathy and How We Connect with Others*. New York: Picador.
Kirshenbaum, Sheril. 2011. *The Science of Kissing: What Our Lips Are Telling Us*. New York: Grand Central.
Koffka, Kurt. 1935. *Principles of Gestalt Psychology*. New York: Harcourt-Brace.
Lakoff, George and Mark Johnson. 1999. *Philosophy in the Flesh: The Embodied Mind and Its Challenge to Western Thought*. New York: Basic.
Lateiner, Donald. 2009. "Greek and Roman Kissing: Occasions, Protocols, Methods, and Mistakes." *Amphora* 8.1: 16–17.
Metz, Christian. 1977 [1982]. *The Imaginary Signifier: Psychoanalysis and the Cinema*. Bloomington: Indiana University Press.
Michotte, Albert. 1946 [1963]. *The Perception of Causality*. New York: Basic.
_____. 1950. "The Emotions Regarded as Functional Connections." *Feelings and Emotions, the Mooseheart Symposium*. Ed. M. Reymert. New York: McGraw-Hill. 114–26.
Morris, Desmond. 1991. *Babywatching*. London: Jonathan Cape.
Mulvey, Laura. 1975. "Visual Pleasure and Narrative Cinema." *Screen* 16.3: 6–18.
Nyrop, Christopher. 1897 [2010]. *The Kiss and its History*. Whitefish, MT: Kessinger.
Perella, Nicolas J. 1969. *The Kiss Sacred and Profane: An Interpretative History of Kiss Symbolism and Related Religio-erotic Themes*. Berkeley: University of California Press.
Pirates of the Caribbean: At World's End. 2007. Dir. Gore Verbinski. With Johnny Depp (Jack Sparrow), Geoffrey Rush (Captain Hector Barbossa), Orlando Bloom (Will Turner) and Keira Knightley (Elizabeth Swan). Walt Disney. DVD. Walt Disney Home Entertainment, 2007.
Pirates of the Caribbean: Dead Man's Chest. 2006 [2007]. Dir. Gore Verbinski. With Johnny Depp (Jack Sparrow), Orlando Bloom (Will Turner) and Keira Knightley (Elizabeth Swan). Walt Disney. DVD. Walt Disney Home Entertainment.
Plantinga, Carl. 2009. *Moving Viewers: American Film and the Spectator's Experience*. Berkeley, Los Angeles: University of California Press.
Rizzolatti, Giacomo and Corrado Sinigaglia. 2006 [2008]. *Mirrors in the Brain: How Our Minds Share Actions and Emotions*. Trans. Frances Anderson. Oxford: Oxford University Press.
Sobchack, Vivian. 1992. *The Address of the Eye: A Phenomenology of the Film Experience*. Princeton: Princeton University Press.
_____. 2004. *Carnal Thoughts: Embodiment and Moving Image Culture*. Berkeley: University of California Press.
Varela, Francisco J., Evan Thompson and Eleanor Rosch. 1991. *The Embodied Mind: Cognitive Science and Human Experience*. Boston: MIT Press.

Melancholy, Empathy and Animated Bodies
Pixar vs. Mary and Max

RICHARD NEUPERT

> If it can be said that cinema is a technological metaphor for the body ... then animation, in its product and its very process, is a metaphor for cinema itself. If cinema is the illusion of continuous motion, animation is the illusion of the illusion, and as such it provides a unique opportunity to study this passionate liaison between the body and the cinema.
> —Barker 136

Contemporary animation builds upon a wide variety of traditions, including comic strips, graphic novels, classical Hollywood cartooning, art cinema modes of storytelling and, more recently, digital media conventions. When it comes to assessing cinematic narratives that elicit emotional responses, including sentimentality, empathy and a sense of intimacy, there may be no better testing ground than the field of animation. Studies now prove that humans readily perceive character traits, including intent to act, gender and emotion, even from very sketchy, abstract cues (Prince 107). Animators, like other artists, exploit these human processes of perception and cognition as they construct and codify these characters and actions, whether from hyper-real elements or less mimetic forms. As Stephen Prince argues, animation routinely relies on our innate ability to perceive emotion from minimal performances (108). In this essay, I analyze two very different modes of animation for how they cue spectators to identify emotions, here melancholy, disappointment and self-doubt, in relatively artificial animated figures. Moreover, I argue that these animated texts can create real empathy within the audience, and that spectators easily recognize intimate traits, even in non-human Pixar characters such as Luxo lamps and tin toys composed of millions of pixels, or crudely formed plasticine clay, as in Adam Elliot's *Mary and Max* (2009). Thus, intimacy, in what follows, involves both the emotions and experiences expressed by animated characters and the affect and/or empathy those characters generate in the viewer.

Classical Hollywood cinema famously and efficiently exploits a vast arsenal of plot devices and stylistic techniques to establish a set of psychological traits and motivations in characters (Bordwell and Thompson 98). When American studios added animation departments, the resulting short cartoons quickly became standardized as condensed classical narratives, with protagonists moving rather predictably through their short stories toward securely resolved termination points. Partly because of their intertextual connections to comic strips, as well as their intended audience of children, Hollywood cartoons often told simplified tales with clearly defined themes and characters. Cartoons were dependent on gag structures, but they were also heavily reliant on sentimental situations to provoke strong, immediate responses (Neupert 2011, 95). Disney's cartoons of the 1930s mastered character animation, providing blueprints for how to structure their stories to elicit maximum emotional involvement from spectators.

For instance, the 1939 version of *The Ugly Duckling* combined a vast arsenal of cinematic visual and audio cues to communicate quickly the sad disappointment when a new born duckling is first rejected by its parents, then realizes it does not even resemble its other family members. In just two minutes, this Disney cartoon establishes one character with whom the spectator can sympathize, while simultaneously distancing us from the mean parents and their other four identical, rude baby ducklings. The naive little white duckling is quickly recognized as the worthy object of our concern. As Torben Grodal has argued, humans "have a hardwired disposition to tenderness toward helpless youngsters" (148). *The Ugly Duckling*'s narrative also follows an intensified variation of a traditional and sentimental "separation-reunion" journey plot built around a child who loses one family, but ultimately finds a new protective home (Tan and Frijda 56). The cinematic cues for the duckling's body, personality, and desire, which result in a series of distinct emotions, all without dialogue, prove the success of Disney's model of sentimental character animation, which is so central to the Silly Symphony series involving orphans and substitute parents (Merritt 6).

During the 1980s, John Lasseter brought many of these same principles from Disney and classical American animation to Pixar. He adapted character animation principles in order to clearly personify their new 3D computer generated figures. However, early computer modeling did not allow for the level of detail and flexibility possible in 2D drawn animation, where subtle facial gestures routinely suggested inner feelings and physical reactions (Neupert 55). CGI characters had to be composed from a rather limited range of rigid geometric shapes, initially without editing for point of view shots or shot/reverse shots. The first Pixar shorts, like many 1930s Disney Silly Symphonies, also had to communicate sentimental situations without the aid of dialogue. They were restricted to action, gesture, sound effects and music. Some of the first Pixar characters did not even have faces. Yet, one of Lasseter's great initial contributions to the history of computer animation was his recognition that one could synthesize strengths from hand-drawn 2D animation with the precision of 3D CGI. He understood that even characters with no specific facial features and only rudimentary head and body shapes could "perform" in ways that audiences would recognize and even assign personality, intention and ultimately emotion to. As Stephen Prince has explained, "[m]uch character animation takes advantage of the human perceptual system's fine-tuned propensity to scan objects and environments for signs of intention and to read these signs often on the basis of scant and incomplete evidence" (107). Animators discovered that even simple shapes could express attitude and emotion. Lasseter and Pixar proved that a cold metallic representation of a lamp or a car could warrant emotional responses similar to those generated by a cel-animated duckling.

But how is it that spectators can conjure up detailed character traits, and even intimate emotions such as melancholy, in overtly artificial, animated figures? According to Ed Tan, cinematic spectators readily respond to both cognitive and affective structures (96). Beyond following the plot of a film, and forging and testing hypotheses as they go, spectators also become increasingly involved emotionally in a narrative thanks to the less rational processes of "affective investment": to become emotionally invested in a movie, we must identify with and develop empathy for some characters (Tan 98). Certainly the most comprehensive account of identification with fictional characters comes from Murray Smith, who explains how we comprehend characters as embodied persons with goals and personalities, even while we also realize quite consciously that they are blatantly fictional constructs (31). For Smith, character depends upon agency, and the ultimate agent, even a fictional, role-playing agent, is, in effect, human. Building on constructivist cognitive theory, Smith posits seven traits for agency: the very first qualification involves a discrete body; the others, including self-awareness, personal emotions, and intentionality, all help the audience recognize personhood within the represented body (Smith 21). Lasseter's early cartoons, including *Luxo Jr.* (1986), *Red's Dream* (1987) and *Knick Knack* (1989), provide insightful test cases for revealing how quickly audiences ascribe emotions, including feelings of desperation and melancholy, to non-human figures.

In each of these short Lasseter cartoons, a simple plot line quickly establishes a central character who breaks out of his or her routine temporarily, and who then encounters a moment of disappointment, even self-realization, after a brief euphoria. During the ground-breaking short experiment *Luxo Jr.*, for instance, the small lamp bounds into the frame, hops up and down on a rubber ball, but then punctures it thanks to "his" rough-housing. As the air escapes from the ball, the small lamp is lowered to the floor. The larger parent lamp shakes its shade (or head), and the little lamp nearly crumples down even lower, accompanied by the sound of creaking hinges that resemble the air wheezing out of the deflating ball. Even at *Luxo Jr.*'s first screening at the computer expo SIGGRAPH, digital pioneer Jim Blinn asked Lasseter whether "the parent lamp was a mother or a father," proving that gender and even family relations are attributes quickly assigned by viewers (Paik 60). Stephen Prince praises Lasseter's job of establishing gender and emotional traits so efficiently:

> The animation endows these [lamps] with personalities and the roles of father and child [...] Squash and stretch, timing, and exaggeration delineate the characters and their emotions. Dad moves slowly, with gravitas, Junior with quicker, chippier actions [...] to convey emotion and thought [106].

The sparse but effective soundtrack also adds "affective congruence," to borrow Jeff Smith's term, as it intensifies the narrative situation, increasing the spectator's empathy for the "child" lamp's temporary shame and disappointment (162). However, the young lamp's joy quickly returns when he reenters, romping with a new, even larger ball.

By contrast, the longer, darker *Red's Dream* exploits the expressionistic film noir plot structure of a mental subjective fantasy in which a unicycle, now abandoned and marked down for quick sale in a bicycle store corner, imagines stealing the show during a clown's juggling act. However, as the dream ends amidst thunderous applause, the unicycle "awakes" to realize it was just a fantasy. The lonely saxophone music, bending unicycle neck/frame and low-key lighting—all help cue the audience's response, which is to recognize the unicycle's disappointment, helplessness and even melancholy isolation. Unlike Luxo, Jr., Red gets no second chance at happiness. Similarly, *Knick Knack*'s frustrated snowman, stuck in the snow globe but lusting after Miss Miami, quickly establishes his character traits and desires as he sets about his goal of liberating himself from his glass home. He activates many of Smith's criteria for engaging the audience, including clear eyeline matches to prove what he is seeing and thinking, as well as direct address glances at the camera to indicate self-awareness and garner our pity. The sad but comic ending, with the snowman now doubly encased in his snow globe and a fish bowl, and also doubly frustrated by a second object of desire, generates mixed emotions. Lasseter jokes that these two shorts, with their non-happy endings, are from Pixar's "blue period" (Young 2011). But clearly, exploring the short format of CGI to generate engaging characters taught Pixar that emotions, especially sadness and even melancholy, were among the quickest ways to involve the audience and make them overlook the artificial aspects of the medium. These may be computer-generated shapes appearing briefly in very short films, but the audience sympathizes with the figures as feeling, cognizant characters, just as in the classical cel animation of Disney's *Ugly Duckling*.

In contrast to the engaging conventional representations and fluid realistic movement of classical Disney or 3D Pixar, stop-motion animation has often been considered rather artificial, with visible marks of production in the frame-to-frame readjustment of the figures and miniature, often toy-like sets. Maureen Furniss has pointed out that in almost all stop-motion animation, "it is difficult to recreate an absolutely realistic sense of movement," and the frame-to-frame animating creates inconsistency and calls attention to the surface and materials of the figures (161). Clay animation, by its very nature, tends toward artifice rather than realism. Further, as Paul Wells has explained, there is a long tradition of caricature and satire in stop-motion animation, further separating it from 3D realism. Moreover, stop-motion clay animation calls attention to its hand-made materiality and is "the most obviously 'artisanal' [sort] of animation" (Wells 106, 117). Yet, for Jennifer Barker, stop-motion animation is a special mode for inspiring "sensuous empathy" in the spectator:

> Stop-motion animation [...] exaggerates the discontinuity according to which motion pictures work and in the process renders even more obvious the discontinuous nature of movement, both cinematic and human [...] Stop-motion animation offers a lingering look at an *extended* arrest of movement [136].

Stop-motion, which has recently made a strong comeback in commercial animation, offers unique qualities that seem to distance it and its characters from the fluid potential realism of cel and CGI animation. Animation historian Philippe Moins has even argued that the resurgence of claymation is partly a response to the sophisticated illusions of volume and bodies in CGI; stop-motion animation is less industrial, less technological, and seems natural and home-made in contrast to Pixar and 3D animation (10). Yet even stop motion plasticine figures can earn a spectator's empathy.

In *Mary and Max*, Adam Elliott, inspired by Aardman's Nick Park, among many others, uses plasticine to create "biographies of 'underdog' characters and employs a mixture of humor and pathos" (Cavalier 346). His brand of stop-motion provides a perfect test case for empathy toward melancholy, if artificial, characters, by producing what Barker would label "a feeling of sensual harmony" (143). *Mary and Max* builds a narrative full of pathos by alternating between Mary Daisy Dinkle, an unfortunate young Australian girl, as she grows and moves from one domestic disappointment to another, and Max, an older, lonely man in New York who suffers from a host of physical and mental ailments. Mary randomly selects Max Horowitz's name from a phone book and the pair exchange bizarre, honest letters and care packages of unhealthy food stuffs over the years. This epistolary narrative springs in part from writer director Elliot's real life exchange with a pen pal in New York; they shared a number of personal, often intimate exchanges.[1] *Mary and Max* becomes, then, a sort of animated graphic novel in the "life narrative" genre. Hillary Chute, writing on comic book traditions, has argued that the graphic novel readily engages with biography and autobiography more than many other narrative genres: "The form of comics has a peculiar relation to expressing life stories [...] that engages with a human subject who is either in extremis or facing a brutal experience" (108). She adds that graphic life narratives are often mapped out visibly on the bodies of the protagonists and are "multivalent with complex relations to embodiment." Thus, graphic life narratives address loss, but are built around an architecture of the body and the self (Chute 112, 116).

Eliot's characters, Mary and Max, made as they are from malleable clay, are material figures in constant flux from frame to frame, and thus their shifting bodily discontinuity makes them simultaneously physically present and yet highly artificial. It is this contradiction of stop-motion bodies that fascinates viewers, as this technique seems simultaneously to challenge and yet encourage viewers to assign emotion and empathy to these normally inanimate, toy-like clay figures. In his work on immobility, Lucien Cortade has noted that affect can be both threatened and reinforced by such moments of awareness of the original stasis of filmed objects, such as clay figures; he has further argued that "within the oxymoronic juncture of movement and immobility perches a definition of modernity" and cinema (130). *Mary and Max* quickly strikes a balance between a satiric perspective on these two characters and a sensitive portrayal of their desperately sad problems and plights, despite their uneven movements and occasionally static poses.

Mary, like the Ugly Duckling, is pitiable and basically alone from the beginning. Her parents are dysfunctional, offering no real support or guidance, and her only constant companion is a chicken that fell off a truck on the way to the slaughter house. Mary is so lonely and confused that she writes to Max for human connection, and early on, she explains that she has no friends and is a constant victim of bullying. Her letter to Max reminds him of how he was bullied as well, which leads to one of his own mental breakdowns. The utilization of Mary's earnest if pathetic voiceover, images of her being harassed by elders and other kids, and then Max's flashback and physical reactions and trauma, all reinforce the characters' fragile emotional states. Their exaggerated facial features—especially the extreme closeups and the artificial beads of sweat and tears—as well as their acknowledgment of the trauma of being teased and bullied, are likely to generate emotional understanding from the audience. The increasingly intimate cinematography and sound work brings the spectator ever closer to the characters, their states of mind and predicaments.

As Ed Tan explains, initial empathy is due to the spectator's understanding of the protagonist's situation, and then during climactic moments, sentiment-provoking stimuli work together to generate a level of high emotion. In *Mary and Max*, the emotion cues include Max's frightened eyes in extreme closeup, a sudden crescendo of music, the mean voices of bullies, and Max's quivering face as he is trapped in an alley before the screen goes black as he shuts out the violent memories [30:35] (Fig. 21). Sympathy is accompanied by the spectator's desire to be close to the protagonist, and while we cannot help movie characters, we nonetheless feel as if we should "share their suffering" (Tan and Frijda 53, 64).

Fig. 21. An extreme closeup of Max's frightened face encourages empathy in Adam Elliott's *Mary and Max* (2009).

Max and Mary repeatedly "warrant" our sympathy and empathy, as they try unsuccessfully to cope with life around them and their inner fear and melancholy. For instance, late in the film, after years of writing back and forth and a series of unfortunate events, Max explains to Mary that he was recently committed to a mental hospital where he received a belated diagnosis of Asperger's Syndrome. His deadpan summary of Asperger's traits—explained in his voiceover while the audience sees flashback examples of his previous oddball behavior—allows a comical montage of "poor Max" examples [49:20]. His account not only aligns us anew with his sad state of affairs, but it produces a new stage of allegiance with Max, who has been struggling against the world without understanding his own condition. Retroactively, his new self-knowledge also makes us even sorrier for Mary, whose luck, in reaching out for some human contact, led her to a man who, ironically, is himself so unable to forge normal relationships.

Moreover, soon after Mary shocks and angers Max by writing about his illness and life in her PhD thesis, the pair become increasingly estranged, distraught and depressed. The epistolary narrative alternates between the two devastated characters, dividing our attention between their very different failures to cope and recover. Mary has gone to college to learn about Asperger's Syndrome and written a popular book that exploits Max's stories. Max, angry, lists all the emotions he feels and then sends her the "M" key from his typewriter, proving he can never write her again. Dumbfounded, Mary destroys all the books, takes to drinking and loses her husband to another man. She even prepares to commit suicide, but her shut-in neighbor in a wheelchair miraculously knocks on the front door at just the right climactic moment [76:10]. His appearance stands in for that of the audience, eager to see poor, long suffering Mary survive and hopefully revive herself. Nonetheless, even though Mary then sets off to New York with her baby in tow, she will never see Max alive, and the separation-reunion plot is never really fully resolved, in contrast to the Disney formula. Max is dead and Mary has lost yet another of her few connections to humanity.

Such emotional climaxes, built around mental and physical trauma at key plot points, prove once again the power of even relatively abstract animation, here clay figures moved between frames, to generate palpable cues for emotion. Affective mimicry results as the audience finally feels empathy for Mary and Max. In contrast to cel animation and 3D CGI, some critics even find that stop-motion animation has the potential to affect the audience more deeply. Jennifer Barker has argued that stop-motion can be especially haptic, "provoking our desire to touch, caress, squeeze, and scrape the images before us" (137). She has even claimed that some viewers become "bewitched by stop-motion animation," precisely because it makes temporality tactile, via "the experience of getting caught up in their rhythm" thanks to the "sensual harmony" (137, 143).

Yet, as we have seen with examples from *The Ugly Duckling* up to the Pixar cartoons of the 1980s, narrative animation often strives to appeal immediately to the audience by exploiting highly emotional situations and plot lines that allow for desperate, vulnerable characters undergoing some highly significant experience. While fear and melancholy trigger our emotional engagement, bursts of joy and triumph are more common affective cues in mainstream animation. But a full range of emotion is, in effect, possible and essential in conveying characterization from a wide spectrum of fanciful, sometimes abstract, animated figures in varying forms and bodies. Intimate psychological moments and fine-tuned personality traits are readily evoked and put into action within animated films that struggle, often quite successfully, to appeal to spectators in ways that rival the more conventional characterization and modes of representation found in commercial, live-action cinema. Animation just seems more amazing and insightful for revealing the processes that allow us as viewers to work so happily at constructing emotional characters out of sparse, even contradictory, visual and audio signifiers.

Notes

1. "I do have a pen friend in New York who I've been writing to for more than 20 years. He does have Asperger's, he is a big man, he is Jewish, he is an atheist" (Pond 2009).

Works Cited

Barker, Jennifer. 2009. *The Tactile Eye*. Berkeley: University of California Press.
Bordwell, David, and Kristin Thompson. 1979 [2013]. *Film Art*. New York: McGraw-Hill.
Cavalier, Stephen. 2011. *The World History of Animation*. Berkeley: University of California Press.
Chute, Hillary. 2011. "Comics Form and Narrating Lives." *Profession*: 107–17.
Cortade, Ludovic. 2008. *Le Cinéma de l'immobilité*. Paris: Sorbonne.
Furniss, Maureen. 2007. *Art in Motion: Animation Aesthetics*. Eastleigh, NJ: John Libbey.
Grodal, Torben. 2009. *Embodied Visions: Evolution, Emotion, Culture, and Film*. New York: Oxford University Press.
Mary and Max. 2009 [2010]. Dir. Adam Elliot. With the voices of Toni Colette (Mary Daisy Dinkle) and Philip Seymour Hoffman (Max Jerry Horowitz). Melodrama Pictures. DVD. MPI Home Video.
Merritt, Russell. 2005. "Lost on Pleasure Islands: Storytelling in Disney's Silly Symphonies." *Film Quarterly* 59.1: 4–17.
Moins, Philippe. 2001. *Les Maîtres de la pâte*. Paris: Dreamland.
Neupert, Richard. 2008. "Kirikou and the Animated Figure / Body." *Studies in French Cinema* 8.1: 41–56.

_____. 2011. "'We're Happy When We're Sad': Comedy, Gags, and 1930s Cartoon Narration." *Funny Pictures: Animation and Comedy in Studio-Era Hollywood*. Eds. Daniel Goldmark and Charlie Keil. Berkeley: University of California Press. 93–108.

Paik, Karen. 2007. *To Infinity and Beyond*. San Francisco: Chronicle.

Pixar Short Films Collection Volume 1. 2007. DVD. Walt Disney Home Entertainment.

Pond, Steve. 2009. "The Weird Brillilance of *Mary and Max*." *Wrap*, December 9. http://www.thewrap.com/deal-central/column-post/weird-brilliance-mary-and-max-11544. Retrieved on 12/2/2013.

Prince, Stephen. 2012. *Digital Visual Effects in Cinema: The Seduction of Reality*. New Brunswick, NJ: Rutgers University Press.

Smith, Jeff. 1999. "Movie Music as Moving Music." *Passionate Views: Film, Cognition and Emotion*. Eds. Carl Plantinga and Greg M. Smith. Baltimore: Johns Hopkins University Press. 146–67.

Smith, Murray. 1995. *Engaging Characters: Fiction, Emotion, and the Cinema*. New York: Oxford University Press.

Tan, Ed S.-H. 2011. *Emotion and the Structure of Narrative Film*. New York: Routledge.

Tan, Ed S.-H., and Nico H. Frijda. 1999. "Sentiment in Film Viewing." *Passionate Views*. Eds. Carl Plantinga and Greg M. Smith. Baltimore: Johns Hopkins University Press. 48–64.

Wells, Paul. 2006. *Fundamentals of Animation*. Lausanne: Ava Books.

Young, John. 2011. "John Lasseter on Pixar's early days." *Entertainment Weekly*, June 16. http://insidemovies.ew.com/2011/06/16/pixar-john-lasseter-burton. Retrieved 8/27/2013.

About the Contributors

Adriano **D'Aloia** is an adjunct professor in the Department of Communication and Performing Arts of the Università Cattolica del Sacro Cuore, Milano, Italy. He is the author of *La vertigine e il volo: L'esperienza filmica contemporanea fra estetica, psicologia e neuroscienze* (2013) and he has published in the journals *Bianco e Nero*, *Cinema* and *Cinéma & Cie*, among others.

Jean-François **Baillon** is a professor of English and film studies at the Université Michel de Montaigne Bordeaux 3 where he launched an interdisciplinary research group on diaspora cultures. He has published extensively on the history of British cinema, gothic and horror film, as well as recent articles on Atom Egoyan.

Zachary **Baqué** is an associate professor at the Université Toulouse Jean Jaurès, where he teaches American civilization and film studies. He has published on David Lynch and other American directors like Frank Capra, Stanley Kubrick and Michael Mann, and his research interests include the representation of American political institutions onscreen, the politics of documentaries and, more generally, the relation between politics and American films.

Christophe **Chambost** is an associate professor at the Université Michel de Montaigne Bordeaux 3. He has published articles on horror films, Westerns and on the representation of journalism. He has also published articles on 19th century American authors such as Bierce, Hawthorne, Melville and Poe.

Raphaëlle **Costa de Beauregard** is a professor emeritus at the Université Toulouse Jean Jaurès where she taught film and visual studies and British and American literature. She is also a Clare Hall Fellow and a founding member of SERCIA. She has published many articles on cinema that combine formal, historical and philosophical approaches.

Thomas **Elsaesser** is a professor emeritus in the Department of Media and Culture of the University of Amsterdam. From 2006 to 2012, he was a visiting professor at Yale University and now teaches part-time at Columbia University, New York. He has authored, edited and co-edited some twenty volumes on early cinema, film theory, German and European cinema, Hollywood, new media and installation art.

Wendy **Everett** is a former reader in film studies and French at the University of Bath and research fellow at the Camargo Foundation, Cassis, France. Her research interests are in European cinema, and she has published widely in the field, including on color, identity and space in European films, fractal narratives of the postmodern and the European road movie. She is a member of the Editorial Board of the *Literature/Film Quarterly* and *The Soundtrack*.

Christophe **Gelly** is a professor of British and American literature and film studies at the Université Blaise Pascal (Clermont 2). He mainly works on film genre, film noir, adaptation, and he has published two book-length studies on Arthur Conan Doyle (2005) and Raymond Chandler (2009).

Grégoire **Halbout** is an associate professor at the IUT of Tours/University François Rabelais of Tours, France. His research interests include classical Hollywood cinema, cultural industries, non-political public sphere and social media, and the representation of minorities in contemporary cinema and TV shows. His book *La Comédie screwball hollywoodienne: Sexe, amour et idéaux démocratiques* was published by Artois Presses Université in 2013.

Marianne **Kac-Vergne** is an associate professor of American and film studies at the University of Picardie Jules Verne, Amiens, France. She has written on masculinity in contemporary Hollywood film genres and other film topics involving gender. Her book *Masculinity in Contemporary Science Fiction Cinema: Cyborgs, Troopers and Other Men of the Future* is forthcoming.

Isabelle **Le Corff** is an associate professor of English and film studies at the Université de Bretagne Occidentale, Lorient, France. Her research interests include Irish and Irish American cinema as well as film in education. She has published many articles and is chief editor of the peer-reviewed e-journal *Mise Au Point*.

Fabrice **Lyczba** is an associate professor of American studies at the Université Paris Dauphine (Paris 8). His research aims at analyzing the pleasures of 1920s Hollywood cinema and the circulations of cinema in American culture through reception studies, audiencing processes and a study of the virtual.

Céline **Murillo** is an associate professor at the Université Paris Nord (Paris 13). She has published on Westerns and co-edited a special issue of *RFEA* (issue 156, January 2013) called "What About Independent Cinema?" Her research focuses on independent and underground American cinema, including Jim Jarmusch and punk films.

Richard **Neupert** is the Wheatley Professor of the Arts and J. Meigs Distinguished Teaching Professor in Film Studies at the University of Georgia. He is author of *A History of French Animation* (2011), *A History of the French New Wave Cinema* (2003/2007) and *The End: Narration and Closure in the Cinema* (1996).

Anne-Marie **Paquet-Deyris** is a professor of American literature and film studies at the Université Paris Ouest Nanterre. She is the co-author of *Lolita: Cartographies de l'obsession (Nabokov, Kubrick)* (2009), co-editor of *Thomas Hardy & John Schlesinger: Moments of Vision—Far from the Madding Crowd* (2011), and editor of issue 136 of *CinémAction* entitled *Cinéma de l'horreur: Les Maléfiques* (2010).

Yann **Roblou** is an associate professor at the Université de Valenciennes, France, where he teaches, among other things, the history, aesthetics and ideology of American cinema. His dissertation centered on violence of language in the films of Stanley Kubrick and he has published a number of articles on contemporary American directors, including Clint Eastwood, Spike Lee, Martin Scorsese and M. Night Shyamalan.

David **Roche** is a professor of film studies at the Université Toulouse Jean Jaurès. He is the author of *Making and Remaking Horror in the 1970s and 2000s* (2014) and *L'Imagination malsaine* (2007). He has also published on horror cinema, Darren Aronofsky, Tim Burton, David Cronenberg, Emir Kusturica, Sergio Leone, David Lynch and Quentin Tarantino.

Isabelle **Schmitt-Pitiot**, Dijon, France, is an associate professor at the Université de Bourgogne. Her interests include cinema and television series. She has published articles on Woody Allen, John Ford and John Huston.

Clémentine **Tholas-Disset** teaches American and English history, business English and media at the Université Paris Est Créteil. Her research focuses on early motion pictures in the U.S., in particular World War I propaganda films, the role of silent films in promoting progressive politics, and the connections between silent cinema and other visual arts.

Index

Adam's Rib (Cukor, 1949) 69
The Adjuster (Egoyan, 1991) 166–67, 169, 174
Adoration (Egoyan, 2008) 169
The Affairs of Anatol (DeMille, 1921) 58
The Age of Innocence (Scorsese, 1993) 5
Agel, Henri 144
All That Heaven Allows (Sirk, 1955) 189
Almodóvar, Pedro 28, ; *The Skin I Live In* (2011) 24, 25
Alper, Gerald 1
Altman, Rick 68
Amalric, Matthieu 29
American Revolution 2 (Howard Alk and Mike Gray, 1969) 105–17
Amselek, Alain 1
Anderson, Wes 27; *Moonrise Kingdom* (2012) 27, 28, 32
André, Emmanuelle 82
Anna Karenina 81
Anna Karenina (Brown, 1935) 79
Anna Karenina (Wright, 2012) 209
Apollinaire, Guillaume 94
Ararat (Egoyan, 2002) 167
Ardenne, Paul 198
Atonement (Wright, 2007) 204–6, 209–10
Avatar (Cameron, 2009) 29
The Awful Truth (McCarey, 1937) 68–69

"Baby Did a Bad Bad Thing" (Chris Isaac, 1995) 150
Bach, J.S.: *Goldberg Variations* 158
Bachelard, Gaston 1–2, 135
Bakhtin, Mikhail 102, 141–42
Ballantyne, Tony, Antoinette Burton et al. 1
Barber, Samuel: *Concerto for Violin and Orchestra*, Op. 14 186, 188
Baridon, Michel 73
Barker, Jennifer 215, 219–20, 222
Bálazs, Béla 20

Barnouw, Erik 108
Barrymore, Lionel 51
Barthes, Roland 102, 136, 140
Basinger, Jeanine 189
Bataille, Georges 141
Baudrillard, Jean 142
Baudry, Patrick 144
Bava, Mario 23
Bayon, Estelle 40, 141–42
Bazin, André 20, 168
"Bear" (McQueen, 1993) 192
Beau Travail (Denis, 1990) 20
Belle de Jour (Buñuel, 1967) 152
Bellour, Raymond 27
Belting, Hans 172
Ben-Hur (Nibol et al., 1925) 50, 55
Benoit, Laurent 91
Bergman, Ingmar 179, 190; *Persona* (1966) 110
Bergson, Henri 82
Berlant, Lauren 1–2, 17–18, 28, 146
Bertensson, Sergei, and Jay Leda 79
Beugnet, Martine 4, 24, 32
Bhabha, Homi K. 175
Bird (Eastwood, 1988) 163
Bishop, Elizabeth 1
Black, Dustin Lance 161
Black Panthers: A Report (Varda, 1968) 117
Blanchot, Maurice 1–2
Blinn, Jim 218
Blow Job (Warhol, 1983) 5
Bolter, Jay David, and Richard Grusin 46
Bombaugh, Charles C. 203
Bonello, Bertrand 24
Boorman, John 190
Bordwell, David, and Kristin Thompson 6, 22, 216; and Janet Staiger and Kristin Thompson 6, 62
Borges, Jorge Luis 150
Boyer, Charles-Arthur 2

229

Index

Braindead (Jackson, 1992) 140
Brakhage, Stan 5
Branigan, Edward 22, 187
Breen, Joseph 64
Breillat, Catherine 24
Brenon, Herbert 54
Brick, Howard 116
The Bridges of Madison County (Eastwood, 1995) 5
Brief Encounter (Lean, 1945) 26, 73–83, 189
Bringing Up Baby (Hawks, 1938) 65–66
Brody, Richard 112
Bromley, James M. 1
Brooks, Peter 48
Browder, Earl 164
Browning, Robert: *The Pied Piper of Hamelin* 177
Brüno (Charles, 2009) 28
Bug (Friedkin, 2006) 133–44
Bug (play) 133, 136–37
Burch, Noel 168
Burgin, Victor 48
Butler, Judith 167

Calendar (Egoyan, 1993) 168, 171, 175
Cameron, James: *Avatar* (2009) 29; *The Terminator* (1984) 119–20, 122–23, 126–27, 129–30
Cardiff, Janet: *Whispering Room* (1991) 173
Carnicke, Sharon Marie 147
Carr Spencer, Virginia 144
Casino (Scorsese, 1995) 25
Cassady, Carolyn and Neal 95
Cavalier, Stephen 220
Cavell, Stanley 61, 69
Chandler, Raymond 85
Chaplin, Charles 51
Chateauvert, Jean 91
The Cheat (DeMille, 1915) 53
Chesal, Robert 181
Chion, Michel 4, 12, 78, 102
Chloe (Egoyan, 2009) 176
Chopsticks (Euphemia Allen, 1877) 77, 81
Chute, Hillary 220
Clam, Jean 1–2, 135
Clark, Kenneth 197
Clean, Shaven (Kerrigan, 1993) 136
Cohen, Paula Marantz 55
Cohen, Sacha Baron 28
The Companionate Marriage (Lindsey, 1927) 65
Cooke, Jennifer G., et al. 1
Coolidge, Calvin 161
Cormack, Mike 79
Corner, John 110–11
Corso, Gregory 94–101
Cortade, Lucien 220

Costa, Pedro 24
Coward, Noël: *Still Life* 83, 189
Crafton, Donald 49–50, 52
Creature from the Black Lagoon (Arnold, 1954) 75
Cronenberg, David: 5–6, 11–12, 121, 165; *A Dangerous Method* (2011) 22, 205, 210; *The Fly* (1986) 119–20, 123–24, 126–27, 129–30; *Videodrome* (1983) 5–6, 12
Cukor, George: *Adam's Rib* (1949) 69; *The Philadelphia Story* (1940) 68; *Tarnished Lady* (1931) 63

Damasio, Antonio 144
Daney, Serge 109
A Dangerous Method (Cronenberg, 2011) 22, 205, 210
Dante: *Inferno* 194; *Purgatorio* 194
Dark Passage (Delmer Daves, 1947) 85
Das, Santanu 1
A Daughter of the Gods (Brenon, 1916) 54
Davies, Terence 8, 179–90; *The Deep Blue Sea* (2011) 183–90; *Distant Voices, Still Lives* (1988) 8, 180; *The House of Mirth* (2000) 183–84; *The Long Day Closes* (1992) 180–82; *The Neon Bible* (1995) 183–84; "Trilogy": *Children* (1976), *Madonna and Child* (1980) and *Death and Transfiguration* (1983) 180
"Deadpan" (McQueen, 1997) 192
Death and Transfiguration (Davies, 1983) 180
The Deep Blue Sea (Davies, 2011) 183–90
The Deep Blue Sea (play) 184–85, 189
De Kuyper, Eric 96, 101
Deleuze, Gilles 4, 8, 20, 98
Del Rio, Dolores 51
DeMille, Cecil B.: *The Affairs of Anatol* (1921) 58; *The Cheat* (1915) 53; *Don't Change Your Husband* (1919) 58; *Male and Female* (1919) 58
Denis, Claire 5, 13, 25, 26, 27; *Beau Travail* (1990) 20; *Trouble Every Day* (2001) 140; *Vendredi Soir* (2002) 26
Derrida, Jacques 169–71
De Sade, Marquis 28
Le Diable boiteux 48
Dishonored (von Sternberg, 1931) 63
Disney 216–17, 219, 222; *Silly Symphonies* 216; *Ugly Duckling* (Cutting, 1939) 216
Distant Voices, Still Lives (Davies, 1988) 8, 180
District 9 (Blomkamp, 2009) 57
The Diving Bell and the Butterfly (Schnabel, 2007) 29
Dix, Dorothy 65
Dixon, Simon 53
Doane, Mary Anne 189

Dr. Strangelove (Kubrick, 1964) 152
The Dodge Brothers Hour 52
Don't Change Your Husband (DeMille, 1919) 58
Douglas, Bill 190
Doyle, Michael William 112
Drew, Robert 115
The Duchess (Dibb, 2008) 209
Dugain, Marc 160
Dyer, Richard 75

Eastwood, Clint: *Bird* (1988) 163; *The Bridges of Madison County* (1995) 5; *J. Edgar* (2011) 156–64; *Pale Rider* (1985) 158
Easy Rider (Hopper, 1969) 108
Eat (Warhol, 1963) 5
Ebert, Roger 107, 109
The Edge of Love (Maybury, 2008) 105, 109
Egoyan, Atom 165–77; *The Adjuster* (1991) 166–67, 169, 174; *Adoration* (2008) 169; *Ararat* (2002) 167; *Calendar* (1993) 168, 171, 175; *Chloe* (2009) 176; *Exotica* (1994) 174–75; *Family Viewing* (1988) 167, 173; *Felicia's Journey* (2001) 169–70, 176; *Next of Kin* (1984) 166–70; *Speaking Parts* (1989) 167–69, 171–72, 175; *The Sweet Hereafter* (1998) 166–67, 177; *Where the Truth Lies* (2006) 169
Ehrenzweig, Anton 186
Eibl-Eibesfeldt, Irenäus 203
Elias, Norbert 22
Elsaesser, Thomas 46, 49; and Malte Hagener 4–5, 13
Empire of the Senses (Oshima, 1976) 20
Epstein, Jean 187
Escott, Harry 20, 144, 187, 200
Exotica (Egoyan, 1994) 174–75
Eyes Wide Shut (Kubrick, 1999) 146–54

Fairbanks, Douglas 51, 55
"The Fall of the House of Usher" 135
Family Viewing (Egoyan, 1988) 167, 173
Farber, David 105
Favazza, Armando 141
Fear and Desire (Kubrick, 1953) 152
Felicia's Journey (Egoyan, 2001) 169–70, 176
Fellini, Frederico 190
La Femme défendue (Harel, 1997) 84–86, 89–92
Ferrari, Pier Francesco, Vittorio Gallese, Giacomo Rizzolatti, and Leonardo Fogassi 211
5th Avenue Girl (LaCava, 1939) 69
Fisher, Helen 204
The Fly (Cronenberg, 1986) 119–20, 123–24, 126–27, 129–30

Forster, E.M.: *A Passage to India* 175
Foucault, Michel 25, 136, 181, 196
The Fountain (Aronofsky, 2006) 8–9
François le Champi 177
Frank, Anne 169
A Free Soul (Brown, 1931) 63
Freud, Sigmund 30, 125, 142, 147, 201, 203
Friedman, Thomas 18
Frijhoff, Willeim 203
Fuery, Patrick 136, 142–43
Full Metal Jacket (Kubrick, 1987) 152
Fuller, Kathryn H. 53
Furniss, Maureen 219

Gabb, Jacqui 1
Gallese Vittorio 211; and Michele Guerra 212
Gallup, Gordon, Jr. 204
Garbarini, Francesca, and Mauro Adenzato 211
Garbo, Greta 51–52, 55, 79
Gaudreault, André 46, 91
Gentry, Curt 162, 164
Gernalzick, Nadja 91
Gibson, James J. 202, 208
Giddens, Anthony 1, 134
Gilbert, John 51–52, 55
Ginsberg, Allen 94–100, 103
Gish, Lillian 54
Gitlin, Todd 116–17
Glassman, Marc 173
The Glory Road 54
Godard, Jean-Luc 116, 179, 190
The Good Fairy (Wyler, 1935) 66
Goodfellas (Scorsese, 1990) 25
Gorbman, Claudia 81
Grandrieux, Philippe 24
Green, Abel, and Joe Laurie, Jr. 58
Greenspun, Roger 110, 116
Gregory, Dick 108, 115
Grieveson, Lee, and Peter Krämer 35, 43
Griffith, D.W. 51
Grodal, Torben 216
Gross, Larry 147, 152

Hall, Ben L. 7, 51–52
Hall, Edward T. 2, 4
Hall, J.A. 130
Hancock, Brannon 27
Handel, Leo 62
Hansen, Miriam 34, 41–42, 58
Harcourt, Peter 168, 171, 176
Harrison, Victoria 1
Hartley, Hal 27
Harvey, Karen 203
Harvey, Keith, and Celia Shalom 179
Hatfield, Elaine, and Richard L. Rapson 1

232   Index

Hawley, Richard 203
Hays, Will H., and the Hays Code 61, 62, 64, 67–68, 106, 117
Heidegger, Martin 21
Heider, Fritz, and Marianne Simmel 207
Hill, Wendy 204
Hilmes, Michele 51–52
Hiroshima mon Amour (Resnais, 1959) 20
Hitchcock, Alfred: *Mr. and Mrs. Smith* (1941) 69; *Psycho* (1960) 136, 170; *Suspicion* (1940) 170; *Vertigo* (1958) 6–7
Homer: *The Odyssey* 152
Hoover, J. Edgar 156–57, 161–64
Hostel I (Roth, 2005) 27
Hostel II (Roth, 2007) 27
Hot Stuff (LeRoy, 1929) 63
Hou, Hsiao-hsien 24
Houdini, Harry 47–48
The House of Mirth (Davies, 2000) 183–84
The House of Mirth (novel) 184
Hughes, Susan M., Marissa A. Harrison, and Gordon G. Gallup, Jr. 204
The Humming Bird (Olcott, 1924) 58
Humphrey, Hubert 107
Hunger (McQueen, 2008) 192–198, 200–1
Hunt, D. Bradford 117
Husing, Ted 51–52

Iacoboni, Marco 211
Iacub, Marcela 70
Ibrahim-Lamrous, Lila 95
Ideal Marriage (Van de Velde, 1930) 65
Inferno 194
The Insider (Mann, 1999) 5
Intimacy (Chéreau, 2001) 8
The Isle (Ki-duk Kim, 2000) 20
It Always Rains on Sunday (Hamer, 1947) 189

J. Edgar (Eastwood, 2011) 156–64
Jacobs, Jason 3
Jacobs, Lea 48
Jacobs, Lewis 43
James, David E. 106, 108, 115–16
Jarman, Derek 5
Jeffords, Susan 119, 131
Jenkins, Henry 46
Jeudy, Henri-Pierre 1, 134
Jivani, Alkarim 181
Jones, Jim 137
Jost, Jon 5
Jullier, Laurent 6

Kaczynski, Ted 137
Kael, Pauline 131
Kallen, Stuart A. 105
Kennedy, Joseph 54

Kerouac, Jack 94–103; *The Vanity of Duluoz* 102
Killer's Kiss (Kubrick, 1955) 152
King, Martin Luther 164
Kirkham, Pat, and Janet Thumim 123
Kirshenbaum, Sheril 203
Kiss (Warhol, 1963) 5
Klossowski, Pierre 28
Knick Knack (Pixar, 1989) 218
Knightley, Keira 202, 204–10
Koffka, Kurt 208
Kracauer, Siegfried 20
Kramer, Peter 49
Kreider, Tim 147
Kreutzer Sonata 81
Kristeva, Julia 1, 134
Kubrick, Stanley: *Dr. Strangelove* (1964) 152; *Eyes Wide Shut* (1999) 146–54; *Fear and Desire* (1953) 152; *Full Metal Jacket* (1987) 152; *Killer's Kiss* (1955) 152; *Lolita* (1960) 152; *Paths of Glory* (1957) 152; *The Shining* (1980) 152
Kusturica, Emir 29

Lacan, Jacques 2, 12, 13, 18, 100, 125, 134, 137, 142, 144, 170, 180, 193–94, 201
Lady in the Lake (Montgomery, 1947) 84–93
Lakoff, George, and Mark Johnson 211
Lalanne, Jean-Marc 161
La Place, Maria 189
Lasseter, John 216–19
Lateiner, Donald 203
Laurent, Béatrice 73
Laurent, Benoît 91, 93
Lebovici, Elisabeth 1–3, 5
Lee, Bobby 112
Le Gall, Didier 144
Le Sage, Alain-René: *Le Diable boiteux* 48
Letter from an Unknown Woman (Ophüls, 1948) 189
Letts, Tracy: *Bug* (play) 133, 136–37
Levinas, Emmanuel 20, 167–68
Levy, Donald P. 119–20
Libeled Lady (Conway, 1936) 68
Lindsey, Ben: *The Companionate Marriage* (1927) 65
Lolita (Kubrick, 1960) 152
London Boulevard (Monahan, 2010) 209
The Long Day Closes (Davies, 1992) 180–82
Love (Goulding and Gilbert, 1927) 51
Love Is News (Garnett, 1937) 69
Lustig, T.J. 135
Luxo Jr. (Pixar, 1986) 216, 218

MacDougall, David 199
Madelénat, Daniel 1, 136, 141, 144

Madonna and Child (Davies, 1980) 180
Male and Female (DeMille, 1919) 58
Mallarmé, Stéphane 27
Malle, Louis 190
Maltby, Richard 35
Maniac (William Lustig, 1980; Franck Khalfoun, 2012) 13
Manovich, Lev 46
Marion, Philippe 46
Marker, Chris 165
Marks, Laura U. 4, 7, 20–21, 25, 98
Mary and Max (Elliot, 2009) 216, 220–23
Masson, Alain 152
McCann, Ben 32
McCullers, Carson 144
McEnteer, James 106–7
McLean, Adrienne 53
McMahon, Laura 26
McQueen, Steve 192–201; "Bear" (1993) 192; "Deadpan" (1997) 192; *Hunger* (2008) 192–198, 200–1; "Queen and Country" (2007) 192; *Shame* (2011) 192–201
McSorley, Tom 166–67, 176
McVeigh, Timothy 136, 144
Meflah, Nadia 154
Mekas, John 94
Méliès, Georges 85
Mellier, Denis 139
Memento (Nolan, 2000) 29
Merleau-Ponty, Maurice 4, 19–20, 168–69
Merritt, Russell 216
Mészáros, Márta 190
Metz, Christian 3, 68, 84, 167, 205
Michals, Debra 106
Michotte, Albert 207
Midnight (Leisen, 1939) 69
Miller, Jacques-Alain 12
Mr. and Mrs. Smith (Hitchcock, 1941) 69
Mix, Tom 54
Moins, Phlilppe 219
Moonrise Kingdom (Anderson, 2012) 27, 28, 32
Morey, Anne 53
Morrey, Douglas 25
Morris, Demons 203
Morris, T.J. 172–73, 176
Mosher, Donald, and Mark Sirkin 119, 129–30
Mulvey, Laura 86, 92, 123, 187, 198, 206
Murat, Laure 2
The Murder of Fred Hampton (Varda, 1971) 117
My Favorite Wife (Kanin, 1940) 70

Naficy, Hamid 172
Naked (Leigh, 1993) 20

Nancy, Jean-Luc 20, 25–27, 139–40
Neale, Steve 157, 163
Nelson, Tollof 171
The Neon Bible (Davies, 1995) 183–84
The Neon Bible (novel) 184
Next of Kin (Egoyan, 1984) 166–70
Night Nurse (Wellman, 1931) 63
Nilsson, Anna Q. 55
Nishime, LeiLani 125
Nixon, Richard 108, 161
Noé, Gaspar 5, 24
Normand, Mabel 53–54, 57
Now, Voyager (Rapping, 1942) 188
Nyrop, Christopher 203

O'Connor, Flannery: *Wise Blood* 144
Odin, Roger 22
The Odyssey 152
Old Boy (Chan-wook Park, 2003) 20
Olsen, Mark 27
Ophüls, Max: *Letter From an Unknown Woman* (1948) 189; *La Ronde* (1950) 152
Orlovski, Peter 94, 96
Ortoli, Philippe 158, 164

Paik, Karen 218
Pale Rider (Eastwood, 1985) 158
The Palm Beach Story (Sturges, 1942) 66–68, 70
Palmer, Mitchell 156
Palmer, Tim 5, 8, 20, 23, 138
Park, Nick 220
Parker, Charlie 163
Parrott, Dominic, and Amos Zeichner 129
Pasolini, Pier Paolo 23; *Teorema* (1968) 167
Paths of Glory (Kubrick, 1957) 152
Peacock, Steven 5–6
Peeping Tom (Powell, 1960) 12, 167
Perella, Nicolas J. 203
Persona (Bergman, 1966) 110
The Philadelphia Story (Cukor, 1940) 68
The Piano (Campion, 1993) 5, 21–22, 32
The Pied Piper of Hamelin 177
The Pillow Book (Greenaway, 1996) 20
Pirates of the Caribbean: At World's End (Verbinski, 2007) 205, 207
Pirates of the Caribbean: Dead Man's Chest (Verbinski, 2006) 210
Pixar: *Knick Knack* (1989) 218; *Luxo Jr.* (1986) 216, 218; *Red's Dream* (1987) 218
Plantinga, Carl 203
Poe, Edgar A.: "The Fall of the House of Usher" 135; "The Tell-Tale Heart" 136
Pond, Steve 223
Pratt, Geraldine, Victoria Rosner et al. 1
Pride & Prejudice (Wright, 2005) 209
Prince, Stephen 215, 217–18

Proust, Marcel: *Swann's Way* 177
Pryluck, Calvin 107, 111–12
Psycho (Hitchcock, 1960) 136, 170
Pull My Daisy (Alfred Leslie and Robert Frank, 1959) 94–103
Purgatorio 194

Quandt, James 23, 24
"Queen and Country" (McQueen, 2007) 192

Rabelais, François 142
Rachmaninov, Sergei: *Second Piano Concerto* 73, 78–79, 81–82
Raguin, Virginia 73
Ramsaye, Terry 54
Rappeneau, Jean-Paul 24
Rattigan, Terence: *The Deep Blue Sea* (play) 184–85, 189
Reagan, Ronald 119
Red's Dream (Pixar, 1987) 218
Reservoir Dogs (Tarantino, 1991) 27
Resnais, Alain 24; *Hiroshima mon Amour* (1959) 20
Ridley-Duff, Rory 146
Rivers, Larry 96
Rivette, Jacques 24
Rizzolatti, Giacomo, and Corrado Sinigaglia 210–11
RoboCop (Verhoeven, 1987) 119–28
RoboCop 2 (Kershner, 1990) 119, 124–25, 127–29
Roche, David 125
Rohmer, Éric 24
Romney, Jonathan 171
La Ronde (Ophüls, 1950) 152
Roosevelt, Eleanor 63, 71, 162–64
Rosenthal, Alan 109
Rosso, Vito 189
Rothapfel, Roxy 51–52
Rothman, William 168
Rothstein, Nat 51
Rousseau, Jean-Jacques 179

Salinger, Pierre 108
Sand, George: *François le Champi* 177
Sands, Bobby 192–97, 200
Sanger, Tam 1
Sargeant, Jack 96, 101, 103
Saunders, Brian 114
Saw (Wan, 2004) 27
Scharrer, Erica 119–20
Schatz, Thomas 62–63, 131
Schneider, Alexandra 49
Schnitzler, Arthur: *Traumnovelle* 147
Scorsese, Martin: *The Age of Innocence* (1993) 5; *Casino* (1995) 25; *Goodfellas* (1990) 24; *Taxi Driver* (1976) 24

Second Piano Concerto (Rachmaninov) 73, 78–79, 81–82
Séguret, Olivier 4–5
Seidman, Steven 64, 68, 71
The Seven Year Itch (Wilder, 1955) 73–83
Seyrig, Delphine 101
Shakespeare 188
Shame (McQueen, 2011) 192–201
Shearer, Norma 50
The Shining (Kubrick, 1980) 152
Silly Symphonies (Disney, 1929–39) 216
Simon, J.P. 87
Singer, Ben 49
Singer, Isabelle 173, 175
Sipière, Dominique 6–7
The Skin I Live In (Almodóvar, 2011) 24, 25
Sklar, Robert 4, 76, 117
Sleep (Warhol, 1964) 5
Slide, Anthony 53
Smith, Murray 217–18
Sobchack, Vivian 5, 7, 19, 21–22, 25, 29, 196, 203, 206
The Social Network (Fincher, 2010) 164
Solondz, Todd 27
Sounac, Frédéric 82
Speaking Parts (Egoyan, 1989) 167–69, 171–72, 175
Spicer, Andrew 85
Springer, Claudia 119, 131
Staiger, Janet 42
Starfield, Penny 73, 147
Steamboat Bill, Jr. (Reisner and Keaton, 1928) 192
Sterritt, David 97
Still Life 83, 189
Stockham, Alice, *Karezza* 65
Stokes, Melvyn 3
Stoler, Ann Laura 1
The Straight Story (Lynch, 1999) 5
Studlar, Gaylyn 53
Sullivan, Francis William: *The Glory Road* 54
Suspicion (Hitchcock, 1940) 170
Swanson, Gloria 58
The Sweet Hereafter (Egoyan, 1998) 166–67, 177
Sylvester, David 135, 143

Talmadge, Norma 51
Tan, Ed 217, 221; and Nico H. Frijda 216
Tanizaki, Junichiro 172
Tarkovsky, Andrei 190
Tarnation (Caouette, 2003) 8
Tarnished Lady (Cukor, 1931) 63
Tarr, Béla 24
Taxi Driver (Scorsese, 1976) 25
Téchiné, André 24

"The Tell-Tale Heart" 136
Teorema (Pasolini, 1968) 167
The Terminator (Cameron, 1984) 119–20, 122–23, 126–27, 129–30
Terror Island (Cruze, 1920) 47
The Texas Chain Saw Massacre (Hooper, 1974) 141
Thalberg, Irving 47–48, 57
Thatcher, Margaret 193
Theodora Goes Wild (Boleslawski, 1936) 69
Théry, Irène 134
Time Regained (Ruiz, 1999) 177
Tisseron, Serge 1, 12, 100
Tolstoy, Leo: *Anna Karenina* 81; *Kreutzer Sonata* 81
Too Many Husbands (Ruggles, 1940) 68
Toole, John Kennedy: *The Neon Bible* (novel) 184
Traumnovelle 147
"Trilogy": *Children* (Davies, 1976) 180
Trouble Every Day (Denis, 2001) 140
Truffaut, François 24
Tschofen, Monique 167, 171

The Ugly Duckling (Cutting, 1939) 216
Uncle Tom's Cabin (Polard, 1927) 51
The Untouchables (Nakache and Toledano, 2011) 29

Vachaud, Laurent 147
Van de Velde, Theodore: *Ideal Marriage* (1930) 65
Van Dyke, W.W. 51
The Vanity of Duluoz 102
Varda, Agnès: *Black Panthers: A Report* (1968) 117; *The Murder of Fred Hampton* (1971) 117
Varela, Francisco J., Evan Thompson and Eleanor Rosch 211
Vendredi Soir (Denis, 2002) 26
Verbinski, Gore: *Pirates of the Caribbean: At World's End* (2007) 205, 207; *Pirates of the Caribbean: Dead Man's Chest* (2006) 210

Vermeer, Johannes 188
Vernet, Marc 168
Vertigo (Hitchcock, 1958) 6–7
Videodrome (Cronenberg, 1983) 5–6, 12
Virilio, Paul 168, 174

Wahl, Elizabeth Susan 1
Waltz, Gwendolyn 58
Ward, Fannie 53
Warhol, Andy: *Blow Job* (1983) 5; *Eat* (1963) 5; *Kiss* (1963) 5; *Sleep* (1964) 5
Warner, Harry 51
Wasson, Haidee 49
Wells, Paul 219
Wharton, Edith: *The House of Mirth* (novel) 184
Where the Truth Lies (Egoyan, 2006) 169
Whispering Room (Cardiff, 1991) 173
White Shadows in the South Seas (W.S. Van Dyke and Robert J. Flaherty, 1928) 51
Wickham, Phil 58
Williams, Linda 8, 29–30, 147, 200
Williamson, Catherine 86–87
Wilson, Emma 171
Winnicott, D.W. 169–70, 176
Winston, Brian 115, 117
Wise Blood 144
Wolfe, Jesse 1
Woolf, Virginia 179
Workers Leaving the Lumière Factory in Lyon (Lumière, 1895) 84
Wright, Joe: *Anna Karenina* (2012) 209; *Atonement* (2007) 204–6; 209–10; *Pride & Prejudice* (2005) 209

"You Belong to Me" (Stafford, 1952) 187, 190
Young, John 219

Zabriskie Point (Michelangelo, 1970) 152
Žižek, Slavoj 29
Zumthor, Paul 102

www.ingramcontent.com/pod-product-compliance
Lightning Source LLC
Chambersburg PA
CBHW051220300426
44116CB00006B/648